Susan and Dan,

Thank you for
all you do for our
country.

Tom

Advance Praise for *The Fall of the FBI*

"An interesting and insightful look into the FBI. This book will give the reader a better understanding of the inner workings of the FBI and integrity of some Agents and the lack of it in other Agents. A very powerful read."

—Joe Pistone, former FBI agent, author of *Donnie Brasco: My Undercover Life in the Mafia*

"Tom Baker, a retired FBI agent who enjoyed a wide-ranging and successful career, describes the chaos that led to the decline of the FBI in recent years. *The Fall of the FBI* is both entertaining and informative and centers on the turmoil that has engulfed the FBI. Baker sheds light on Director Bob Mueller's disastrous culture change and Director Jim Comey's failed leadership in the Russia Collusion case."

—Joe Wolfinger, former FBI Assistant Director, author of *Rico: How Politicians, Prosecutors, and the Mob Destroyed one of the FBI's Finest Special Agents*

"Tom Baker is a legend in the FBI: the first agent on the scene of the Reagan assassination attempt, wizened veteran of hundreds of other criminal cases, large and small. When he writes on the calling and compromise of the FBI's institutional culture, as in his frequent commentary for the *Wall Street Journal* and here, in *The Fall of the FBI*, Baker commands unrivaled authority—and the undistracted attention of all patriots who care whether the United States remains a nation of laws."

—James Rosen, chief White House correspondent for Newsmax, author of *The Strong Man: John Mitchell and the Secrets of Watergate*

"Thomas J. Baker's more than three decades of distinguished service in the FBI validates his participation in major historic events and views of a declining Bureau. A thousand former FBI Agents wish they had the courage displayed by Tom in writing *The Fall of the FBI*. He reveals not only one or two former Bureau bad apples but his writing skill has the reader nearly smelling the stench of an entire orchard rotting in decay. A deeply researched serious work of nonfiction, it is a must read for all concerned with preserving our democracy."

—Paul Letersky, former FBI Special Agent, author of *The Director: My Years Assisting J. Edgar Hoover*

"The failures and political corruption of the FBI have become undeniable in recent years. The incredible insight from Thomas Baker's thirty-three-year career at the Bureau and his eye-opening reporting make *The Fall of the FBI* a book only he could have written, and it's essential reading for the rest of us who want to know what went wrong and wonder if the FBI can be saved."

—Mollie Hemingway, Editor in Chief of *The Federalist*,
author of *Justice on Trial: The Kavanaugh Confirmation
and the Future of the Supreme Court*

"Baker's must-read book is both timely and critical for the turbulent times in which we live. A touchstone for FBI historians and law enforcement organizations alike, *The Fall of the FBI* is essential reading and should be considered one of the most powerful and thought-provoking FBI books ever written!"

—Kenneth Strange Jr., former FBI and DOJ Special
Agent in Charge, author of *A Cop's Son: One G-Man's
Fight Against Jihad, Global Fraud, and the Cartels*

"Tom Baker's book is a must-read for those desiring to witness firsthand the career of a legendary FBI agent, as he brings the reader along from his days at the FBI Academy and beyond: kidnappings, airplane hijackings, espionage…even the attempted assassination of a sitting president. The author then tackles the thorny issues plaguing the FBI today, recognizing his beloved Bureau is 'drifting away from its law enforcement moorings.' Tom Baker's stories are compelling, his insight is enlightening, and his conclusions are cogent."

—Greg Dillon, former FBI agent, author of
The Thin Blue Lie: An Honest Cop vs. The FBI

"For those of us who grew up admiring the FBI and were shocked by the agency's behavior in the Russia Hoax, this is the book to read. Thomas Baker, a retired FBI official, tells us why this happened, how an American legend was gradually unraveled by incompetent management, dishonesty, and loss of, well, decency itself. Mr. Baker grew up in the agency, and in the old style rose to the management level, only to see his and his colleagues' work devalued by the likes of James Comey and his coterie. Now we have an FBI that spies on Americans. It's time for Congress to investigate and return the FBI to its former level of respect."

—Peter J. Wallison, former White House Counsel, author *Ronald Reagan: The Power of Conviction and the Success of His Presidency*

"There are a million stories in the life of an FBI Agent. Some can be, some should be, and others the FBI hopes are never told. Tom Baker, in his compelling book, *The Fall of the FBI* takes the reader through highlights of his remarkable career and offers an insight to what the FBI has meant to America. He also tells the story of other, more recent incidents, that do not reflect what the FBI has been. He offers suggestions on what must be done to restore this storied institution back to where it should be to protect, not sully, our nation."

—Richard A. Marquise, former FBI Special-Agent-in-Charge, author of *Scotbom: Evidence and the Lockerbie Investigation.*

"The FBI was the world's greatest law-enforcement agency. To get back to being great, it has to get back to being a law-enforcement agency: criminal investigators nonpareil, committed to the Constitution's guardrails, not wannabe spies scheming to circumvent them. That is Thomas J. Baker's *cri de cœur*, compellingly delivered with the strength of more than three decades as an agent, from the trenches to the heights of what the Bureau does best: fight crime. That sound you hear is those of us who love the FBI—what it was and what it still can be—cheering.

—Andrew C. McCarthy, former federal prosecutor, *New York Times* bestselling author of *Ball of Collusion: The Plot to Rig an Election and Destroy a Presidency.*

"Tom Baker clearly understands the importance of an independent and objective federal law-enforcement authority. In this memoir, he expresses his concerns for the organization in which he served for more than three decades, and for which he clearly feels deep affection. His experience bridges the Hoover era with the post-Comey Bureau, providing a unique perspective. A cautionary tale told with humor and insight."

—Marc Ruskin, former Brooklyn assistant district attorney, legislative aide to U. S. Senator Daniel Patrick Moynihan, adjunct professor at the John Jay College of Criminal Justice, author *The Pretender, My Life Undercover for the FBI*

"As I read this wonderful and entertaining book, all I could think to say was... 'well, this is certainly long overdue.' It's about time that someone with Tom Baker's vast experience, skills, and integrity presented a close-up insider's view of the world's greatest investigative organization. Baker shows us, especially through all of the high profile cases, why the Bureau has enjoyed so many decades of respect and admiration; and yet only to see it descend in recent years into political intrigue and demoralization. This book should not only give insight, pride and hope to every rank and file agent in the field, but more importantly, to every American who still loves what the FBI stands for: Fidelity, Bravery, and Integrity."

—John F Picciano, former FBI agent and New York trial attorney, author of *Liam's Promise*, a work of historical fiction about the TWA Flight 800 crash off Long Island in July 1996

"Tom Baker draws on his years of experience within the Bureau to present a superb examination of America's foremost law enforcement agency. From his amazing first-hand knowledge of historic cases like the Reagan assassination attempt and the death of Princess Diana to his insightful views on how to remedy the recent shortcomings of the agency that he so loves, I found *The Fall of the FBI* to be an informative and thought-provoking read."

—Philip Jett, author of *The Death of an Heir* and *Taking Mr. Exxon: The Kidnapping of an Oil Giant's President*

"Tom Baker, citing the total lack of character apparent in some of the FBI's most recent so-called leaders, raises the question as to whether we are treating the symptom (getting rid of a few bad apples) and ignoring the problem (the changing FBI culture). Sharing thirty-three years of FBI experiences during his illustrious career, Tom provides keen insight into a leader's most important responsibility—culture management.

—Richard M. Ayres, former FBI agent, former Executive Director of the FBI National Executive Institute Associates, author of *Leading to Make a Difference: Ethical, Character Driven Law Enforcement*

THE FALL
OF THE FBI

HOW A ONCE GREAT AGENCY
BECAME A THREAT TO DEMOCRACY

THOMAS J. BAKER

BOMBARDIER
BOOKS

Published by Bombardier Books
An Imprint of Post Hill Press
ISBN: 978-1-63758-624-2
ISBN (eBook): 978-1-63758-625-9

The Fall of the FBI:
How a Once Great Agency Became a Threat to Democracy
© 2022 by Thomas J. Baker
All Rights Reserved

Cover Design by Matt Margolis

Post Hill Press
New York • Nashville
posthillpress.com

Published in the United States of America
1 2 3 4 5 6 7 8 9 10

For Anne

"We must do the work the American people expect of us, in the way the Constitution demands of us."

Judge William H. Webster
FBI director 1978–1987

TABLE OF CONTENTS

Part II—The Bad: Injustice

Part III—The Ugly: The Fall of the FBI

Thomas Dineen, my maternal grandfather, was a police officer in the city of Brooklyn, when it was its own city. His oldest son, Frank, was a NYPD officer and then an investigator in the Army's CID during World War II. His other son, Bill, was a detective with the NY Central Railroad Police and then a NYPD officer. The stories of my uncles' adventures fueled my passion for law enforcement.

AUTHOR'S NOTE

After hearing one of my FBI adventures, some have suggested, "You ought to write a book." Perhaps, but the question remains: Why *this* book?

Over the past few years, I became concerned about abuses by our FBI. Abuses caused by a change in culture or poor leadership. In trying to find the answer to "what went wrong" I turned to Yuval Levin's *A Time to Build*. His analysis of the failure of institutions today, in some respects, answered the question.

His work provided another insight: We are formed by our institutions. Reflecting on what Levin wrote, I realized his analysis was true in my case. Family, church, and school formed my character and beliefs. Like thousands of others, I took that formation with me into the FBI, where I continued to be formed.

Everybody starts out in life, particularly in our professional lives, with some preconceived ideas. Some of these ideas change as we grow and evolve; some never change. Some are ideals we hold onto to guide us; some are lost to disillusioning experiences along the way.

My maternal grandfather was a policeman in Brooklyn, New York, when it was its own city. His sons—my uncles—were police officers in New York City. As a youth, I heard their stories and shared their pride in bringing the "bad guys" to justice. I had a positive view of the justice system. A naively idealist view, some might say. In my thirty-three-year FBI career, and in my continued association with the criminal justice system since, I have come to the realization that justice is far from perfect.

This book is divided into three parts. First, the adventures, which I hope you will find as entertaining as I found my uncles' stories. Second, the injustices I have witnessed in the FBI and in life. The third part covers recent dysfunctions of our FBI, with possible solutions. In other words, the good, the bad, and the ugly.

In working through the FBI's fall, I had the opportunity to pen several opinion pieces for *The Wall Street Journal* and other publications. The bulk of Part III is based on those opinion pieces.

Still, despite the ugliness and injustice that surrounds us today, I remain an optimist. It is always, as Ronald Reagan put it, "Morning in America."

INTRODUCTION

Americans have lost faith in the Federal Bureau of Investigation, an institution they once regarded as the world's greatest law enforcement agency. I spent many years with the FBI, and am deeply troubled by this loss of faith. Specific lapses have come to light, and each is thoroughly discussed in this book. But why did they happen? What changed? The answer begins days after the 9/11 attacks with a cultural change at the Bureau.

Culture is the issue. The Department of Justice Inspector General's reports damningly document a pattern of deliberate omissions, misstatements, and outright falsifications in material presented to the United States Foreign Intelligence Surveillance Court (the FISC) by three different investigative teams. This widespread behavior describes a culture—not just the work of a "few bad apples." In what is certainly an understatement, the Inspector General (IG) concluded the Bureau's actions "fell short of what is rightfully expected from a premier law enforcement agency." That may be because they were acting and thinking as an intelligence agency, rather than a law enforcement agency.

To understand how far the Bureau has fallen, I show in these pages the good—albeit sometimes imperfect—role played by the FBI and FBI agents in past decades. It was quite often, as I hope you will see from my firsthand experiences, a fun-filled adventure. While at the same time, the reader will also see the reverence the Bureau had for the Constitution and the concern agents held for the rights of Americans. It was once the norm.

PROLOGUE

Camp David, Maryland,
September 15, 2001

Three and a half days after the attacks of September 11, 2001, Robert Swan Mueller III, newly appointed director of the FBI, was summoned to the presidential retreat in the wooded Catoctin Mountains of Maryland. Muller had held the job for a little more than a week.

He was at Camp David that Saturday morning to give President Bush the FBI's report on the attacks. The investigation—codenamed "PENTTBOM"—would become the largest one ever conducted by the Bureau. In just three and a half days it had already identified the nineteen hijackers as well as their roles, nationalities, travel documents, and histories. Their Al-Qaeda connections and links to bin Laden were in the Bureau's crosshairs. Mueller, as he later acknowledged, was confident in the report. The Bureau had done what it does best—investigate.

President George W. Bush, in a leather bomber jacket, was sitting at the head of a big square conference table in the rustic oak cabin. National Security Advisor Condoleezza Rice was sitting at the president's right. Other key administration figures, all ruggedly dressed, were scattered around the room. Robert Mueller, in his starched white but-ton-down shirt, confidently briefed the president and his team on the Bureau's accomplishments.

Expecting praise or thanks, Mueller was taken aback when the president coldly commented, "I don't care about that. I just want to know how you're going to prevent this from happening again." Later that morning, CIA Director George Tenet presented a proposed plan of action. At the conclusion of Tenet's presentation, Bush exclaimed, "That's great!" and turned toward Mueller saying, "That's what I want to hear." Mueller was humiliated.

So, for reasons that seemed justified at the time, Mueller set out to make the FBI an "intelligence-driven" organization. Unintended con-sequences followed. The organization I had served for the proceeding thirty-three years would undergo a cultural change during the Mueller/Comey years, culminating in the ugly disaster of the Russian collusion investigation, code-named: "Crossfire Hurricane."

CHAPTER ONE

ROTTEN APPLES OR ROTTEN CULTURE?

ortunately, the principal miscreants of Crossfire Hurricane were cast out of the FBI. James Comey, the former FBI Director who hovered over the mess from its inception in the spring of 2016 until his firing by President Trump on May 9, 2017, was the first to go. Next was FBI Deputy Director Andrew McCabe, then the acting director. He was fired by Attorney General Jeff Sessions on March 17, 2018, after an investigation by the Justice Department's Inspector General discovered he lied to investigators on four occasions—three of which were under oath. Next, Deputy Assistant Director Peter Strzok, who had initiated the Crossfire Hurricane investigation, was literally shown the door as he was escorted out of the Hoover Building on June 15, 2018 after another IG report. Strzok was finally officially fired on August 10, 2018 by Deputy Director David Bowdich. The dismissed malefactors have all published books, which make no apology for the damage they've done to the Bureau and our country.

This book is a response to their fiction.

Ridding the Bureau of these rotten apples initially gave many people hope, but now it's clear their dismissal was not enough. The question remains: How did it happen?

Senator Marsha Blackburn of Tennessee and Attorney General William Barr engaged in a bit of a colloquy on May 1, 2019, at a hearing of the Senate Judiciary Committee. By then it was apparent that both the FBI's Russian collusion case and Robert Mueller's subsequent Special Counsel Inquiry were grievously misconceived. Their dialogue directly concerned the fundamental question, "How did this happen?" And Senator Blackburn concluded it was the result of an "unhealthy work culture" at Bureau headquarters.

During the summer of 2021, Department of Justice (DOJ) Inspector General (IG) Michael E. Horowitz announced the results of several investigations that blasted the Bureau's lax culture. Additional reporting only added to this bleak picture.

On July 1, 2021, a female FBI field supervisor filed a lawsuit in federal district court in Nevada alleging sexual harassment by the Las Vegas Assistant Special Agent in Charge (ASAC), and another supervisory agent. The ASAC had tried to pressure her into a sexual relationship, so she sought help from the office's employee assistance officer, the other Supervisory Special Agent (SSA). Instead of helping, however, this supervisor sent a photo of a rainbow-colored dildo between his legs to her Bureau-issued cell phone. The suit also set forth numerous vulgar messages from the SSA concerning alcohol abuse, mishandling of weapons, and—like the infamous Peter Strzok/Lisa Page texts—repeated misuse of Bureau-issued cell phones for obscene purposes.

The female agent in Las Vegas had also reported her concerns to the Bureau's Equal Employment Office. In light of the SSA's frequent alcohol abuse, she was particularly concerned that he kept a loaded shotgun near his desk. Her detailed complaint documented the unprofessional atmosphere among management in the Las Vegas office and the continuing cultural rot in the Bureau.

At 8 a.m. on Sunday morning, July 11, 2021, the official FBI Twitter account (@FBI) posted a tweet that had many former agents shaking their heads and many on Twitter making comparisons to the Stasi and other totalitarian security services. The tweet read: "Family members and peers are often best positioned to witness signs of mobilization to violence. Help prevent homegrown violent extremism. Visit this website to learn how to spot suspicious behaviors and report them."

Asking all Americans to report their family members for signs of "suspicious behaviors" is scary stuff. Louis J. Freeh, as FBI Director in a pre-9/11 world, required that all agents in training visit the Holocaust Memorial Museum in Washington, DC. There it is documented what happens when people inform on their neighbors. Freeh wanted new agents to understand the dangers of the police power of the state being turned against its own people.

Whoever in the FBI sent those tweets had missed that lesson.

On July 14, 2021, the IG issued a report on the FBI's mishandling of the allegations against Dr. Lawrence Gerard Nassar, the physician for both US Women's Gymnastics and Michigan State University's Gymnastics. He was accused of sexually abusing hundreds of young women and girls. The truly heartbreaking aspect of this report was the Bureau's lack of care or concern for the victims, which allowed Nasser's depredations to continue.

The IG found that the FBI's Indianapolis office had failed to respond with the urgency the allegations required. They also made fundamental errors when it finally *did* respond, and failed to notify the appropriate field office (the FBI's Lansing Michigan Resident Agency, located near the campus of Michigan State University and Nassar's residence). They also failed to notify state and local authorities. After eight months of inactivity by the Indianapolis office, the FBI's Los Angeles office received similar information. The IG found the Los Angeles office also failed to take action to notify the appropriate field office or state and local authorities.

The FBI's Lansing Michigan Resident Agency only become aware of the allegations about Nassar when Michigan State University Police acted. They'd received similar complaints about Nassar, which led them to search his residence, where they discovered child pornography.

At this point, over a year had passed since complaints were first made to the FBI, and Nassar had continued to "treat" gymnasts at Michigan State University, a high school in Michigan, and a gymnastics club in Michigan. The Michigan investigation found that Nassar had sexually assaulted hundreds of victims and possessed thousands of items of child pornography.

He was convicted in both federal and state courts and is currently imprisoned in Florida on a federal sentence of sixty years—the statutory maximum—for child pornography violations. His two state sentences—over a hundred years each—for child abuse are to be served consecutively.

A de facto life sentence.

In the IG's review of the FBI's handling of the Nassar matter, the lack of attention or concern by the management of the Indianapolis office is stunning. Crimes against children are supposed to be an FBI investigative priority. A decades-long undercover operation code-named "Innocence Images" focuses on crimes involving the sexual exploitation of minors. Interstate travel for purposes of sex with a minor is a federal crime,[1] as any FBI Special Agent should know.

The IG specifically cited the FBI Indianapolis interview of a gymnast on September 2, 2015, in which she alleged sexual assault by Nassar. That interview wasn't documented until February 2017. There's a long-standing Bureau rule—the five-day rule—and every agent knows it: The results of an interview must be memorialized on form FD-302 within five days.

Both a Supervisory Special Agent (SSA) and the Special Agent in Charge (SAC) were cited for their "false statements" in the Nassar case—or what most people would call lies. The IG reported that the victim interview summary, which the SSA drafted seventeen months after the interview, contained materially false statements and omitted material information. The IG also charged that when questioned, the same SSA twice made manifestly false statements to the IG's team. In

---

[1] Title 18, U.S. Code, § 2252.

addition, the IG found that the SAC made materially false statements about the Indianapolis investigation during his interview with the IG team, and then he twice falsely denied specific contacts with the US Olympic Committee when asked by the IG's team.

Perhaps most tragic of all was the IG's assertion that at least seventy more athletes were subject to abuse in the time that elapsed before Nassar's arrest by state authorities, while Nassar's victims had claimed the number abused in that period was 120 young women and children. IG Horowitz concluded that in the Nassar case, "Numerous FBI policies were violated."

The rules were there, but the problem was with the attitude and culture.

The harshly critical July 14, 2021 IG report on the FBI's handling of the Nassar case quickly led to media coverage of the abuse suffered by the gymnasts and others. Some of the victims spoke out publicly about what they had suffered. This led, in turn, to the inevitable congressional hearings.

The Senate Judiciary Committee held a public hearing on Wednesday, September 15, 2021. Current and former gymnasts testified about the abuse they endured from Nassar, under the guise of medical treatment, when they were girls. The televised hearing was highly emotional. The gymnast who first reported Nassar's crimes to the FBI testified that "this conduct by these FBI agents...who are expected to protect the public is unacceptable, disgusting, and shameful." FBI Director Christopher A. Wray had the admittedly difficult task of testifying at the same hearing. The initial bungling of the Nassar case had occurred under the troubled tenure of his predecessor, James Comey—but it was his mess to clean-up now. The Indianapolis SSA, cited in the IG report for mishandling and ignoring the complaint against Nassar, was fired just days before the Senate Committee hearing.

Lawyers for the victims took their shots, calling the SSA's firing "long overdue," but questioned the timing of the Senate hearing. Senators joined in: Speaking directly to Wray, Richard Blumenthal of Connecticut, for example, mused, "Someone perhaps more cynical than

I would conclude it was this hearing here staring the FBI in the face that prompted that action."

Wray was clearly on the spot, as his testimony had followed the young victims' gut-wrenching accounts. Accordingly, he began appropriately enough by apologizing to them. Two of the offending agents no longer worked at the FBI, he stated, and they were "not representative" of the Bureau's work. He offered variations of "the bad apples are gone" theme numerous times in response to Senators' questions. Most of the Senate hearing—lasting four hours—was broadcast on national television. It was watched with rapt attention by a huge audience, including me and many other concerned former agents. It was becoming clear to many of us that what was ailing the FBI couldn't be solved by a few more firings.

The culture itself had to change.

On Thursday, September 16, 2021, the day after Wray's hours-long Senate testimony, the Former Agents Society had a luncheon meeting at The Springfield Golf & Country Club in suburban Virginia. FBI Director Wray was the luncheon speaker and guest of honor. Most everyone of the nearly a hundred attendees had watched the previous day's testimony on television. We were anticipating a readout from Wray in our closed-door gathering. Disappointingly, he made no mention of it and gave a fairly standard speech, one he could have given at any time to the Rotary or the Elks Club. The elephant was in the room yet he managed not to acknowledge it. He did, however, repeat the buzzwords bequeathed by Mueller: The FBI was now an "intelligence-driven" organization.

Standing among other former agents, just outside the country club's door, watching the black Chevy Suburbans with the director's entourage pull away, there was a definite sense of disappointment. One guy said he didn't know what he was going to tell his neighbor, who was always asking him for further explanation of the Bureau's misdeeds. Another wondered what he could possibly tell his wife, who was waiting at home, anxious to hear what the director had said.

Except Wray hadn't said anything about the topic du jour.

Later, on Saturday, October 23, 2021, the FBI Deputy Director, Paul Abbate, speaking to an audience of several hundred people at the Former Agents Society national conference in Scottsdale, Arizona, was more forthcoming. Many in the audience were angered by the behavior of the two agents cited in the IG report regarding the gymnasts' complaints. Paul Abbate explained that only one of them was fired because the other had "beat the clock" by taking retirement before administrative action could be taken against him. Abbate maintained that had the other agent remained in the Bureau, he too would have been fired. As Abbate continued fielding numerous impassioned questions, he expressed his own utter puzzlement at why these two failed to respond to the gymnasts' complaints. Once again, "rotten apples" were expunged from the Bureau, but there was still no examination of why these rotten apples kept surfacing from the bottom of the barrel.

On July 20, 2021, the IG issued a summary of misconduct by "a former senior FBI official" who had numerous unauthorized contacts with the media leading up to the November 2016 election. That report referenced an earlier May 29, 2019 finding of misconduct (again, it involved unauthorized contact with the media) on the part of a deputy assistant director. The case touched on both the Clinton email scandal *and* the Trump Russian collusion narrative. These two reports cited a half dozen other FBI officials for similar misconduct. It expressed deep concern about a permissive cultural attitude within the FBI.

On July 22, 2021, the IG reported findings of misconduct by FBI Assistant Director in Charge of Congressional Affairs, Jill C. Tyson. The FBI's Inspection Division had referred the matter to the IG after receiving information alleging she was engaged in an inappropriate relationship with a subordinate. The IG's investigation found that she did have a sexual liaison with a subordinate, and that the affair disrupted the workplace by interfering with the ability of other FBI employees to complete their work. The IG also specifically discovered that Tyson made hiring and organizational decisions involving the subordinate.

On Monday, August 2, 2021, the IG reported on yet another investigation of a special agent who had had an inappropriate relationship with a support employee. During the investigation, the IG learned that Special Agents (SAs) sometimes used photographs of young female support staff to pose as minor children or sex workers to entice sexual predators on various social media websites. The SA in question was found to have asked the support staff employee to "provide him with provocative pictures of herself for an online UCO (undercover operation)." The SA said he was just "fishing" on social media sites and was not recording which sites he visited. He and his Supervisory SA were unable to furnish the IG with any documentation of how the photographs were obtained or used. The IG criticized this casual use of support staff as online sexual bait and expressed concern that the images could still float around on the web, potentially placing those employees in danger. The IG also specifically noted that these practices conflicted with the Attorney General's Guidelines for FBI Undercover Operations.

On August 3, 2021, the special agent, who was the public face of the investigation of the alleged kidnapping plot of Michigan Governor Gretchen Whitmer, was charged by local authorities in Kalamazoo, Michigan with one count of "assault with intent to do great bodily harm." He was accused of assaulting his wife by banging her head against a nightstand and choking her. They were fighting after their attendance at a swingers' party earlier that same evening. According to the charging documents, when police arrived on the scene, the agent's wife had bloody lacerations on the right side of her head and "blood all over her chest, clothing, arms, and hand," as well as "severe" bruising to her neck and throat. She told police her husband had gotten on top of her, grabbed the sides of her head, and smashed it into a nearby nightstand numerous times. She tried to grab his beard to get him off her when he started to choke her. She then grabbed the agent's testicles, which ended the fight.

This same agent, in an echo of practices that came to light in the Russian collusion fiasco, also used his official phone to unleash diatribes against the former president and his supporters, calling Trump a "piece of shit" and far worse. He showed incredibly bad judgment with his obscenity-laced online tirade. Lessons from the earlier mess were either not learned, or worse yet, not taught.

To add to his sins, the agent was working as trainer in a gym, specializing as a CrossFit coach. In the past it would be unheard of for an agent to be allowed to work a second job. It still is, as it should be, since agents are on call at all times. But under the current permissive culture, rules seem to be flouted.

The wifebeater agent was deeply involved in all aspects of investigation of the Governor Whitmer kidnapping plot. He testified in federal court at the preliminary hearing in the case, signed off on the criminal complaint, was the affiant for multiple search warrants, and was involved in numerous interviews. In September 2021, he was dismissed from the Bureau.

In the local Kalamazoo court, the former agent entered into a plea agreement for the assault on his wife. At his December 20, 2021 sentencing, his wife—the victim—spoke in his defense and said she forgave him. Perhaps another sad example of the "battered-wife" syndrome. The obviously frustrated prosecutors said they had to agree to the plea because his wife refused to cooperate in the case against the agent. He pleaded no contest and was sentenced to two days of time already served, plus court fines and fees.

But this wifebeater was not the only problem agent on the case, nor the only problem with the Whitmer case itself.

A second agent, who was deeply involved in running an informant central to the kidnapping conspiracy, had also become a problem. He had incorporated a private security firm as an LLC in New Mexico and spent much of 2019 bragging online about his FBI terrorism cases in order to attract clients to his business. Named "Exeintel," it chased million-dollar contracts promising potential clients that it could identify terrorist threats to their businesses. The Twitter account—@ravagiing, identified as belonging to Exeintel's CEO and linked to the company's website—had previously posted comments tied to the agent's ongoing terrorism investigations even before the cases went public.

In January 2019, the second agent's Twitter account featured a post about a group of Somalis who were being investigated for providing material support for terrorists, specifically ISIS. In a post just days after the men's arrests, the claim was made that Exeintel "had been tracking this group since last year" and crowed that "agents handling this case are INCREDIBLE!" The tweets on the case gave away more, including screenshots of encrypted messages from the prior October, which included the name of one of the suspects. A link to the Facebook page of the suspect's cousin had been sent as well.

Even more problematic, two weeks before the raids and arrests, on September 24, 2020, this second agent tweeted: "Soon....MICHIGAN Soon." Then on October 7, 2020, just hours before the arrests @ravagiing tweeted: "Don't worry Michigan I told ya A LOT more coming soon."

In this crucial Michigan case, two of the key agents were engaged in outside employment, and one of them owned and operated a business that presented a clear conflict of interest. All of this is clearly prohibited by Bureau rules—and manifestly ignored in the current culture.

And then a third key agent in the Michigan kidnapping conspiracy appeared tainted. The agent had testified in some preliminary hearings and was identified as one of the handlers of a key informant in the case. Then it came out that he had been accused of perjury in a previous case. That past allegation had never been resolved. On Friday, December 17, 2021, federal prosecutors advised the court that none of the three agents in question would be used at trial.

The FBI investigation of the alleged plot to kidnap Governor Whitmer has itself become problematic. The defense of entrapment was being bantered about. In the aftermath of the Bureau's famous ABSCAM cases of the early 80s, guidelines were put in place—and strictly followed—that eliminated entrapment as a viable defense. Basically, there is no entrapment if the government can show the defendant was predisposed towards the crime. Agents were cautioned and trained not to cross over that line of enticing someone who was "not otherwise disposed" to committing the crime. What has been disclosed in this matter certainly raises the possibility that one or more informants went too far in shaping the events of the conspiracy.

Defense attorneys in Michigan then asked the court to allow hundreds of passages from government recordings to be introduced—apparently to bolster an entrapment defense. Many of the quotes suggest the defendants were uneasy with the idea of kidnapping, and even confused about the goal. The second agent to be removed from the case is quoted in a text to his informant, just a week before he led a surveillance of the governor's residence: "Mission is to kill the governor specifically."

In the aftermath of ABSCAM, we believed entrapment had become a non-issue. Maybe not.

There were only four defendants facing federal charges in the alleged plot, and it is widely reported that there were as many as twelve FBI informants and two undercover agents (UCAs) among the alleged plotters.

The whole thing reminds me of the joke—or the criticism from some quarters—about the FBI and the Communist Party (CPUSA) during the 1950s. The Bureau had so many informants in the CPUSA they were the majority of members at the meetings of each cell. The not-so-funny joke was it was only the dues of the government-paid informants that kept the party going.

What is also not so funny is that the alleged kidnapping plot was weaponized by Democrats in the 2020 presidential election. Nor is it funny in our democracy that a couple of ultimately acquitted defendants endured eighteen months imprisonment.

Later, in April 2022, the trial of the alleged kidnapping plot ended with zero convictions. The defense of entrapment was discussed for the first time in years with a degree of credibility. Disclosures in the Michigan case likely convinced jurors that informants and undercover agents helped shape the conspiracy.

On August 4, 2021, in another matter, the IG released a summary report of misconduct by "a former FBI Unit Chief," who had failed to repay a $25,000 loan from a financial institution and then failed to report the debt—as well as other financial delinquencies—to the FBI.

The unit chief then pressured a subordinate to loan him $12,000—and again refused to repay. Among other findings, the IG cited the misuse of the subordinate's time and the unit chief's "lack of candor," which others might just call lying. The unit chief—a headquarters-level manager—resigned while under investigation. Another rotten apple out the door.

But why did he think he could get away with this kind of behavior?

On Tuesday, August 16, 2021, a special agent assigned to the New Orleans field office pleaded not guilty to several counts of sex crimes against children, including, "aggravated crimes against nature and indecent behavior with a juvenile." His most recent FBI duties included investigating child pornography and other crimes against children.

Arrested in Louisiana in June, a judge ordered him held without bond in Ascension Parish where he harmed two victims under the age of seventeen. The judge also declared the agent "a threat to the public at large." He faces similar charges in East Baton Rouge and Orleans parishes in Louisiana. An investigation of his conduct is pending in Florida. In Tyler, Texas, a warrant charges that he repeatedly exposed himself to teenaged girls and sent inappropriate text messages, which documented his depravity. Although not as searing as his offenses against young girls, the misuse of his government cell phone to document his predatory behavior has an echo of other recent instances of cultural rot.

On Saturday, August 13, 2021, a special agent assigned to the Louisville Kentucky field office turned himself in at the Woodford County Jail. Two days earlier, a local judge had signed off on an arrest warrant, which charged the agent with "assault-domestic violence and strangulation." He was released on a $5,000 bond. Earlier, on July 9, 2021, an emergency protective order was issued against him, and he had to surrender his firearms.

On Monday, August 23, 2021, in a separate incident, the Assistant Agent in Charge (ASAC) of the New Orleans Division was arrested at her home and accused of domestic violence. Deputies from the St. Tammany Parish Sheriff's office went to the home in response to the agent's wife's pleas for help. They found the ASAC had beaten her wife.

They then arrested the ASAC for domestic abuse and battery. The accused agent had spent almost her entire career in intelligence work and was the second-highest ranking agent in the New Orleans field office.

Lastly, on August 27, 2021, a former section chief, previously assigned to the FBI Laboratory Division in Quantico, Virginia, was arrested following a criminal complaint charging him with theft of government property. According to the complaint, he falsely certified in the FBI's time and attendance system that he worked approximately 876 hours that he had not worked. The investigation of this fraud was conducted by the IG's team. A headquarters section chief could be characterized as a high-ranking executive. As with the case of two of the problem agents in the Michigan case, this section chief was apparently distracted by his ownership and operation of an outside business. In this case, it was the Perigeaux Vineyard in St. Leonard, Maryland, a winery.

All these foregoing incidents were reported over just a few weeks in the summer of 2021. They demonstrate the deep and profound rot in FBI culture. Sexual affairs disrupting the workplace and supervisors pressuring subordinates for money. Senator Marsha Blackburn's declaration on May 1, 2019, about an "unhealthy work culture" at Bureau headquarters was prescient.

But firing a few miscreants is obviously not enough. Mueller's change in culture away from a "swear to tell the truth" law enforcement agency is at the root of the problem. To appreciate how far the FBI has fallen, we must see how great it once was.

PART I

THE GOOD

SOMETIMES IT IS LIKE THE MOVIES

CHAPTER TWO

AND SO, IT BEGAN

In choosing to enter law enforcement, I shared the same ideas as others who enter the field and, for that matter, much of the public. I believed justice was even-handed, that those accused were guilty, and that everyone in jail deserved to be there.

I assumed my idealism was shared throughout law enforcement.

That last point was the first to change. I very quickly learned cynicism was widespread, and not everyone in law enforcement wanted to do the right thing.

In my last semester at Fordham University, I had decided on two things going forward. The first was I would marry my love, Anne. The second was I would join the New York Police Department (NYPD), which was then starting to professionalize by recruiting college graduates. Happily, I achieved the more important of those two goals, but the other was a different story. One evening during my final spring in college, I stopped in the local tavern for a beer before going home. In those years, it was legal to drink at age eighteen in New York, and so we did. A young man, perhaps five or six years older than me, was at the other end of the bar. I only vaguely knew Eddie Murphy, but I knew he was a cop.

Engaging him in conversation, I wanted to gain any insights I could and share the news of my plans to start at the police academy that September. As we chatted, it became obvious Eddie was an extreme cynic. He believed everything was "fixed" and everyone was "on the take." And he wanted part of the action. He specifically said the only place to "make a buck" for someone like him was in plainclothes.[2] That was his goal. He thought I was crazy to want to join the NYPD. He told me with a college degree, I could work for the FBI for a year or two and then go on to become an agent.

Since then, I have learned an occupational danger for any type of law enforcement is cynicism: believing everything and everybody is evil, rotten, or corrupt. I met many in law enforcement who had soured. But none as badly as Eddie Murphy.

Although I was shaken by Eddie's deep cynicism and frank espousal of corruption as a career path, I took his suggestion about the FBI seriously. The very next morning, I took the subway to its New York office on East 69th Street, walked up to a reception desk, and obtained an employment application. And so, it began.

By 1967, I was working in the FBI Photo Laboratory on 69th Street, waiting to begin new agents' training at the FBI Academy in Quantico, Virginia. Anne and I had been blessed in February with the birth of our first child, Thomas. In a division of labor that continues today in our marriage, Anne was handling all the medical bills and related health insurance claims. She also frequently signed my signature to expedite matters. At the time we had a disputed bill from the hospital, and Anne, not wanting to bother me with any details, had been handling all the correspondence.

About that same time in 1967, Richard J. Baker arrived in the FBI's New York office, known then and now as the NYO. He was a new SAC (Special Agent in Charge). His position was a rather big deal, and it commanded a great deal of respect. On one of his first days in the office,

---

[2] Plainclothes, in the parlance of the NYPD, were groups of officers who enforced laws against vice (e.g., gambling). This is not to be confused with Detectives, which is a different career path.

after finding suitable housing, his secretary arranged a series of phone calls with utility companies for telephone service, and so on. As he was taking these calls, another came in from a collection agency. They asked to speak to "Mr. Baker," and the switchboard put the call through to *that* Mr. Baker, the newly arrived SAC. A minute or so into the call with the bill collector, he startled his secretary by booming "Baby Boy Baker!?!"

Mere moments later, the new SAC was standing beside me in the Photo Laboratory. In an office as large as New York, this is not an everyday event. He asked, "Is everything all right?" He seemed genuinely concerned. I, on the other hand, was terrified. Discipline was draconian in that era's FBI, and a clear credit report was a minimum requirement for employment. Causing a Bureau executive concern was also something to be avoided at all costs. I repeatedly assured "Mr. Baker" we would pay all our bills. I visualized my burgeoning career as an agent ending before it began—all because of some errant hospital bill from my son's birth. I immediately called Anne and pleaded my case: "Pay the bill. Just please pay the bill."

I would meet SAC Richard J. Baker again.

CHAPTER THREE

MISTAKES MADE, LESSONS LEARNED

D espite the close call of the baby boy Baker billing incident, I was accepted for new agents' training. In the fall of 1967, I reported to FBI Headquarters, then housed in the block-long Justice building on Pennsylvania Avenue in Washington DC. The brutalist-styled building named for J. Edgar Hoover was years away from completion, as was the "new" FBI Academy on the Marine base in Quantico, Virginia. So, unlike today's agent trainees, who spend months of training at the self-contained academy in Quantico, our one classroom was in the Justice building. We lived in boarding houses on Capitol Hill. Our only visits to Quantico were for firearms training a few days at a time.

Young and idealistic, I was not at all intimidated when entering the massive Justice building through its twenty-foot tall, art-deco metal doors. I was excited. Our fifth-floor classroom had quite a history. In July 1942, it was used by the military tribunal that tried eight Nazi saboteurs. The 1959 Jimmy Stewart movie, *The FBI Story*, even filmed several scenes there. I met Mr. Stewart when he was a guest at the FBI's

75th anniversary gala. At a pre-dinner reception, when the movie was mentioned, Stewart broke into a rather physical demonstration of how he learned to shoot the famous Thompson submachine gun for the film. Taking in the very tall and slim Stewart, with that utterly unique, hesitant catch in his voice was like watching someone do a Jimmy Stewart impression.

In that historic classroom we received weeks of lectures on the US Constitution, particularly its first ten amendments, the Bill of Rights. The instructors were outstanding agent attorneys who conveyed to us their reverence for that document. Unlike many of my classmates, who were recent law school graduates, I had not previously heard all this in detail, and I soaked it up like a sponge. My attorney classmates surprised me when they commented that these lectures were far better than anything they had heard in law school.

The Bill of Rights, particularly the Fourth, Fifth, and Sixth Amendments were not presented as obstacles we had to overcome, but as something we should embrace and cherish. One legal instructor gave each of us a pocket copy of the Constitution. There was a genuine emphasis on the FBI's role—and our responsibility as agents—in protecting Americans' civil rights. These lessons would come flooding back during the ugliness of "Crossfire Hurricane."

During the final stages of training in that era, new agents went to the Bureau's Washington field office to be paired off with an experienced agent for a week of on-the-job-training. By that point we had been sworn in, issued our sidearm, and suitably trained not only with firearms but in defensive tactics and arrest techniques as well.

I was fortunate to be paired with Laurence Edwin Danbom. He'd been in the Bureau for over twenty years and was a quarter-century older than me. Larry Danbom seemed like a giant of a man, over six feet tall with shoulders much wider than mine. He had been an All-American fullback at Notre Dame. He was also very smart, having graduated with academic honors. He was well known in the nation's capital. Walking with him on L or K Street, we paused several times as he chatted with impressive-looking men in well-tailored suits. One was Edward

Bennet Williams, then the president and part owner of the Washington Redskins. Danbom introduced me, as he and Williams swapped inside football gossip. Nearly a quarter-century later, Williams again briefly crossed my path when his law firm defended John W. Hinckley, Jr., the would-be assassin of President Ronald Reagan.

Jimmy Stewart, the star of the film *The FBI Story*, at the FBI's 75th anniversary celebration, broke into an explanation of firing the famous Thompson submachine gun. His familiar halting delivery, with the signature catch in his voice, reminded us of someone doing a Jimmy Stewart impersonation.

J. Edgar Hoover was still the FBI boss, and the Bureau was bound by his many rules, some of which, even then, we thought ridiculous. For example, agents were prohibited from drinking coffee while working. In DC, Hoover actually sent inspectors out to hunt down coffee drinkers. Human nature being what it is, this made stopping for coffee almost a daily test of manhood. On the first morning with Larry Danbom, we stopped at the National Shrine of the Immaculate Conception in Northwest Washington. I had no idea why—initially the grizzled veteran was not wasting words or explanations on this new kid. We started walking up the main steps into the sanctuary. I thought this odd, since Danbom, despite being a Notre Dame graduate, was not Catholic. Once in the vestibule, however, he made a sharp turn, with me following in his wake, and headed down the stairs.

We entered a large public cafeteria, and I joined him in the food line. This was a test. And it wasn't just coffee, it was a formidable breakfast: generous heaps of eggs, sausage, bacon, and toast. Larry Danbom was a big man. We took our trays to a table and sat down facing each other. He started talking; I had passed the test. Looking over his shoulder, I spotted someone entering and warned sotto voce:

"I see a guy coming in who looks like an inspector."

Without looking up, Danbom replied, "Real tall, black hair?"

"Yeah," I responded.

"That's Dick Marquise."

Richard T. Marquise was Larry's friend and fellow agent. Years later, I would work with a much younger and somewhat shorter Dick Marquise, who ran the investigation of the Pan Am Flight 103 bombing over Lockerbie, Scotland. One of many father-son pairings in the Bureau. Today there are father-daughter pairings as well. Listening to those two FBI veterans was a great experience. As Yogi Berra might have said, you can learn a lot by just listening.

It wasn't all just listening, either. There was a lot of action in the district. Bank robberies were a daily occurrence. When the call went out over the Bureau radio that a bank robbery had happened or—better yet—was in progress, agents within a reasonable distance were expected to respond. And we did. Arriving at the scene with police sirens blaring was exciting for us new agents. We were also impressed to see the senior agents collaborate and manage the crime scene. They knew what to do and quickly went about their business.

The Federal Credit Union at St. Elizabeth's Hospital was robbed the week I was with Larry Danbom. St. Elizabeth's is not a stand-alone hospital. It's more like a small town: numerous buildings on what was a 300-acre campus, with nearly 8,000 patients and 4,000 employees. It later obtained notoriety as the place where John Hinckley was confined. It's a psychiatric facility.

Larry and I quickly arrived at the scene of the robbery on St. Elizabeth's campus. I spotted many of my fellow new agent classmates arriving with their more experienced partners. The more senior agents took on the "inside" work, processing the crime scene and interviewing the tellers and other key witnesses. We were sent off to canvass for witnesses who might have seen anything of value. Despite our youthful enthusiasm, we already realized this was often a fruitless undertaking.

I was on a gently descending road that curved under a stone archway. As I rounded a corner, I encountered a thin middle-aged man, leisurely washing a car with a sponge. I displayed my credentials, informing him the bank up the road had been robbed. I asked if he'd noticed anyone suspicious, and he replied he had indeed. *This might be good*, I thought to myself. I started writing in my notebook. He went on to say the man he saw was wearing a mask, had a pistol in one hand, and a money sack in the other. This was almost too good to be true. I had an eyewitness!

"When did you see this man?" I asked.

"Just now," he responded.

"How long have you been here?"

In a calm and reasonable tone, he replied, "Oh, about 150 years."

And then, "Napoleon put me here."

Several of my classmates had similar experiences that day. "St. E's" was, after all, a mental health facility. In the coming years, I would encounter others who appeared reasonable but then said bizarre stuff.

MOVING SOUTH

At the completion of agent training in February 1968, along with several of my classmates, I was transferred to Jacksonville, Florida. Anne and I were excited about Florida and striking out on our own as a young couple. The truth was, we would have been happy going anywhere. Bureau policy was for agents to remain only a year in the first field assignment.

It was meant to be a time of learning and growth. Departing after a year gave the maturing agent an opportunity to leave behind any mistakes made. And we made plenty.

There was a general template for an agent's first year. You'd work with a senior agent for a few weeks, somewhat like the one-week experience in the Washington Field Office. Before the year's end, certain items had to be checked off: testifying in federal district court, presenting cases to an assistant US attorney, presenting a case to a federal grand jury, and developing at least one criminal informant. You were also expected to help the senior agents on their major cases, e.g. bank robberies, kidnappings, and extortions. We did so with great enthusiasm.

Every morning, we had new cases waiting in our inbox. Soon we all accumulated a caseload, which included a variety of criminal investigations, many of them minor offenses. We often worked in pairs, particularly when there was the possibility of arrests or other dangerous situations. But some days I was alone, interviewing complainants, victims, or possible witnesses. I often knocked on doors to ask neighbors about a fugitive or possible suspect.

Among my new cases was an impersonation complaint. A woman living in a bungalow at Jacksonville Beach had phoned in. She said, "a kid" had been to her home the previous day pretending to be an FBI agent. He showed her something stamped "FBI" and "seemed really nosey," but she couldn't recall his name. I, however, recognized *her* name. I had visited her because her neighbor might have been the girlfriend of a fugitive. I was "the kid!" I wondered if another agent was pulling a gag, but nobody knew I had contacted her. I was young and I knew I looked young, but this was embarrassing. I kept this one to myself and closed the "impersonation" case administratively. Fortunately, that was something I had already learned.

Among the miscellany of criminal offenses were cases of con men defrauding senior citizens. There were—and still are—numerous variations on social security frauds. One suspect was victimizing seniors throughout the southeastern states. I was assigned a lead to interview

"Captain" Kelsey, one of the victims. Kelsey had worked on the tug-boats in the port of Jacksonville most of his life, hence the honorific "Captain."

His home was on the northwest edge of Jacksonville. By the time I reached it the street paving had disappeared, and I was driving on hard-packed red clay. The large wooden house—three stories tall—looked freshly painted and had a wraparound porch. There were several cars—some very old, some brand new—parked helter-skelter around the front of the house. As I got out of my vehicle and walked toward the door, I noticed a few clusters of Black people on the porch. They looked like they were dressed for Sunday church.

I climbed the stairs to the porch, and as I approached, the front door opened and a woman, neatly dressed in a black dress, stepped towards me.

"Can I help you?" she asked.

"Yes," I responded. "I'm here to see Captain Kelsey."

"I'm his daughter," she said turning. "Follow me."

The large room was full of similarly dressed people. I was the only white person. In the center of the room was Captain Kelsey—in his casket. What could I do? I stepped forward and stood beside the coffin, looking down on him and, as is my custom, said a prayer for his soul. After a decent minute or two, I turned and left, telling his daughter on the way out I was sorry for her loss. Some leads never get covered.

POLICE RELATIONS

By the fall of 1968, I had established law enforcement contacts and made some friends in the counties surrounding Jacksonville. One was the remarkable John Henry Whitehead, sheriff of Union County. When I came into his very rural patch, he was already a long-serving sheriff; he served thirty-three years by the end of his career. Whitehead was a gentleman, well versed in all manner of human frailties. A Navy combat veteran of World War II, he looked and spoke like a lawman, command-ing respect but not fear. He knew his county like the back of his hand, as well as most of its residents. Most importantly, to this first-year FBI agent, he was more than willing to help when I had a lead to "locate and interview" one of the denizens of Union County. Today, Union County still has a Sheriff Whitehead: Brad, John's grandson.

My boyhood friend, Claude Dubos, was now a New York City police officer and an avid hunter. He came to visit us in Florida and perhaps do some whitetail deer hunting. When Sheriff Whitehead heard of Claude's visit, he invited us to join a hunt at his ranch. I soon learned his hunts were rather renowned, and that it was an honor to be invited.

Claude and I showed up in the pre-dawn darkness at the agreed upon crossroad. Whitehead was there with a pickup truck full of braying hounds. Dogs were used to hunt deer in Florida, something unknown to us New York nimrods. About four policemen from Jacksonville were also guests of the sheriff. An additional two or three men, clearly under his command—ranch hands, deputies, maybe both—were tending to the truck and the hounds.

Introductions had not yet been made in the dim light. But enough was said—it didn't take much—for all to know that Claude and I "weren't from 'round these parts." Sheriff Whitehead was barking orders, it was his show, and he was in charge. He instructed where to take the hounds and when to release them. One of the dog handlers said he'd drive the hounds in the truck.

Whitehead quickly responded, "No, you won't. You walk 'em over," he ordered. "Dawgs are like policemen," he continued. "Once you start letting 'em ride around, they'll never get out and work again."

I chuckled. Claude laughed out loud. Even in the dim dawn, we could see these Jacksonville cops looking daggers at us. Later that day, once they learned Claude was a cop, they warmed up. Laughter about cops was tolerated—from another cop. By that point, we were enjoying an informal but generous lunch at the ranch.

The sheriff's rustic ranch was on the top of a small hill—there aren't any big hills in Florida. We gathered around picnic tables and barbecue pits. Only a few yards from the tables was an enclosure of tall flat boards strung together with wire. Inside the enclosure was a black bear. A really big bear.

Claude and I were fascinated by the bear; the others had seen it before. They handed us sugarcane, cut into one-or two-foot stalks. We each—tentatively at first—held our breath and pushed the sugarcane stalks through the inches-wide openings in the boards. Before long, we were shoving the sugarcane directly into the bear's mouth. He was now standing on his hind legs, front paws braced on the boards. We were eye to eye. The bear munched ravenously on the sugarcane, a frothy white foam running from his mouth and dripping off his chin.

The fur on the bear's body flowed in a pattern that left a tiny bald spot in the center of his chest. Whitehead said, "Oh he loves it when you pet him there." We looked at him. He encouraged us, "I swear, he'll lie down and purr like a kitten." Claude took a breath, reached between the wooden slats, and touched the spot.

The bear let out a mighty roar, slamming its massive body into the rickety wood, causing the whole enclosure to shake. Claude and I leapt back in terror. We likely screamed as well. Our "audience" howled with laughter. Some were rolling on the grass convulsed in fits. Although no deer were taken that day, the others agreed it was more than worth it just for that moment. We were not so sure.

AN ASSASSINATION AND A LESSON

On April 4, 1968, Dr. Martin Luther King, Jr. was murdered in Memphis, Tennessee. Reaction across the nation was immediate and widespread. The FBI launched a massive investigation to identify and apprehend the killer. While that ultimately successful effort was underway, Alfred Daniel "A.D." Williams King, the slain leader's only brother, was in Jacksonville organizing a mourners' march, which was to start at the Civic Auditorium.

It was three days after King's death when the march got underway. Twenty-five hundred people is a big crowd anywhere, but a march this size was a real challenge for this Florida town. Riots had broken out in other American cities, and major unrest had been ongoing for three days in the nation's capital. Hundreds of buildings were burned, thirteen people were killed, and the violent crowds got close to the White House. The unrest would continue through the next day. Somewhat understandably, national leadership wanted all demonstrations covered. The Jacksonville field office sent all the agents assigned to civil rights and internal security to "monitor" the huge gathering.

Were they there to protect the demonstrators, watch out for civil rights violations, or gather intelligence? The FBI's role was not clear. The Attorney General Guidelines were still years away.

On the march day, we learned the Ku Klux Klan would be staging a counterdemonstration. The Klansmen arrived from rural counties in cars and trucks and were staging in vacant lots only a few blocks north of the federal building. Their march towards the civic auditorium would take them right past our building. The few agents still in the office, myself included, were sent onto the street. We were now to "monitor" (whatever that meant) the Klan march.

There were less than a half dozen of us. We spread out on the street alongside the Federal Building, where some of our Bureau cars were parallel parked. There were not many people on the street, and we were clearly recognizable as FBI in our business suits and ties. Within minutes, the Klansmen arrived. They were not wearing their infamous white robes. Not much of a "march," just fifty to one hundred guys shuffling along. All men, all ages, many in plaid work shirts and bib overalls, some carrying brown bag lunches and thermoses. I was posted near the end of the street where they would pass last.

Motion caught my peripheral vision and I turned left to face the commotion. At that very instant, I caught the sight of an agent landing a classic right hook to the jaw of a Klansman. That's all I saw. I ran towards the scene, twenty to thirty feet away. When I got there, the agent and Klansman were locked together in a bear hug. With the help of a third agent, we yanked them apart and handcuffed the Klansman. His friends were cursing and screaming at us, but none of them moved in to fight us. We hustled the Klansman into the building and up to our office, where we fingerprinted and photographed him. He kept claiming the agent had hit him; we advised him he was being arrested for assaulting a federal officer.

George McBride, the agent who landed that perfectly executed right, was a lot older than me, everybody was. But McBride was full-head-of-white-hair old and well past retirement age. Yet, I saw him land that punch. He breathlessly gave us a full explanation right there, which I would hear repeated many times right up till it was rendered as testimony in federal district court in that very same building months later.

McBride explained that he knew this Klansman and the others, as for years he'd covered Nassau County, Florida, which many of these characters called home. As the Klan marchers were parading down the street, one tossed something under a Bureau car parked along the curb, which turned out to be the balled-up brown bag he had used for his lunch. McBride took a step forward and called to the Klansman, by name, "Hey, what did you toss under there?" At that, the Klansman swung a roundhouse right, which our white-haired George claimed he blocked with his left forearm, then classically followed with the right to the jaw.

In the back of my mind, I just did not believe him. I had seen the older agent hit the Klansman. I knew there was a lot of bad blood between these old-timers and the Klan; they had been sparring for years. I believed George had just popped him. But I kept my own counsel.

For the charge of assault, a blow does not have to land. Taking a swing at someone is assault; landing the blow is battery, and it certainly seems more serious to a jury if a blow is landed. A notorious Klan lawyer, Jesse Benjamin Stoner Jr., came down from Atlanta to defend his confrere. "JB" Stoner was widely known—cover of *Life* magazine notoriety—and he attracted more attention to the government's somewhat weak case.

Just as the Klansman's trial for assault was getting underway, there was the proverbial last-minute bombshell. Unbeknownst to us, the intelligence unit of Jacksonville City Police had been observing the march from the second floor of a store directly across the street from where I had been standing. They were focused on the Klan marchers as they came down the street—focused with a 16-millimeter camera. They made the film available and it showed the jurors—and me—in living color how the entire episode unfolded.

Exactly as the veteran FBI agent testified: The Klansman threw the first punch.

I was wrong to suspect George McBride. You can't always believe your own eyes. You may not have all the facts. That was the most important lesson I learned.

CHAPTER FOUR

BURIED ALIVE

I n the aftermath of the 1932 kidnapping of the Lindbergh baby, a law was enacted that made kidnapping a federal crime[3] and the investigation of kidnapping for ransom quickly became an FBI specialty. Although such crimes were rare, we had trained for them from our first days at Quantico. As a newly minted agent, I was involved in one such case while assigned in Jacksonville, Florida.

THE CRIME

The Barbara Jane Mackle kidnapping began, ironically, in the middle of a mother's efforts to protect her daughter. It was December 1968, and the Hong Kong flu pandemic had spread across the world. In the United States alone, the disease would kill 100,000 people. Barbara Jane Mackle, a twenty-year-old student at Emory University in Atlanta, Georgia, was among those who had become sick.

---

[3] The 1932 Lindbergh Kidnapping Act, Title 18, United States Code, § 1201.

Her mother, Mrs. Jane Mackle, wanted to get her out of the dormitory and back to the family home in Coral Gables, Florida, for the Christmas holidays. Mrs. Mackle picked up Barbara and began the 670-mile drive to Coral Gables. While still in Georgia, they stopped for the night at a Rodeway Inn. At around five o'clock in the morning on Tuesday, December 17, someone knocked on the door of their room. As Mrs. Mackle would later recall, a man and a boy were standing outside. The man said he was with the police, and the pair came inside. They forced Mrs. Mackle to the floor of the motel room and tied her up. Then they took her daughter and drove away.

The man who attacked them was Gary Steven Krist. An escapee from a California state prison, the then twenty-three-year-old had managed for the past two years to live under the assumed name of George Deacon. The boy—contrary to Mrs. Mackle's impression—was not a boy at all, but a woman named Ruth Eisemann-Schier, who had met Krist while working at the University of Miami's Institute of Marine Science. She was intelligent and clever. Born in Honduras to Austrian immigrants, Eisemann-Schier was fluent in Spanish and German as well as English.

The two kidnappers took Barbara to a remote area in Georgia, near the town of Duluth, where they had prepared a coffin-like reinforced box in a shallow grave. They put her inside, closed the lid, and filled in the trench with dirt. Leaving her buried alive, they walked away.

The box had small air holes connected by tubes to the surface, however, along with a small battery-powered lamp that soon failed, leaving Barbara imprisoned in the darkness. They also left her a plastic bottle of water.

An awfully long countdown began.

THE INVESTIGATION

The FBI became aware of the kidnapping later that morning, after Krist made a ransom demand: he wanted $500,000 to be delivered in Miami. It seemed highly likely the two suspects would travel from Georgia to

Miami to collect the money. Their most probable route would take them down Interstate 95, right through Jacksonville—where I was a new agent.

We soon had an all-hands-on-deck meeting and received orders from our supervisors. The city of Jacksonville was divided into sectors for canvassing. I was sent to the north, while others were sent east, west, and south to check out the motels along the interstate. We had some information to go on from Barbara's mother. She provided descriptions of the man and the second person, whom she still thought was a boy.

All day long, our team of agents checked motels and gas stations, looking for a man and a boy, perhaps traveling with a young woman. In the process, we alerted managers and employees at these locations to be on the lookout for these people of interest. Between hard-working agents and alert citizens, we soon had eyes everywhere.

But it was all to no effect. No one reported seeing the kidnappers. By six that evening, the focus of the investigation had shifted to the expected scene of the ransom payment—Miami.

The Jacksonville office was asked to get ten or twelve cars to Miami—350 miles south—along with agents to work the case, which in Bureau parlance was now designated a "Special" (the rare major case investigation to receive extra resources and attention). I was one of about a dozen agents assigned to drive a car to Miami that evening. There was only one person to each car because Miami wanted the cars as much as they wanted us agents. We were given strict orders. In those days, especially as new agents, we followed our orders. We were told to get there as fast as possible.

RACE THROUGH THE NIGHT

It was a hair-raising experience. A dozen of us spread out on Interstate 95, driving south in the dark at nearly ninety miles per hour. At several points, the Florida Highway Patrol cut in to stop us reckless speeders—before learning who we were and what we were doing.

They then escorted us in a series of relays. Thank God they cleared a path for us, although we still got very spread out throughout the night. My hands gripped the steering wheel so tightly for so long, I didn't think I could open them again.

In Miami, confusion awaited us. As in most major cases, multiple FBI field offices were involved. Today the FBI has a template or at least a checklist for running things. This "Special" seemed to me to be run by the seat of the pants. By the time we got there, the Miami agents, who had been working nonstop for a long time, handed off a variety of routine leads to us. Bill Baker, no relation, who had also raced through the night, was assigned the boring but key task of recording the serial numbers on the ransom bills.

Early that evening, there was an unsuccessful attempt at a pay-off on the Tamiami Trail, Route 41, on the outskirts of Miami. It was interrupted by two uniformed police officers unknowingly driving into the pickup site. A car the kidnappers had used was abandoned as they fled on foot. The registration in the car was under the name of George Deacon, which turned out to be the alias Krist had been using. Fingerprints found in the car would eventually lead to his true identity.

I was sent with some other agents to join the search of the nearby area. A witness thought he had seen someone throw something out of a car window. We were told to search along the edge of the road for anything of interest.

As I was walking up and down the side of the Tamiami Trail, I realized I didn't know who had given me these orders. In fact, I did not know who most of the other agents were. There were agents from the Tampa and Jacksonville divisions, as well as the people from Miami, who I assumed were giving us the orders.

It turned out this one fellow—with a lot to say—was Billy Vessels. He had been a football star at The University of Oklahoma and was now employed by Robert Mackle, the victim's father. Vessels was both a bodyguard and right-hand man to Mackle. I remember walking along the side of the road and hearing a couple of agents asking, "Who is this guy?"

When they learned who he was, they asked if anyone had checked out Vessels. It turned out he had absolutely nothing to do with the kidnapping, but initially we were suspicious because none of us had been thoroughly briefed as the massive investigation was quickly thrown together.

Robert Mackle was the kind of man who would have his own bodyguard. He was a multimillionaire land developer, with properties on both coasts of Florida. The Mackle family home in Coral Gables was a mansion. Among the Mackle developments were the Spring Hill and Deltona communities, and Mackle Island in Biscayne Bay. Richard Nixon, who was preparing to take office after winning the presidential election just a month earlier, had his vacation home on Mackle Island.

The incoming president knew Robert Mackle. FBI Director J. Edgar Hoover, then in his forty-fourth year of running the Bureau, also knew Mackle. So, a central figure in this case was an extremely wealthy and well-connected man. All crime victims should be treated equally, but the reality is when somebody is wealthy and well-connected, it puts extra pressure on an investigation.

Today, $500,000 might seem not much of a ransom for a multimillionaire's daughter. But when adjusted for inflation, its value comes to about $4 million in today's dollars.

After the debacle of the first payoff, a full day went by before the kidnappers made contact again—even though Krist and Eisemann-Schier knew Barbara Mackle was trapped underground all the while, with only small tubes to bring air into her coffin.

THE RANSOM DROP

Agents were in the Mackle mansion on Biscayne Bay the next evening when the family finally received new ransom instructions. Robert Mackle—who had, at the kidnappers' instruction, driven the car with the money during the first payoff attempt—was now totally exhausted. In a call with the kidnappers, an agreement was reached that Billy Vessels would be the driver this evening.

We gathered under the lights of a shopping center parking lot. There were nearly forty of us agents there. Again, no one fully knew who was who. By this time, at least three days into the case, most of us were from other divisions, mainly Jacksonville and Tampa (most of the Miami agents had been sent home to sleep, because they had been up so long.) Unlike the Miami agents, we lacked the familiarity with the streets and neighborhoods. An inspector from Washington, Rex Schroeder, was now running the case. With Billy Vessels standing beside him, he stood on a car under the parking lot lights to explain the plan and our instructions.

The kidnappers had instructed Vessels to come alone, driving Robert Mackle's limousine, bringing the $500,000 ransom in a suitcase. A swarm of journalists and photographers were covering the unfolding story, as well, so there was fear the payoff would be interrupted again.

The events were set to unfold in a tiny neighborhood in Coral Gables; Schroeder did not want to use too many cars and create a scene. He announced we would have two teams. The first to act would be the blocking team, which would stop photographers from following the payoff car. Next would be the pursuit team, which would follow the payoff car at a distance.

After telling us this rather brief plan, he pointed to two agents in the crowd and said, "You'll be the blocking car." I was one of the two selected. The other was Bill Baker, also from the Jacksonville Division. So, we would have two Bakers, neither of whom knew the local streets, working in tandem. Then Schroeder gestured to two other agents to drive the pursuit cars. Unlike the previous evening, at least I now knew who was giving us orders.

To perform our blocking role, Bill and I positioned our cars facing each other from the bottoms of driveways on opposite sides of the rather narrow street leading from the Mackle home. We were to wait for the limo to pass and then block any pursuers. Details of how to do this were left unsaid, but it had to be done.

The kidnappers had specified Billy Vessels should drive the limo alone. But in Schroeder's secret alteration of that plan, an agent named

Billy Kittle was hidden in the trunk. Using a walkie-talkie, Billy Kittle relayed what Vessels began saying as they pulled out of the driveway. So, to add to the confusion, we had a Billy in the front and a Billy in the trunk.

Kittle, much senior to me, was also from the Jacksonville Field Office, where he was a firearms and defensive-tactics instructor. He had quickly become the right-hand man to Schroeder, the inspector who had been sent down from FBI Headquarters in Washington to run the show.

We were all listening in our vehicles as the limo left the house and Kittle described going down the driveway and turning right. A few seconds later, they came through the darkness right past my car. As soon as the limo passed, I drove forward. Bill Baker also inched out in the opposite driveway; we touched bumpers in the middle of the road, creating an instant barricade.

Sure enough, another vehicle suddenly appeared and screeched to a halt, almost crashing into us. It was a small car carrying a photographer. We had blocked him. But then he backed up and drove onto the lawn beside me. So, I reversed back up the driveway, blocking him again. This went on two or three times with the paparazzi trying to get past us, as Bill Baker and I screeched up and down the driveways to block him. Eventually, he did a fast turn in the street and went back the way he came. The limo had gotten away safely.

We then listened to the surveillance reports from the pursuit cars, which were now several blocks out into the larger neighborhood. According to the plan, we moved toward the main action.

The payoff was successful. Billy and Billy's car delivered the money to the two kidnappers, while the pursuit cars were still at a distance. Then the question became what happened to the car with the kidnappers and the money after it left the payoff site. By radio, Billy Kittle relayed Billy Vessels' sketchy description of the kidnappers' car. One of the pursuit cars had followed it—at a distance—to a street entrance. The agents thought the kidnappers' car would emerge from the other end of the street.

It turned out the kidnappers had this part of the evening very well planned.

FLIGHT OVER WATER

When the agents in the pursuit cars turned down the street, they found it led nowhere. The street dead-ended in a cul-de-sac on a spit of land jutting into Biscayne Bay. Where the pavement ended, there was a circular, waist-high wall, and beyond that a drop to the water. The kidnappers had abandoned their car and escaped.

I came upon that scene just a minute or two later. There were already three or four agents strung out along the wall on this very dark night. They were just standing at the waist-high wall, looking down into the even darker water. The kidnappers had disappeared.

We learned later the two kidnappers had become separated. Krist, with the money, sped off in a boat; Eisemann-Schier disappeared. Very shortly, we were all instructed to go to another rallying point. Schroeder had already started to arrange the next phase of the plan.

We were told the kidnappers must be out on the water in a small boat. We had a rough idea of what it might look like, but we needed boats ourselves to search for it. Some of us were sent to a US Coast Guard station while others were sent to the Miami Harbor Police. I ended up with another FBI agent in a small fast boat, operated by Coast Guard personnel.

We spent the rest of that night on Biscayne Bay stopping small boats. The Coast Guard turned their searchlight on them, while we agents stood ready with our drawn weapons. In the process, we stopped some people who started throwing stuff overboard: it turned out they were poachers stealing from other people's crab traps. Interrupting a few of these little poaching operations and really scaring them seemed like hot stuff to this relatively new agent. I was later told far more hilarious stories of others breaking up romantic interludes on the waters of Biscayne Bay.

But while we were having this adventure, Barbara Mackle was still buried.

DIGGING IN GEORGIA

On December 20, having successfully gotten the ransom money, Krist made one phone call to the Atlanta field division. In those days, they still used human operators plugging cords into a physical "switchboard" to connect phone calls. As was almost always the case at the time, the operator who answered was a woman. Krist identified himself as "the kidnapper" and then stated, "I'm only going to say this once." The operator was alert enough to write down what he said: "Here's where the Mackle girl is buried." Thank God for that quick-thinking woman who made those notes. Krist hung up and never called back. The Atlanta agents immediately went to the area to start a search.

It was a rural area around Berkeley Lake. Krist's instructions weren't clear, so teams went out looking at two or three different places. Tom Renaghan, a friend of mine who was then an agent in Atlanta, was at Berkeley Lake that day. Around two in the afternoon Renaghan with another agent, Bill Colombell, was about fifty or a hundred yards away from the main group of searchers, when they heard a noise. They moved towards the sound and discovered a spot where the ground looked like it had been disturbed. They lacked any proper digging tools, but they quickly got to work, digging with their bare hands. They knew Barbara had been buried a long time and did not want to experience the horror of uncovering the young woman just hours or even minutes after she had died. They desperately tore at the soil.

In his description years later, Renaghan clearly still felt strong emotions. The spot they found was indeed the place where the kidnappers had entombed their victim. The agents got down to the surface of the box and realized they were digging in the right place. But they also knew that by now she had been buried for well over three days. In fact, it would turn out she had been underground for eighty-three hours.

They did not know what they would find as they pulled off the lid.

But there she was. Barbara's eyes and mouth were open, and she looked right at them. They would repeat, years later, that they were overcome by emotion at the recovery. They said she didn't seem at all frightened.

Colombell took Barbara in his arms. He carried her back to their car, which was between fifty and one hundred yards away. Later, when reflecting on that day, they both recognized the power of their emotions and adrenaline. Although gym regulars, neither had ever curled a hundred pounds. Yet, with arms in the curled position, Barbara—who weighed at least that much—was carried all those yards.

She said she never lost faith and believed she would be rescued.

Later, people who processed the crime scene in the Atlanta division found the water the kidnappers had left with Barbara in her coffin contained a powerful sedative. This was to keep her calm, quiet, and still. She was thus a little bit drowsy when she was found. Considering what she had been through—and she was ill with the Hong Kong flu even before she was kidnapped—she was not in such bad shape.

But both kidnappers were still at large.

THE MANGROVE MESS

Krist, on the water, continued his flight around the tip of Florida and up the West coast of the peninsula. Along the way, he purchased a new boat with some of the ransom cash. The serial numbers on the currency, earlier recorded by Bill Baker, confirmed he was the kidnapper and helped in tracking him down. He was pursued to Punta Gorda, where an exhausting search ensued, eventually focusing on Hog Island.

Agents, mostly from the Tampa division, searched day and night in the swamp. As they tired, it was again necessary to call in reinforcements from other offices. Back in Jacksonville, the SAC picked my friend, Jim Siano and another agent to go immediately to join the search. They went to a nearby private airport and boarded a small plane to fly them down to Punta Gorda. Upon arrival they each teamed up with a deputy sheriff who knew the area. After midnight on another very dark night, Siano and the deputy got onto an airboat and headed off to Hog Island.

As they were heading out with a spotlight on the front of the airboat, the deputy noticed some tracks and started pulling the boat over toward the shore. Siano got into the water and approached the island by foot. He worked his way onto the island through mangrove trees, whose roots grow above the surface of the water. The deputy kept the searchlight pointed alternately on and in front of him.

As Siano was picking his way through the area, trying to find the tracks again, there was a gunshot. He moved toward the noise and came upon Krist, who was trying to hide under one of the mangrove trees. Siano realized Krist was in poor condition as he handcuffed him. Making it back to the boat was a major challenge. Krist was exhausted, so Siano carried him through the vines and mangrove roots.

Just as an agent had carried the victim out of the mud in Georgia the previous day, so now an agent carried one of the perpetrators out of the muck in Florida.

After getting Krist onto the boat, Siano and the deputy took the prisoner back to a landing on the mainland. There, Schroeder, the inspector from Washington, and his now sidekick and number two, Kittle (the senior agent from the Jacksonville office), took over. They took Krist into their own custody, put him into an FBI vehicle, and took off.

Jim Siano had almost singlehandedly apprehended this kidnapper, yet the glory of the arrest was snatched from his hands. I seldom saw anything like this again in my FBI career. And I knew then that when the time came, I would never behave like those managers.

Krist was convicted in 1969 and sentenced to life in prison. Surprisingly, he was paroled after only ten years of imprisonment to obtain a medical degree. Krist, like so many criminals, was described as charming. That may have been a factor in his early pardon.

He finished medical school and went on to practice for a few years. In 2003, authorities revoked his medical license and he then got involved in dealing cocaine with the use, once again, of small boats.

In 2006, Krist and four accomplices were apprehended off the coast of Alabama in a sailboat loaded with cocaine. US District Judge Callie Virginia Granade of Mobile sent Krist to prison for sixty-five months, the maximum she could impose for cocaine smuggling.

When Krist finished that sentence, he wanted to move to Georgia where his wife lived on a farm. The farm had an underground bunker, where he originally had a cocaine laboratory. The federal probation authorities in Georgia refused to be responsible for his supervision unless he agreed to fill in the bunker and wear a GPS monitor, and Krist refused. So, he continued to live in Alabama on a sailboat docked on Dauphin Island. One day he sailed off. He went to Venezuela and then Cuba, where in August 2012 he was arrested and flown to Miami. When he arrived in Miami, he had over $11,000 on him. Judge Granade revoked his parole and again sentenced him to the maximum available: forty months.

Released again in July 2015, Krist is now living in rural Auburn, Georgia.

BACK TO BASICS—FINGERPRINTS

Unlike her co-conspirator, the second kidnapper, Ruth Eisemann-Schier, vanished. The hunt for her continued, however, and she became the first woman to appear on the FBI's "Top Ten" list of most wanted criminals.

It seemed Eisemann-Schier had completely disappeared. It was not until two and half months after the kidnapping, in February 1969, that she would finally be apprehended. She was found working as a carhop at a luncheonette in Norman, Oklahoma, near The University of Oklahoma.

What tripped her up was the same thing that led us to the identity of Gary Steven Krist, who had been using a different name at the time of the kidnapping: fingerprints. The Bureau had taken the latent prints found in the first abandoned car in Miami with the "Deacon" registration and searched them against the ten-print cards in the old identification division. That is how we learned the true name of Krist, whose ten-prints were on file from his previous arrests. But Ruth Eisemann-Schier had never been arrested or fingerprinted. It would have to be a different approach for her.

In the months she spent as a fugitive, the FBI's identification division started their own "special." They decided to search all new incoming ten-print cards from females, both civil and criminal, against the unmatched latent prints recovered from the kidnappers' cars. Everything then was done manually—an incredibly manpower-intensive operation. It was worse than searching for a "needle in a haystack," since the haystack might not even contain a needle.

But when Eisemann-Schier applied for a job as a nurse's aide at the university hospital in Norman, she had to have her fingerprints taken as part of the application process. She may have felt confident that she had no fingerprint records in the United States at that time, and so agreed to have them taken.

Just six days after submitting her prints, though, the identification division made the match. Eisemann-Schier was arrested.

She was sentenced to ten years but was released after four and deported to her native Honduras. Now a grandmother, Ruth Eisemann-Schier, still using that name, is living by the sea in Tegucigalpa, Honduras.

Jim Siano—the agent who grabbed Krist—and I would remain friends and have other adventures.

Bill Baker, who recorded the ransom's serial numbers and was the other half of the blocking team, rose in the FBI ranks to become an assistant director. He would later hold a similar position at the CIA. We have remained friends, too.

Tom Renaghan, who dug up the victim with his bare hands, would also remain a friend. Together in Washington, DC, we would confront criminals and politicians, who were sometimes one and the same.

Virginia "Ginnie" Granade, the federal district judge who twice sent Krist to prison, is someone I came to know years after the Mackle case—and before she became a judge—when I was working in Mobile,

Alabama. She was an assistant US attorney and a great law enforcement partner.

The laborious work of the old Identification Division, as noble as it was, has been greatly streamlined by the Automated Fingerprint Identification System (AFIS) and now Next Generation Identification (NGI), whose birth at the FBI's Criminal Justice Information Services Division (CJIS) in West Virginia I assisted at as a consultant.

And the FBI's management of major cases has vastly improved.

CHAPTER FIVE

MARCHING ORDERS FROM A SAINT

I was working in Washington and serving as a director on the board of the Fordham University Club of Washington, DC, when we got word that Mother Teresa would be visiting Washington.

It was early in 1982; Mother Teresa had been awarded the Nobel Peace Prize two years earlier. She was coming to DC to visit President Ronald Reagan and to receive an honorary degree from one of Washington's universities. This visit was to occur sometime in May or June.

The Fordham Club sent a request to Mother Teresa asking to honor her at our annual dinner with the Brien McMahon award. She said she would accept the award, but did not want a dinner and requested instead that any dinner funds be given to the poor.

The board immediately agreed and then wondered, "What do we do?"

What would be the appropriate setting to present the award?

Father Gilbert Hartke of Catholic University generously offered the use of the Hartke Theater on the Catholic University campus. Word of Mother Teresa's visit also reached some other members of the DC community.

Milton Kronheim, owner of the eponymous liquor company, which was then the major liquor distributor in DC, provided wine for the reception after Mother Teresa's talk. Joe Danzansky, an owner of Giant Foods Inc, which was then an independent chain, provided bread and cheese. I think it is worth noting these two businessmen were members of DC's Jewish community. It is a testimony not only to their generosity but also Mother Teresa's ability to move all people to do good.

The award presentation was a daytime event on May 31, 1982, on what turned out to be a warm sunny afternoon. Tables were set up on the terrace, just outside the Hartke Auditorium, for this modest— in keeping with Mother Teresa's request—reception of bread, wine, and cheese.

Anne could not attend that weekend—she was at Walter Reed Hospital as an Army Reserve nurse. So, my then thirteen-year-old daughter, accompanied me to the event. Father Hartke was there with his friend—and former McMahon Award recipient—the actress Helen Hayes.

Mother Teresa addressed the club membership in the auditorium. It is a relatively small, tiered theater. I will never forget the sight of this very tiny woman facing all of us sitting in rows above her and her remarks to us:

> *"Don't try to be like me.*
> *You are not called to do what I do.*
> *You all have important jobs here in Washington.*
> *That is what God wants you to do.*
> *Do your work here well.*
> *You are husbands and fathers.*
> *God is calling you to be a good husband and*
> *a good father.*

Do that, it is what you must do, and it is very important.
That is what you are called to do."

And then:

"If you want something, just ask for it."

Mother Teresa spoke English in a simple, direct way, using only short declarative sentences.

Later, at the reception on the terrace, she walked energetically among the guests, smiling the whole time. She had a large white bag hanging from her arm. (The bag was like some I'd seen carried by brides at weddings.) Attendees were placing envelopes in the bag as Mother Teresa passed by.

One interchange I recall vividly from the reception:

Immediately after depositing an envelope in Mother Teresa's bag, a woman joined the group where I was standing. She knew several people and chatted with them about how she was managing since being widowed a year ago. She said just the week prior, in her kitchen in Northern Virginia, she had been reviewing her finances. She realized her husband had left her financially well off and she really didn't need all her savings. She also said she wasn't a fan of organized charities. As she was sitting in her kitchen pondering what to do (really praying), she said aloud "If Mother Teresa was here, I would give her five thousand dollars." At that very moment, her kitchen phone rang. "How would you like to meet Mother Teresa?" asked her friend on the line. She looked at us and said, "Five thousand dollars—I knew where it was going."

Takeaways from that day:

There are a lot of good people in the world.
Small miracles happen all the time.
What each of us do is important.
If you want something, just ask for it.

CHAPTER SIX

BRAVERY AMONGST CHAOS

I n the late 1960s the United States suffered a rash of aircraft hijackings now largely forgotten. Almost since the dawn of commercial
aviation, there have been federal laws addressing crimes in the air.
They evolved from older laws concerning crimes on the high seas.
Hence, "Aircraft Piracy," the colorful federal term for aircraft hijacking
or skyjacking.[4]

Also lost in history is an exciting case, which should be right up
there with Captain Sully and all the other commercial pilots recognized
as heroes. This one is special for several reasons. One is that my friend,
Special Agent Jim Siano, is also a hero in the case. I played a minor role.

TWA Flight 486, a Boeing 727 aircraft, originated in Phoenix and
was headed to Washington National (now Ronald Reagan Washington
National) Airport on June 4, 1970 with Arthur Gates Barkley on board.

---

[4] Title 49, U.S. Code, § 465.

THE AIRCRAFT HIJACKER

Unlike prior aircraft hijackers, Arthur Barkley's motive was not to get a one-way trip to Cuba. Barkley was in the habit of traveling to Washington, DC to make a case that the IRS owed him $471.78. He finally asked the Supreme Court to consider his evidence. They declined.

That slight was the last straw for Barkley. Early on the morning of June 4, 1970, he kissed his wife goodbye and said, "I'm going to settle the tax case today."

There was no airport screening in 1970. The brawny forty-nine-year-old in a rumpled plaid sports jacket wasn't searched in Phoenix; he was able to get on the flight with his weapons. As flight #486 passed over Albuquerque, New Mexico, Barkley entered the cockpit with his .22-caliber pistol, a straight razor, and a steel can full of gasoline. He threatened to incinerate the passengers unless he was given $100 million. The pilot radioed ahead about the hijacker and his demands.

TWA officials were baffled by Barkley's demand for ransom. Up until that point, American skyjackers had only been interested in obtaining passage to Cuba. No one had envisioned a hijacker trying to swap passengers for money. There was a crew of six plus fifty-one passengers—men, women, and children—on the plane.

Without considering the long-term implications of submitting to extortion, TWA decided to simply give in to (a portion of) Barkley's demands. The airline managed to round up $100,750 in cash from two banks near Dulles International Airport, where Barkley had forced the plane to land. TWA hoped and assumed Barkley would settle for this smaller amount.

Instead, Barkley was enraged at being short-changed. He dumped the cash on the floor of the cockpit, ordered the plane to take off at once, and radioed back a message that he addressed directly to President Richard Nixon: "You don't know how to count money, and you don't even know the rules of law."

All that happened before the FBI was even aware of the hijacking. TWA either didn't think to notify or chose not to notify the FBI.

Apparently, the FAA at Dulles was also slow to react and coordinate with others. So, as we were first alerted and told to head out to Dulles, we didn't know what had already transpired: The plane with the hijacker had come and gone and a ransom of sorts had already been paid.

THE FBI RESPONSE

Barkley had the plane circle the airport for two hours. By this time, TWA officials had decided to tell the FBI about the ongoing aircraft piracy and to let the Bureau run the show. Soon most of Alexandria field office agents were at or on their way to the airport. One of the first agents to arrive took up a position in the tower so we could monitor communications with the plane.

The SAC was Jack McDermott, an outstanding leader and a very strong personality. He was among the first to arrive at Dulles Airport. The folks at headquarters, he pointed out, were "thirty miles away. We are not going to run every decision past them," he said.

We watched the plane circling. The tower informed us it would make another landing. Meanwhile, we were to get money together and put it on the runway because the hijacker had threatened if the money wasn't on the airstrip, he'd dive the plane into the White House.

We wanted to make sure the plane landed at Dulles, so we had agents running all over the airport trying to get suitable bags for the money. The pressure to quickly locate bags added to the tension. They found some duffle bags—postal sacks—in the baggage area. We filled them with torn-up newspapers, to look like they were full of cash. Barkley would see we had put the "money" out there for him. We lined the runway with one hundred mail sacks, each allegedly stuffed with $1 million, then we had the tower tell the pilot where the money was located. We also had them ask the pilot to land the plane on that specific runway so the hijacker could see the "money sacks."

Then we simply waited for the plane to land.

As soon as the Boeing 727 landed and rolled to a stop, the FAA police shot out the tires from a distance with rifle fire to disable the plane so Barkley couldn't crash it into the White House.

Instead, additional confusion ensued. A passenger reacted to the gunfire by kicking open one of the jet's emergency exits and scrambling out over a wing. A flight attendant, on her own initiative, lowered the center rear exit stairs, something unique to the 727. The flight attendants had earlier resorted to what was then widespread airline practice: free drinks for all when passengers were confronted with some inconvenience. Passengers, many of them quite inebriated after drinking their way through most of the hijacking, began scrambling out that rear exit. Since Barkley was in the cockpit, he did not know this was happening.

Meanwhile, SAC McDermott and a group of agents had driven onto the tarmac, directly behind the plane, so they were not visible from the plane's cockpit. They got out of the vehicles and waited underneath the plane. At that point, the cars were also under the aircraft. We decided to wait a bit to see if Barkley would come out himself or have someone get the money. The front passenger door of the plane eventually opened. Then we heard a gunshot! We couldn't wait any longer. Agents boosted Jim Siano from the roof of a car up to the doorway of the plane where he sort of jumped and was pushed up to grasp the edge of the opened door.

While Jim was still holding on to the door frame, Barkley stepped out from the cockpit, where he had just shot the pilot in the stomach. Barkley saw Jim and began firing, engaging in a gun battle at awfully close range. Jim's return fire hit Barkley's hand, which was gripping the frame of an interior door he was using as cover. Jim then swung further into the cabin. As he moved in, the hijacker jammed his gun into Jim's stomach and pulled the trigger. The gun misfired. Jim was then able to pin Barkley—who was about six feet tall, 220 pounds, and in pretty good shape—to the floor of the plane and handcuff him.

The pilot, Captain Dale C. Hupe, had just made a heroic effort himself to thwart the hijacking. When Barkley shot him, the bullet passed through his abdomen and exited out his back without seriously injuring any vital organs.

Barkley jammed that same gun into Jim's stomach, pulled the trigger, and it misfired. It was amazing because he had already fired it several times. He shot Captain Hupe and, as Jim was hanging, holding onto the door, he had fired shots directly at Jim.

I took custody and control of the firearm and brought it back to the office in Alexandria. Eventually, we sent it to the FBI Laboratory.

Among other issues, the lab needed to figure out why the revolver misfired when Barkley pulled the trigger with the barrel pointing into Jim's stomach. The laboratory's explanation was that it was a Rohm, 22 caliber, a small weapon of inferior quality—the same make and model, in fact, that John Hinckley would use a decade later to shoot President Ronald Reagan.

Jim Siano with Arthur Barkley, the perpetrator of the first skyjacking for ransom. Siano, the hero that day, brought the prisoner back; I took care of the gun. (Everett Collection Historical / Alamy Stock Photo)

The laboratory also concluded Barkley had the weapon in his pocket on the flight and some of the hairs and fibers from his pants pocket mixed with the oil of the gun. That in turn got into the firing mechanism, so when the trigger was pulled, the hammer did not go forward with enough force to ignite the cartridge. In other words, Jim was saved by lint.

Most of the agents stayed at Dulles for many hours conducting the crime scene investigation and interviewing numerous witnesses, including the six members of the flight crew and the fifty-one passengers. Many of the witnesses—passengers—were not only shaken-up and confused by the experience, but some were just plain drunk. At least one witness told the interviewing agent he departed the plane because "they ran out of booze."

Barkley's hand was bandaged on site at Dulles. Jim Siano and I then took him to the office of the US Magistrate in Alexandria for his arraignment hearing. At that point, Barkley clearly explained his motive. He felt he was owed money from an injury he had as a truck driver. In his confused mind, the IRS and the government were responsible for paying the money he was due. This was his "reasoning" for hijacking the plane. I have found on other occasions as well, people can say the weirdest things in a calm and reasonable-sounding voice. Barkley was obviously not in his right mind. He was tried in November 1971 and committed to a psychiatric hospital in Georgia.

Jim Siano was a hero that day, and Jack McDermott demonstrated great leadership. Virtually every one of the approximately fifty agents assigned to the Alexandria field office played some role in the incident. The outcome was an overall success. Yes, the pilot and the subject were wounded, but there were no fatalities. Catastrophic damage was prevented.

Arthur Gates Barkley was the first of many American skyjackers whose primary interest was money. Within a year or two, most of the nation's air hijackings would be for ransom.

THE BACKSTORY

This case exposed many problems that would need to be addressed going forward. There had been a complete lack of cooperation and coordination between the airline, the airport, and the responsible government agencies, both the FBI and the FAA. There was also widespread media criticism of all involved. TWA was criticized, and in turn, the airline criticized the FAA for shooting out the tires of the aircraft.

During the next few years, protocols were ironed out and memoranda of understanding written. The major airlines and the FBI ran drills together. In the FBI, specialist jobs, such as hostage negotiator, evolved. Sophisticated SWAT teams were formed. Today, there's no Hoover-era expectation that the SAC will lead the charge in these situations.

But that was still the expectation on June 4, 1970, back when Jack McDermott did lead the charge. J. Edgar Hoover was still alive, and we were unsure of his reaction. Just a month before, there had been another major incident. A TWA aircraft under the control of a hijacker was on the ground in New York City. At a certain point, as that crisis unfolded, the agent in charge of the FBI's New York office, John F. Malone, took the lead. Using a little-known hatch above the cockpit, he dropped down into it, in his business suit and wing-tipped shoes, armed only with his revolver, and managed to end the standoff. Malone, a dignified mature man, had undertaken a physically arduous task. Many saw him as a hero.

But TWA president Charles C. Tillinghast made a public pronouncement criticizing the FBI's handling of the New York incident. Hoover, as was his wont, responded in kind, and there was the inevitable clash between those giant egos culminating in Hoover sending out an "SAC Letter," which all agents were expected to read. It basically said that we, the FBI, should have nothing more to do with TWA, an instruction many of us thought untenable.

And those standing instructions had echoed though some of our heads throughout the Barkley incident. No doubt they were at the

THE FALL OF THE FBI
· THE FALL OF THE FBI ·

forefront of McDermott's thinking, which made his forthright state- ments and actions that day even more courageous.

The day after the hijacking at Dulles, McDermott called an all- agents meeting in which he read us a somewhat obsequious letter he was sending to Hoover that morning. The letter stressed how proud Hoover could be of the actions of the fine young agents in Alexandria. Frankly, we thought it rather odd. Days went by without a word from FBI Headquarters to Alexandria, pro or con, about the case of aircraft piracy.

I was due to attend a week-long in-service class at FBIHQ the following week. McDermott called me into his office one day and explained that when agents are at headquarters for an in-service, they can request a meeting with the director. He had made an appointment for me, he said.

MEETING MR. HOOVER

My only face-to-face meeting with Hoover was that day in early June of 1970. I was then transferring from Alexandria to New York City and asking for a meeting with the director was the furthest thing from my mind. But Jack McDermott had given me a mission: listen for any remark from Hoover regarding Alexandria and our handling of the pre- vious week's skyjacking.

Those assessments never came.

J. Edgar Hoover addressed me as "Baker," no "Mr." or "Tom." He spoke very rapidly. "Baker, I see you're under transfer to New York. That's our toughest assignment, but most important assignment."

He then started rambling on—and I couldn't get a word in edgewise. He described, as if I already knew about it, an evening at his home. John Ehrlichman and H.R. Haldeman, then two of President Nixon's closest advisors, had come to his house in DC's Forest Hills neighborhood for dinner. I got the impression the visit had taken place in the preceding weeks or month. It sounded like a typical evening for four guys of that era: whiskeys with water, then steaks.

· 55 ·

Hoover mentioned he first had drinks with the visitors in his living room. Then "Clyde joined us" (Clyde Tolson, long-serving deputy director). They had steaks for dinner, then descended to the finished basement for after-dinner drinks at the bar, also typical of the era.

Hoover seemed surprised and annoyed when the press showed up outside his front doorstep at the end of the evening and "Nixon's boys" urged him to step outside with them into the blinding lights. But he said, "I would not" as he felt his "face was flush from the bourbons and water." Waving his hands at the sides of his face, he rapidly repeated, "bourbons and water."

We later learned that Ehrlichman and Haldeman's mission that evening was to suggest to Hoover that he resign, but apparently they could not get a word in edgewise, either. Hoover would die in less than two years, on May 2, 1972, and Ehrlichman and Haldeman, key players in the "Watergate" affair, would be in prison within three years.

Days following Barkley's skyjacking, I met with FBI Director J. Edgar Hoover. He did not say a word about the recently resolved skyjacking; he did hold forth about a recent evening with "Nixon's boys."

President Nixon visited Captain Hupe in the hospital and had the wounded hero to the White House. Turns out, they had been friends for decades. Perhaps that's why Hoover never imposed any negative consequences on McDermott or our Alexandria office.

By the end of June, I left Alexandria for New York and new adventures.

CHAPTER SEVEN

BACK TO THE BRONX

I n the summer of 1970, America was smack in the middle of anti-Vietnam war, New Left-driven, radical unrest and the FBI, in turn, would be at the center of that maelstrom.

One of the keys to restoring calm, as then-president Richard Nixon saw it, was quashing the Weatherman Underground, a small but violent spin-off of the Students for a Democratic Society (SDS). Although the Weatherman Underground engaged in many forms of violence, their preferred tactic was small-scale bombings. (They were limited by budget, not appetite for destruction.)

I, along with several other agents, was transferred from Alexandria to New York City that summer. With the situation in the nation, we had assumed all agents going into New York would be put on "security work"—something I did not want to do. I had enjoyed the excitement of criminal investigations in Jacksonville and Alexandria, and had developed the self-confidence to believe I was good at it.

The New York FBI Office—known as the NYO—was headed by an assistant director rather than by a SAC. It had far more personnel than any other office, the only one with over a thousand agents.

Consequently, it was divided into several divisions, each of which was headed by a SAC. New York was the first—and for a long time the only—field office so organized. The SAC of the Organized Crime Division in 1970 was Richard Baker.

Before the Monday I was to officially report to the New York office, I went to New York City. My parents still lived in the Bronx, so I was able to stay at their apartment. The next day, I took the subway to East 69th Street, just as I had over five years ago. Then it had been to pick up a job application on the advice of Eddie Murphy. Now I was doing as Saint Mother Teresa would advise me a decade later: "If you want something, just ask for it."

It turned out the NYO's Organized Crime Division was on the 6th floor. I went up there and politely told the SAC's secretary I wished to speak to the boss. She had me wait some time before I was told to go into his office—a big, impressive corner one overlooking 69th Street and 3rd Avenue. An equally impressive executive was installed behind the big desk, trim and mature-looking in his blue Brooks Brothers suit.

Standing before that desk and that man, I went right into my prepared and rehearsed pitch:

"You get agents assigned here all the time who don't know the Bronx from Brooklyn. I do."

I was telling SAC Dick Baker something he likely already knew.

"I can hit the ground running; these other fellas will take a year or more before they even begin to know the city." And so on, in as earnest and sincere a voice as I could muster.

"Mr. Baker," I implored, "I am reporting next Monday morning and I really want to work Organized Crime."

When I finished speaking, Dick Baker asked, "How is baby boy Baker?"

More than three years later, SAC Richard Baker would recall the baby boy Baker incident. As for the immediate matter at hand, though, he made no commitment.

But when twelve agents reported to the NYO the following Monday morning, eleven were assigned to the Security Division. I was the only one assigned elsewhere, to the Organized Crime Division. It was a blessing in more ways than I then knew.

As the 1970s unwound, pressure continued—often all the way from the White House—to "do something" about the violence of the Weather Underground and similar New Left groups. The agents in the NYO's Security Division, which I had avoided being assigned to, *did* do something. However, the tenor and will of the country changed as time moved forward.

The entire Security Division of the NYO came under great scrutiny as the establishment turned against President Nixon. The agents and supervisors who "did something" such as searches and wiretapping of the radicals now fell under the investigative spotlight themselves. In fact, almost every agent who worked on security matters in the early 1970s became the subject of prosecutorial attention.

Recriminations and ill will festered for years. Friendships were terminated; hundreds of thousands of dollars in legal bills were accumulated. John J. Kearney, the supervisor of the NYO's squad 47, was indicted in 1977 on five felony charges for the actions of his agents against those domestic terrorists in 1970 through 1972. Two high-ranking Bureau executives, Edward Miller and Mark Felt, were also convicted in November 1980 for violating the civil rights of Weatherman Underground members by approving the searches. Only a presidential pardon from the newly elected Ronald Reagan in 1981 spared them from prison.

And I was spared by being assigned to the Organized Crime Division in 1970. But it was even better than that. I was assigned to Squad 54 under Supervisor Guy Berado. He had been one of the original agents working Organized Crime (OC) in New York, long before there even was an OC Division. I learned my craft and a lot more from Guy and from the agents I worked with in New York. And I immensely enjoyed my three years there.

At that point in mid-1970, the FBI's organized crime program was transitioning from an intelligence to an operational undertaking. The Apalachin conference in November 1957, a sort of "summit" for

American Mafiosi, was the catalyst that got the FBI's attention. The Bureau's focus had initially been on gathering intelligence on the Mafia. Called for a decade or more the "Top Hoodlum Program," it was just that, a focus on the leaders. The Bureau carried out photo surveillances of Mafia gatherings often, as in the movies, at funerals and weddings. They also arranged the installation of microphone coverage of their homes and offices, which could never be used as evidence as there was not yet any authorizing legislation. But impressive organizational charts of each Mafia family—photos included—were created.

There were not then federal laws specifically targeting the mob. That would soon change. The "Top Hoodlum Program" was superseded by the "Criminal Intelligence Program" or CIP, which placed an emphasis on informant development.

In 1968, Title III[5] would take effect, allowing for the use of wiretaps in federal criminal cases. The principal organized crime that intersected with the FBI's jurisdiction then was illegal gambling. So, the Organized Crime division was somewhat of a hybrid during this transitional period between simply gathering intelligence and making cases against the mob. Five of the squads in the division were each assigned one of the five Mafia families of New York. Squad 54 had the Lucchese family. That was our intelligence mission. We also had responsibility for bookmaking cases.

When I joined Guy Berado's squad in the summer of 1970, they were just starting a bookmaking case targeting a "wire-room" in East Harlem. Being the absolute newest of the new guys, I was assigned to the monitoring team. For nearly eight hours a day for several weeks, I wore headphones to listen to the runners and bookies. It was a literal headache. It was also a fast education in sports and horse bookmaking. Done under Title III, this was a legal wiretap, which would yield evidence for use in court. It was required that an agent listen as the recordings were made. Under the "minimization" rules, if we heard

---

[5] Of the Omnibus Crime Control and Safe Streets Act; Public Law 90-351; Codified as Title 18, U.S. Code, § 2581.

any personal, i.e., non-criminal conversations, we were to turn off the recording for a few minutes. In this case that rarely happened. This was non-stop gambling.

The violation was classified by the FBI as "Interstate Transmission of Wagering Information;" ITWI on the file jacket, pronounced "it-we." The decade-old statute was based on the Wire Act.[6] We were monitoring a wire-room with many phones in a storefront on East 111th Street. They were receiving "line" information—betting odds—from the odds makers in Las Vegas. They were also "laying-off" their excess bets with other bookies in New Jersey and Pennsylvania. Clearly, this was interstate transmission of wagering information. The wire-room was run by "Funzi of East 111th Street." That much was also clear. Not to be confused with Funzi Tieri, around the corner on Pleasant Avenue, who was a member of the Genovese crime family. We believed our Funzi was with the Lucchese crime family. East Harlem was that kind of neighborhood.

Finally, the day came to shut down the wire and move on with the case. A search warrant was obtained for the storefront wire-room and arrest warrants for Funzi and several others. Because of the problematic neighborhood, extensive planning went into the raid and arrests. It was another learning experience to watch Supervisor Berado put this operation together.

With the help of the US Postal Service, a large postal van carried most of us to the storefront on East 111th Street. The agent driving the van, Jim Thornton, was in a postman's uniform, cap and all. Only after we had successfully entered the storefront would additional agents rush to the scene in their cars. In the event the postman ruse did not work, we had sledgehammers and a battering ram in the postal van. Huddled amongst this paraphernalia, the tension was palpable as the van bounced northward over Manhattan's streets.

It worked. We all rushed in. I had been listening to these guys for so long I felt I knew the bad guys we were arresting. Thornton, a big man, immediately returned to the truck. Grabbing a shotgun nestled

---

[6]   Title 18, U.S. Code, § 1084.

THE FALL OF THE FBI

among the sledgehammers, he posted himself in the middle of the side-walk with the shotgun at port-arms. It had the desired effect. We were there for a while. Carting off the arrestees, collecting and bagging the evidence from inside the wire-room took time.

At a certain point, three guys in worn-looking sports jackets came ambling across the street towards us. I happened to be standing beside Berado at that moment. One of the three asked "Who's in charge?" I instinctively glanced towards Guy, who began to answer. Only one of our visitors spoke. He identified himself as an NYPD lieutenant and told us they were "Manhattan North Plainclothes." Guilt was manifest in their body language, shuffling feet, and all but the lieutenant looking at the ground, none of them making eye contact with any of us. The lieutenant asked some questions: How long had we been on this? Did we have an observation post? Guy said "yes," vaguely gesturing to some high-rise buildings further south. I knew we did not have any such look-out post.

Then the big question: "What was the handle, their take?" The truth was we did not know; these things were difficult to estimate, particularly with the bookies always talking in code. But Guy Berado convincingly responded with a number, much larger than I would have imagined. Our visitors shuffled off. Once they were out of earshot, I asked Guy how he came up with that number. He acknowledged he didn't have any idea; he just wanted to stir up some trouble between the mob and these corrupt plainclothes cops.

That October, President Richard Nixon signed the Organized Crime Control Act of 1970 into law[7] to declare "total war against organized crime." The law, authored by US Senator John L. McClellan, a Democrat, and signed by the Republican president, set forth its purpose as "the eradication of Organized Crime in the United States." That statute had thirteen titles, some of which would have lasting significance. Title IX of the Act was called "Racketeer Influenced and Corrupt Organizations," now known as RICO. That title would be continuously

---

[7] Public Law 91-452. Codified as Title 18, U.S. Code, § 1961.

expanded by various judges' rulings and exploited by prosecutors and investigators in the coming years. A powerful tool and a continuing source of controversy, RICO has become the weapon of choice in the ongoing war on organized crime.

Of more immediate importance to us in New York City, at that moment in history, however, was the Act's Title VIII, which created the federal violation[8] of Illegal Gambling Business. It required only that the government show five or more people were involved for thirty or more days in a gambling operation. No interstate aspect had to be shown. Most significantly, there was now a specific provision placing public officials, e.g., police officers, who facilitated this illegal gambling business in the crosshairs. We were about to move even further away from mere criminal intelligence into investigations much more focused on securing convictions.

Also, in October 1970, the Knapp Commission hearings got underway in New York City. The Commission was formed to identify the extent of corruption in the New York City Police Department. The hearings were shocking to many. But they confirmed what we on Squad 54 already knew, that the Plainclothes Divisions were riddled with corruption. The Knapp Commission would issue its final report on December 27, 1972. It provided Squad 54 with lots of work and lots of leads. Ironically, it also led to closer cooperation with units of the NYPD, particularly the PMAD (Public Morals Administrative Division), which oversaw the plainclothes officers.

The war against organized crime, declared by the 1970 crime bill, would progress, pretty much at the same pace as Squad 54's progress against the Lucchese family, bookmaking, and police corruption. My own education continued as well. In New York, I would take part in more raids and arrests, develop my own informants, and secure Title III electronic coverage in a case of my own.

Guy Berado also made me one of his relief supervisors. No pay raise, but the first step into FBI management. The relief fills in for the

---

[8]   Title 18, U.S. Code, § 1955.

supervisor and has the authority to approve outgoing communications and assign new leads and cases.

In that role I found myself reading an incoming informant report. From it I learned two plainclothes officers in the Bronx were protecting a specific wire-room. One of those plainclothes officers was Eddie Murphy. I was not surprised; Murphy had achieved his goal—to make a buck. I opened and assigned the case to the next available agent. Later, the case was "deferred to local authorities," when it was learned the Bronx County DA was already investigating this wire-room and its corrupt police protectors. Eddie Murphy was indicted in Bronx County and thrown off the police force.

I never told the case agent, nor anyone else at the time, that this felon recruited me to the FBI a half dozen years earlier.

The FBI National Academy—The NA

The FBI National Academy is a professional course of study for US and international law enforcement managers nominated by their agency heads because of demonstrated leadership qualities. The program serves to improve the administration of justice in police departments and agencies at home and abroad and to raise law enforcement standards, knowledge, and cooperation worldwide.

Leaders and managers of state, local, county, tribal, military, federal, and international law enforcement agencies attend the FBI National Academy. Participation is by invitation only, through a nomination process. Participants are drawn from every US state and territory and from international partner nations.

Sessions of approximately 250 officers take undergraduate or graduate courses at the FBI campus in Quantico, Virginia. Classes are offered in a diverse set of areas and officers participate in a wide range of leadership and specialized trainings. Officers share ideas, techniques, and experiences with each other and create life-long partnerships that transcend state and national borders.

from the FBI website

CHAPTER EIGHT

THE TRAINING DIVISION

My next stop after New York was Quantico, Virginia, now known to the world, thanks to movies and TV shows, as the home of the FBI Academy. Having earned a master's degree in Police Administration from the John Jay College of Criminal Justice, in New York City, I was just what they wanted.

In 1973, the "new" Academy, as it was known for some time, had only been opened a year. In a corner of the sprawling Marine Corps base, among the wooded rolling hills of Virginia, a modern academic institution had been raised up. Most think of the Academy as the training ground for new agents, which it is, but the main activity there is training for state and local police. The major police program run by the FBI is the National Academy. Most of the classes presented to the National Academy are recognized by the University of Virginia for undergraduate or graduate college credit, so instructors must have the appropriate academic credentials. Management Science is one of the principal topics taught at the National Academy.

THE NATIONAL ACADEMY

The National Academy began in the 1930s in response to the Wickersham Commission's recommendation that professionalization of law enforcement across the US could be greatly advanced through centralized training. With support from the Congress and the Department of Justice, the "National Police Training School" was established. With a strong tradition of local policing in America and a cultural bias against a national police force, it was not too many years before the word "police" was dropped and the name National Academy was adopted—or now "The NA"—as it is known by law enforcement cognoscenti.

Shortly before my arrival in the training division, an initiative in field police management training started. Every FBI field office has a cadre of agents who, in addition to their investigative duties, serve as police instructors to state and local agencies. Most often these field police training classes are concerned with practical "hands-on" topics such as evidence collection and crime scene investigation. This new initiative in management training would be offered to police leaders at sites throughout the nation by instructors from Quantico.

For nearly five years, I taught management at the National Academy while also traveling around the county in a team with another agent/instructor, offering police management training. I learned so much more than I imparted. Clearly, I learned about police management issues. But most importantly, I continually saw the commitment of police leaders at every level to do what is right. They already considered what they were doing as a profession, not just a job. For many of the NA students it was a sacrifice to be separated from their families for months, but they wanted to learn and improve. Meeting these good officers was a powerful antidote to my experience in New York.

The then FBI Director, Clarence M. Kelley, took a great interest in police training. Early in his career as an FBI agent, he had been an instructor at Quantico. In his second career, he was a long-serving chief of police in Kansas City before being appointed FBI Director in 1973.

As a police chief, Kelley was part of the Major Cities Chiefs (MCC) group and remained close to them as FBI Director. They expressed to him—and he understood—that it is difficult to get the necessary professional development while heading a large police agency. There is no one to turn to; it really is lonely at the top. The pressure of running a major city police department precluded attendance at the National Academy. It was a great program for those who had already gone, but the program was three months long, which is too long an absence for a serving chief.

THE NATIONAL EXECUTIVE INSTITUTE

In early 1975, FBI Director Kelley told Gerald Shanahan, the chief of the Management Science Unit at the FBI Academy—and my immediate boss—to work with the Major Cities Chiefs to develop a high-level executive training program. What emerged from that collaboration was the National Executive Institute (NEI), a program specifically tailored to the needs of the executives of the largest police agencies. Over the course of each year, the NEI class met for three separate one-week sessions. This alleviated the need for the chief executive to be absent for a prolonged period. In addition to the commissioners, chiefs, and sheriffs from major jurisdictions, occasionally an FBI executive would attend with them. And as at the NA, you wouldn't see the word "police" in the title of the National Executive Institute (NEI), in acknowledgement of America's abhorrence of a national police force.

I was one of the agents in Shanahan's unit who did the routine work on this new program. I attended to the needs of the speakers and the chiefs, such as picking them up at Washington DC's Union Station or national airport. It afforded me a lot of one-on-one time with these impressive individuals. I attended their social hours and, most significantly, sat in—with my mouth shut—on their sessions. *Their* mouths were not shut, so again, I learned a lot. There were some giant egos, however, particularly in that first group. But they seemed happy to be in a room with their peers, where they could air their problems. The antidote for "lonely at the top" had been found.

Michael Codd, commissioner of the NYPD, attended that first NEI session along with John F. Malone, the assistant director of the NYO. I picked them up at Union Station. Edward M. Davis, the long-serving Chief of the LAPD was at that first NEI class as well. It was fascinating to hear the discussions from the two opposite coasts—and contrasting policing styles—echoing across the room.

The future of policing in America was being brought to the fore in that room, due in no small part to the outstanding speakers Gerry Shanahan and Clarence Kelly had recruited. Some of them were visionaries who forced us all to think anew and—for those times—radically.

Ernest van den Haag certainly required radical thinking of his listeners. He was the intellect behind the revival of capital punishment in the United States. His book, *Punishing Criminals*, was published in 1975, just as the NEI got underway. Van den Haag also advocated for long-term imprisonment of predatory criminals as the most effective path to public safety. Widely implemented in the ensuing decades, it is still a controversial proposition.

Herman Kahn, the futurist from the Hudson Institute, presented an optimistic scenario regarding America and the world's changing conditions. In the face of an expanding population, he foresaw a boundless potential for progress due to capitalism and technology. Kahn was one of the first futurists and he certainly got those executives thinking and debating.

Herb Cohen, who is sometimes called the "The World's Best Negotiator," provided information and techniques that could be put into immediate use by police executives. Cohen was a favorite at FBI management training programs for years. His book, *You Can Negotiate Anything: The world's Best Negotiator Tells You How to Get What You Want*, has also been a bestseller for years.

By far the presenter who had the most profound effect on these chiefs and on policing in America was James Q. Wilson, then of Harvard. In the Management Science Unit, we all had read his 1968 text *Varieties of Police Behavior: The Management of Law and Order in Eight Communities*. As with Ernest van den Haag's *Punishing Criminals*, James

Q. Wilson's much better-known work, *Thinking About Crime*, would appear just in time for that first NEI session in 1975.

Wilson was just then forming his thinking around what would become known as the "Broken Windows" theory. The discussions he led with this first NEI group of chiefs would help advance it. Sitting in that conference room was like having an ear to the keyhole of the thought processes, which would dramatically change policing for the remaining quarter century.

The Broken Windows theory sprang from the observation of both social psychologists and officers on patrol. If a window in a building is broken and is left unrepaired, other windows will soon be broken. Wilson claimed it is true in affluent neighborhoods as well as in rundown areas. Unrepaired broken windows are, according to Wilson, a signal no one cares, and so breaking more windows costs nothing to the criminal.

This insight would be developed by some of the chiefs in that room into an understanding that to reduce serious crime, law enforcement must begin by addressing minor crimes. One of the earliest and most successful practical adoptions of the theory was in the New York City subways. Those who entered the transit system without paying were known as "fare jumpers," as they entered the system by jumping over the turnstile. It was treated as a minor offense that usually received little or no police attention.

Once strict enforcement against fare jumping got underway, the number of truly serious crimes in the trains and on the station platforms dropped significantly. This was later extended to a war on graffiti and what became generally known as quality-of-life crimes. As James Q. Wilson further refined his theory, America's police chiefs found more practical applications.

In the 1982 updated edition of *Thinking About Crime*, Wilson added a chapter about his Broken Windows theory and its applications. In it he cites the contributions of Clarence Kelly and Chiefs Edward Davis of Los Angeles and William Kolender of San Diego—all members of that first NEI class.

At the conclusion of that first NEI session, John F. Malone retired from the FBI. Gerry Shanahan, who had shepherded Clarence Kelly's idea into reality, retired from the FBI in 1977 to become the director of the Iowa Department of Public Safety. Edward Tully succeeded Gerry as the program administrator, and he would be associated with it for decades. Also, in 1977, I departed Quantico to join the FBI's inspection staff.

But my association with the NA and NEIA programs was not over yet.

CHAPTER NINE

AMERICAN HUSTLE: THE MOVIE VS. THE REAL DEAL

L ike so many major cases, there were many people involved in what is referred to as ABSCAM: a sprawling series of investigations, which started as an undercover operation targeting financial crimes in New York, and ended with the filming of cash bribes being paid to members of congress in Washington. The FBI codename "ABSCAM" was originally a contraction of "Arab scam." After some Arab and Islamic groups complained, the Bureau revised the explanation for the contraction to "Abdul scam" after Abdul Enterprises, a mock company set up for the sting operation.

The Hollywood version of the case, *American Hustle*, both a critical and commercial success, got parts of the story right. It also got ten Academy Award nominations. In the 2013 film, one agent is portrayed as "doing it all." In real life, there are many agents and prosecutors who can say, "It was my case" or it was "my idea." To paraphrase what President Kennedy said about the Bay of Pigs fiasco: "Success has many fathers, failure is an orphan."

So, too, with major cases.

I do not claim to be a father, godfather, or even a stepfather of ABSCAM. But I did cross trails with this case and know it involved a lot of people in FBI headquarters, field offices, and US Attorneys' offices. It also spun off other investigations and was used as a backdrop for unrelated cases.

In early 1977, I was a member of an inspection team examining the operation and performance of the Indianapolis Field Office. In the FBI, service on the inspection staff is a requisite for career advancement. The inspection staff looks closely at the operation of each component of the Bureau and rates the efficiency and effectiveness of that office and its leadership.

During inspections of other field offices in the preceding months, I was to scrutinize one squad or resident agency. This time it was different. I was assigned a single case. I also was given a mild suggestion, perhaps a warning, that this matter was a bit of a "problem child," which might need to be "reined in" or "shut down." Sometimes hints like these came from the management of the very office under inspection, from weak leaders seeking the visiting team to do their dirty work. But just as likely, the warnings may have sifted down from a headquarters entity that simply was feeling queasy.

OPERATION FOUNTAIN PEN

Essentially, I was appraising the work of two young agents, Jack Brennan and James J. "JJ" Wedick. They were already some months deep into an undercover life, which was something new in the Bureau. And though I was inspecting only one case, it encompassed volumes of files. This was "Operation Fountain Pen" (OPFOPEN), Major Case #1. The very first case to receive the Major Case numeric designation.

The veteran *Wall Street Journal* reporter Jonathan Kwitny had written extensively throughout the 1960s and 70s about an international network of financial con men and their predations. He published the results of his reporting in *The Fountain Pen Conspiracy*, a collection of true crime stories, which could serve as a training manual for super-swindlers and the investigators chasing them. The case name Operation Fountain Pen (OPFOPEN) was thus an homage to Jonathan Kwitny.[9]

I thought of *The Odd Couple* upon meeting Brennan and Wedick. Married, Jack was a smiling, deceptively slow-talking southerner. But his mind was always on full speed. JJ was a slim, hyperactive, fast-talking bachelor. His bio was almost my own. JJ had grown up in the Parkchester section of the Bronx, where he was an altar boy at St. Helena's parish. He then went to Fordham University and began his FBI career in the New York office. But as fate would have it, I would grow closer to Jack in the future, not JJ.

After reading the voluminous files—while doubting anyone else had read all of them—and interviewing each of the two agents at length, I was blown away by the breadth and daring of OPFOPEN. These two agents traveled the world in the company of the king of all con men, Philip Karl Kitzer. But they had had no training in undercover work. They were ducking into public bathroom stalls to change the tape on their body recorders. They had zero "backstopping," i.e. the resources and support that would later become commonplace in undercover work. They didn't even have aliases; they were both using their real names and their own American Express cards—and I was thoroughly seduced by their daring. Not only was I not going to shut this undercover operation down, I fully endorsed it.

The case became emblematic of the evolution of the FBI in a more complex world with smarter criminals. It also validated the need for the kind of backup and support that is almost always routine in major undercover operations today. Although this case was truly Jack and JJ's, like most major undertakings, it was a team effort, eventually involving many FBI field offices and US Attorneys' offices. It spun off cases both large and small, most significantly ABSCAM, the FBI undercover

---

[9] A complete account of OPFOPEN is found in David Howard, *Chasing Phil* (Crown Publishing, 2017).

operation of the late 1970s and early 1980s that led to the convictions of seven members of congress and inspired the film *American Hustle*.

THE BIRTH OF ABSCAM

On May 8, 1977, two agents from "Nowhere Indiana," as New York agents would later label them, walked into the FBI's New York office. They had just been undercover at a high-powered criminal meeting in an office on Central Park South and wanted to report what they'd seen. In *American Hustle*, Philip Karl Kitzer, portrayed as a white-haired odd-ball named "Karl," is shown at that meeting. In the real deal, Jack and JJ were there as well.

At the NYO, they initially had a hard time getting anyone to listen to them. Finally, they were able to buttonhole a few New York agents, which in turn provided probable cause for a wiretap, which led to the recording of conversations of Mel Weinberg, another master con man, who would be a key to ABSCAM and is portrayed as "Irving" in *American Hustle*.

Clearly, when Jack and JJ strolled into the New York office that day in May, ABSCAM was born.

As OPFOPEN continued the danger to Jack and JJ grew as more Mafia types, including hit men, were drawn into their circle. Kitzer was arrested in October 1977. It took more than two months, but finally he was persuaded to join the government's team. All those incriminating recordings paid off. He then became a witness for the government and testified in a number of trials. More than 130 individual cases were spun off from OPFOPEN, which yielded some fifty convictions.

MOVING SOUTH, AGAIN

Less than a year after meeting Jack and JJ in Indianapolis, I was a supervisor in the Mobile, Alabama field office leading a squad that focused on white-collar crime violations. From my first day in Mobile, in the tide of incoming communications that crossed my desk, one name kept coming up: Sidney J. Gerhardt.

Gerhardt was a lifelong resident of that old southern city; he was related to a well-respected family in Mobile's commercial circles and his name was popping up in other field offices around the country as well, as a lender or simply a "steerer" who got would-be borrowers into loans that never materialized.

In our small office in Mobile, only a few agents routinely handled financial crimes. I initially assigned the Gerhardt leads to two very senior agents who were long-term residents of the city. They completed their leads by reporting Gerhardt's explanations that the proposed borrower was just not qualified. In other words, Gerhardt was giving agents the same excuse he used with his victims, and the agents were buying the story line. Reputation meant a lot in old Mobile. It sure seemed to mean a lot to those senior Mobile agents. But even a "model citizen" can be a crook.

Meanwhile, Jack Brennan transferred from Indianapolis in November 1977 and joined my squad in Mobile. After he finished his undercover work, someone in the Bureau's hierarchy was kind enough or smart enough to send Jack back home to Alabama. That was exactly what Jack—and certainly his wife, Becky—wanted, and I was more than happy to have this smart financial crime guy with his fresh outlook on my squad.

For although the undercover phase of OPFOPEN had closed, its work continued. For at least the next year, Jack spent weeks at a time away from Mobile testifying in various courts. Philip Karl Kitzer, our valuable cooperating witness, was then being held at the Federal Prison Camp on the grounds of Maxwell Air Force Base in Montgomery, Alabama, and he needed moral support, so Jack took frequent drives on Interstate 65 to Montgomery to shore him up. Often, when Kitzer was transported by the US Marshals to other cities to testify, he was lodged in a local lockup, where, he told Jack, he was often abused. Jack was torn up about it. They had clearly formed a bond.

Jack and I were becoming friends as well. On the weekends we would head to Mobile Bay for fishing or shrimping. Out on the water, Jack unburdened himself and shared what he and his family endured during OPFOPEN. The long separations seemed even worse than the danger. There was no official post-assignment counseling then. Our trips out on the water would have to do.

When Jack arrived in Mobile, he immediately saw Sidney J. Gerhardt for what he was, an "advance-fee artist." Advance fee, a popular con at the time, was briefly but very accurately portrayed in an early scene in *American Hustle*. It was a tricky con to prosecute successfully because the government would have to show intent and demonstrate there was never any intention to fund the loan.

Ever the undercover agent, Jack saw a way to gather the evidence using undercover tactics. Gerhardt would have to admit to a coconspirator that the loan was never going to be funded. We were able to get agents from New York, who had undercover roles in ABSCAM, an operation with full backstopping. This assistance was possible because Jack Brennan, with his knowledge of the ongoing case, was in Mobile. The undercover agents from New York came with aliases and a whole lot of phony backup, something Jack and JJ never had. This played out over time, some of it by mail, some of it by phone. Hence, federal cases against these fraudsters most often featured charges of Mail Fraud and Fraud by Wire.

Ultimately, the government secured indictments against Gerhardt and several other con men in Mobile. By the time the case[10] came to trial in the Southern District of Alabama, I was in Washington DC on my next assignment but I was incredibly pleased to return to Mobile to testify in that trial and help secure the convictions of Gerhardt and his associates. By that time, Philip Karl Kitzer was routinely testifying as an expert witness for the government. In the Gerhardt case, his explanation

---

[10] *United States v. Sidney Gerhardt and Joseph Adornato*, No. 82-CR-8 (S.D. Ala. 1982).

of the various ways an advance fee scheme works made it possible for the jurors to see though the smoke and mirrors of the fast-talking con men.

Kitzer explained that an "advance fee" was presented to a victim as a charge for processing the loan paper. Con men would often write loopholes and trick language into the commitments. Frequently they inserted a line near the end of a lengthy document stating that all of the would-be borrower's paperwork had to be completed "to our [the ersatz lenders'] satisfaction." Then the con men would endlessly ask for more documents from the borrower. They had what they called "the excuse of the week" to explain delays. In the end, Kitzer testified, the con men would tell the victim, "You didn't do what you said you would" and "It's your fault the deal didn't work." A classic example of blame the victim.

"SUCCESS HAS MANY FATHERS, FAILURE IS AN ORPHAN"

After a few years, I departed Mobile to become the Criminal ASAC in the Washington Field Office (WFO). Before my arrival, the office had received major funding for an undercover operation in DC targeting local public corruption in the construction industry, but it had failed to produce the hoped-for results and had now become an orphan.

It was then the idea of the White-Collar Crimes Section Chief at FBI Headquarters, Joe Hannagan, to fold the backstopping props of that orphaned WFO operation into ABSCAM. That turned out to be a very clever idea. The props included a leased house on W Street NW in the very upscale Foxhall neighborhood of the District. That house, wired for film and sound to rival any Hollywood studio, was where the more noteworthy payoffs to congressmen were eventually made.

I vividly recall standing in the W Street house—shortly after the wave of ABSCAM arrests and press releases—with Joe Hannagan. We were looking around the opulent property, with artwork on the walls and a generously stocked wine cellar, when Joe, an accountant, looked at me and said, "You know, you're gonna have to clean up this mess." Later there may have been some raised voices and a bit of finger-pointing, but never ever an agent beating a supervisor over the head with a phone as shown in *American Hustle*. I would have remembered that.

Cases grew in all directions from ABSCAM; no one single person oversaw everything. This led Judge William H. Webster, the FBI director at the time, to famously characterize ABSCAM as "a loose cannon on the deck of the Ship of Criminal Justice." I recall one coordinating conference, held in a large room above the stage of the theater at the FBI Academy in Quantico, with barely enough room for all of us to fit in, and that meeting was just FBI personnel. The Supervisors and agents from the Long Island end of ABSCAM brought our WFO team up to date at that meeting. The scope of this growing operation was impressive and challenging.

Later, as we got nearer the prosecutorial stage, there were several meetings in DC that involved the Department of Justice and various US Attorneys' offices. AUSA (Assistant US Attorney) Thomas P. Puccio from the Eastern District of New York, who the New York agents affectionately called "The Pooch," was there for these meetings. His slick black-haired character is, to me, one of the few easily identified in *American Hustle*. At these case conferences I watched Puccio—with a mixture of annoyance and admiration—as he "ate the lunch" of DC's US Attorney's Office. He left them with just two congressmen to prosecute, while he got four plus the US senator, even though most of the actual payoffs took place in DC—in the house on W Street NW. Puccio had the District's USA smiling and thanking him for these crumbs. There are all kinds of con men.

At another prosecutorial coordinating conference in DC, Mel Weinberg—the "Irving" character in the movie—was present. When we broke for lunch, which for security reasons was at the Officers Club in the Washington Navy Yard, Mel and one of his agent handlers from Miami rode with me. This was just before cell phones became ubiquitous, and I was among the first to have gotten a phone installed in my car. I recall showing off the car phone as we drove to lunch. After, as I was chatting with someone at the restaurant door, I looked out to see Mel sitting in the car talking on my car phone. It was some uncomfortable time before I was sure none of the numbers he called were connected to some new con.

The portrayal of Mel as "Irving" in the movie was close to the real deal in several other ways. Just like Irving, Mel had both a wife and a girlfriend in his life assisting him with his crimes, and eventually supporting his work as an informant for the FBI. This made life particularly challenging for his handlers.

ABSCAM had led to arrests of members of congress, it had garnered widespread publicity, and racked up tremendous costs—so the aftermath of the operation necessarily absorbed the attention of the highest levels of the Bureau and the Justice Department.

First, the defense claimed that their clients had been entrapped. Ultimately that defense did not work for the accused in ABSCAM, but the issues raised did directly lead to the creation of the January 5, 1981, Attorney General's Guidelines for FBI Undercover Operations, which has since been updated numerous times. The guidelines and related training were so rigorously enforced that for decades entrapment seldom became a viable defense in FBI cases. Sadly, that changed when entrapment raised its ugly head in the recent Governor Whitmer kidnapping plot fiasco.

In ABSCAM, leaks to the press about the case as it broke led to the inevitable leak investigations, which resulted in the disciplining of even high-ranking executives. And congress (along with the press, of course) examined the use and management of criminal informants in ABSCAM's wake.

Mel Weinberg, whose personal life was every bit as complicated as Irving's in *American Hustle*, caused many a headache for the Bureau. During the various trials, Mel was living in a government-owned home in Florida when his wife complained to FBIHQ that he had taken the stove (also government property) from the home and given it to his girlfriend.

We were dealing with a guy who would steal the proverbial hot stove.

Advance Fee Scheme

An advance fee scheme occurs when the victim pays money to someone in anticipation of receiving something of greater value—such as a loan, contract, investment, or gift—and then receives little or nothing in return.

The variety of advance fee schemes is limited only by the imagination of the con artists who offer them. They may involve the sale of products or services, the offering of investments, lottery winnings, "found money," or many other "opportunities." Clever con artists will offer to find financing arrangements for their clients who pay a "finder's fee" in advance. They require their clients to sign contracts in which they agree to pay the fee when they are introduced to the financing source. Victims often learn they are ineligible for financing only after they have paid the "finder" according to the contract. Such agreements may be legal unless it can be shown the "finder" never had the intention or the ability to provide financing for the victims.

from the FBI website

CHAPTER TEN

"THE PRESIDENT HAS BEEN SHOT!"

An assault on the President of the United States is a shock to the political and social fabric of the nation. Inevitably, the law enforcement agencies that should have prevented it and those who investigate it fall under scrutiny.

In November 1963, the assassination of President John F. Kennedy devolved into a law enforcement fiasco with conflicts between the FBI, the Secret Service, the Dallas police, and others who would conduct the investigation. It was not yet a federal crime to kill a US president, but in response to that attack, a law was enacted in 1965 making assaulting the president a federal crime, and the new statute was clear: The FBI[11] would lead the investigation.

Eighteen years later, on Monday, March 30th, 1981, President Ronald W. Reagan was shot and wounded, and because of that statute, I became the manager of the investigation of that assassination attempt.

---

[11] Title 18, U.S. Code, § 1751.

THE SITUATION THAT DAY

On that March day in 1981, the international situation was extremely tense. The public was only vaguely aware of how tense.

Ronald Reagan, the new President, had deliberately undertaken a stronger, more aggressive stance towards the Soviet Union. At the same time, the Soviet Union was in a standoff in Poland against Solidarity, a Labor movement that was pushing for more Polish independence. It is now public, but at the time few knew that the Soviet Union was poised to undertake a military invasion of Poland.

The FBI had been tasked to activate all resources and assets targeted at the Soviet Union. If we came up with any new information concerning the Soviets or their intentions, we were to make that information available immediately to the national decision makers. The WFO was particularly tense because of the large diplomatic presence in the District of Columbia.

The US government knew Soviet submarines armed with ballistic missiles were stationed off our coasts. They usually stayed a specific distance away, but in the twenty-four hours preceding March 30, their "picket line" of ballistic submarines moved much closer to the US coastline, setting off alarms at the Pentagon and the White House. This helps us to understand why, in the hours immediately after Reagan being shot, some administration officials—including Secretary of State Alexander Haig, who famously declared "I'm in control here"—were so excitable.

The vice president of the United States, George H.W. Bush, had been in Texas. Later in the day, when returning to Washington DC, his plane did not have secure communications, so he was out of touch with the developing situation.

It was a very unusual day for the FBI. Director William H. Webster, the SAC of the Washington Field Office, Ted Gardner, and other top staff were at a remote location at the bottom of the Delmarva Peninsula on an executive retreat, and consequently they too were out of touch with the unfolding situation.

WFO had two ASACs (Assistant Special Agent in Charge)—one running the Counterintelligence Division, while I ran the Criminal Division. Many of the initial leads that day went to the Dallas and Denver divisions because the shooter had lived in Texas before traveling to Washington, while his family lived in Colorado. Since all the FBI SACs were at the retreat with Director Webster, we turned to other ASACs as we followed leads across the country. Gary Penrith, the ASAC in Dallas, was not only my counterpart but a friend. Knowing each other proved to be a huge positive during the response to the attempted assassination.

The benefit of training was evident that day. I knew and had trained with the other ASACs in major case management and command post procedures. The Bureau had a program called the "Executive Development Institute" which addressed these very topics. The value of major event management, where law enforcement agencies collaborate to plan for events like the Olympics or the Super Bowl, was also apparent. Many of us had worked on President Reagan's inauguration. The biggest lesson of the day was to know your counterparts in other law enforcement agencies, as well as key people in the community before the big unknown event.

"THE PRESIDENT HAS BEEN SHOT!"

President Ronald Reagan was shot at 2:30 p.m. on Monday, March 30, 1981. I was in my Bureau car, having just left a meeting at FBI Headquarters. I was listening to music on the radio when the announcer broke in with news that President Reagan had just been shot at the Hilton Hotel.

I immediately called WFO to ask, "Which Hilton is the incident at?"

Nobody knew about it.

There are two Hiltons in Washington: the Washington Hilton at Connecticut and Florida Avenues, and the Capital Hilton at K and 16th

Streets. But when I asked, "Which Hilton?" the radio dispatcher replied, "What are you talking about?"

"The big incident!" I yelled, "Which Hilton is it at?"

Again, "What incident?"

Agents are supposed to be discreet when speaking on the radio, but finally I bellowed, "The President has been shot outside the Hilton Hotel!"

Later, we learned the assassination attempt happened just as I was listening to the radio. There were reporters with the president when he was shot, so the news was immediate.

Both Hiltons were north of my location, so I raced uptown until I got word it was the Washington Hilton, where I arrived in three or four minutes. In those precious minutes, I had begun a mental checklist of what to do and where to start. I assumed there would already be at least half a dozen FBI agents and other law enforcement there. And I knew the law—an assault on the President is the FBI's investigation—but I still feared a turf war.

I was the first FBI agent to arrive.

It was an extraordinarily chaotic scene. I tripled parked my car because everything was blocked. Ambulances with sirens blaring were arriving from all directions. Two US Marine Corps helicopters—self-dispatched—were hovering just above the roofline between the high-rise buildings. The noise was deafening.

After the assassination of President Kennedy, the FBI, Secret Service, Dallas police, and others battled over the prisoner and jurisdiction in a way that was profoundly unprofessional. In fact, it may have been the mishandling of the prisoner, Lee Harvey Oswald, was what allowed him to be so easily shot and killed by Jack Ruby. In any case, the mishandling of the prime suspect fueled the many conspiracy theories around JFK's death.

That assassination, which I like so many others witnessed on live TV, was at the front of my mind. As I was drove to the scene, I was thinking to myself: *We must handle this right. This shooting is historic. We must do this investigation correctly.* In talking to others involved that day, including the Secret Service, everyone had that same commitment in their mind: We could not repeat the mistakes of November 1963.

Fortunately, the Secret Service was also trained to the new set of rules in the 1965 federal statute, which gave the FBI jurisdiction once the president had been assaulted.

Captain Jimmy Wilson, the commander of the Washington Metropolitan Police Department (MPD) homicide unit, strode toward me with a clear envelope, the revolver[12] they had just taken from the shooter. I asked him to keep the weapon to shorten the chain of custody. The FBI laboratory was sending a crime scene truck; he could hand it directly to them.

Captain Wilson told me Officer Swan had wrestled the weapon away from the shooter, and they had the shooter in custody. Officer Swan, a uniformed police officer, is visible in the photo of the crowd taken just before the shooting. Over the years, the Secret Service and others have claimed they took the weapon from the shooter. Another example of how something gets repeated, and eventually is accepted as fact. It was Officer Swan who pulled the gun from the assassin's hands.

The MPD took the shooter to the Homicide Section at police head-quarters while telling me, "We're holding him for you to interview." I dispatched two agents to question him: Henry Ragle and George Chmiel. Both were known as excellent interviewers and were on their way.

Robert Powis, the SAC of the Secret Service's Washington Field Office, approached next and declared, "You're the FBI. You're taking charge of the investigation now." Those were his opening words. I was relieved, my fears were unfounded. There was no in-fighting. No dispute. No conflict about jurisdiction. We were all in it together. Perfect cooperation ensued.

The second FBI agent on the scene was Glenn Tuttle. Fortunately, I knew him and asked him to be my scribe, to stay with me and write down all my instructions. There were over 500 agents in WFO, so it was

---

[12] The revolver went to the Washington field office, not the laboratory; it had been in WFO's evidence room for decades.

a great break to already know Tuttle. We knew it was vitally important to document what was happening. We would need a record of what was clearly a historical case. Tuttle stayed with me the entire day and did an outstanding job, which was key to how the day unfolded.

The scene in front of the Hilton quickly became even more crowded when people from the White House arrived and the media descended. Thankfully, the Hilton Director of Security, Alexander "Al" Fury, gave us a suite of rooms near the ballroom entrance where the shooting happened to use as a forward command post.

THE FORWARD COMMAND POST

A forward command post is standard FBI and law enforcement practice. You've seen it in movies—various agents and officers gathered around their communications equipment. Ideally, it's set up at, or very close to, the scene of the crime. The initial investigation is run from the forward command post. Today the setup is far more sophisticated. The FBI and major police agencies have mobile vans they dispatch and use as forward command posts. We didn't have that capability, but we did have good training and community relationships.

We were able to set up a forward command post at the Hilton thanks to our relationship not only with the Secret Service and the police, but with Al Fury and Bill Smith, the Hilton General Manager. A crisis scene is not the time nor the place to start exchanging business cards. In my first few months in DC, I invested the time to meet my counterparts and private security contacts. They knew I was FBI. Without those relationships on March 30, I might have been reduced to tugging on people's sleeves in the crowd, "Hey, I'm from the FBI!—Please listen to me!"

Knowing the people in the community, such as the manager and chief of security at the Washington Hilton, paid off. Their first words were, "We'll give you a command post." The two suites they gave us—the Edison and Farragut rooms—were right near the scene of the shooting.

Al Fury took charge of setting up the rooms near the crime scene. Having been a detective lieutenant, he knew what we needed. He cleared out unnecessary items of furniture. He had the entire staff of the Hilton at his disposal. They put in two long conference tables and flip charts. They put in two TV sets, so we could monitor the news reporting. They also set up a dozen separate phone lines on the desks around the room.

While we organized the forward command post, the Hilton staff set up a separate room across the hall where agents and police officers who didn't have an assignment could stand by. The Hilton provided coffee urns in the second room, which helped keep extra people out of the command post.

Throughout the day, we had periodic meetings in the forward command post to update the investigation. Bill Cronin, a section chief from the FBI laboratory, Deputy Chief Alfonso Gibson from the MPD, several senior Secret Service agents, and a White House representative all attended. It was somewhat of a joint command post.

We had open lines to the Denver, Dallas, and Washington field offices as well. One agent was designated as the lead coordinator in the forward command post. He kept a log of who had been assigned leads at the scene and what leads the other offices were handling. Another agent stayed on an open line from the forward command post to WFO, relaying developments to a command post in the field office.

There is always the dual challenge of trying to get leads out and information in. We were getting calls from FBI Headquarters, the White House, the media, and others. All were asking for updates as we were trying to get the investigation moving. It was a significant hindrance and slowed things down. Since that day in March 1981, more discipline has been introduced into command post procedures and decision makers are better shielded from distractions.

MAJOR EVENT MANAGEMENT

The FBI had been preparing for the presidential inauguration in January from a security standpoint: how we would share intelligence, who would have what responsibilities, and how we would set up command posts. This was done relatively informally through a planning committee at the field office level. As the ASAC in charge of criminal matters, I had been the FBI representative to the security planning committee for President Reagan's inaugural—which included the Secret Service, the US Park Police, the US Capitol Police, and the Washington MPD.

We agreed on a leadership exchange for inauguration day. The three principal agencies—FBI, Secret Service, and MPD—would have officials at each other's command posts. I was assigned to the Secret Service command post for the entire day in January 1981. The Secret Service and MPD had people at our Washington Field Office; Secret Service and the Bureau were at the Police command post. This afforded excellent liaison and enabled prompt resolution of any miscues. In retrospect, along with the planning sessions for this major event, the inaugural day experience itself helped me become familiar with the law enforcement partners with whom I would work with in the crisis.

The importance of building relationships is one of the key lessons from that day, which applies to law enforcement at every level today. Knowing your counterparts and as many key people in the community as possible really pays off.

CRISIS MANAGEMENT

In a crisis, to the extent possible, a leader must calm the public's fears. At the same time, the public's need to know is a major aspect of crisis management. On the drive to the Hilton, I thought about the message I wanted to deliver: "The FBI is here" and "The FBI is investigating the case." In the newspapers the next day, that is how I was quoted. That was the only message I wanted to get out. Other than that, I did not get involved with the press at the scene. Mine was a sort of on-the-sidewalk press statement, not an interview. I limited myself to that one statement.

Today everybody today knows that the shooter, John W. Hinckley Jr., was a mentally disturbed young man. But at that moment, we did not know that. We did not know who else might be involved. We did not know if someone else was going to be attacked. We did not know who coordinated the attack or why. We knew somebody had just tried to kill the President of the United States. Was it a conspiracy? Were other officials in peril? The heightened international tensions were of grave concern, so we treated the initial investigation as a crisis, a major crisis that would change and evolve into a major case investigation.

Al Fury, the Washington Hilton's Director of Security, took this photo of those waiting outside the Hilton minutes before President Reagan was shot. John Hinckley, the would-be assassin, has an impassive expression while all others are smiling and laughing. Photo taken by Al Fury and later donated to the Ronald Reagan Presidential Library & Museum.

The agents took Hinckley from the MPD to the Washington Field Office to interview him. On the way over they advised him of his rights. When they sat down with him, they gave him a written warning and waiver form, which he signed. His wallet was searched and he was photographed and fingerprinted.

MAJOR CASE INVESTIGATION

Al Fury, a retired detective lieutenant from the MPD robbery squad, had worked with the FBI on bank robberies over the years.

Because of his presence at the scene before the shooting started, Al, the hotel's security manager, played a pivotal role. As the president was readying to depart the Hilton, Al observed the growing crowd of reporters and others outside, and offered to have the Secret Service bring the President out though the garage to avoid exposure to the uncontrolled crowd. He was outspoken in his disappointment with their decision not to heed his advice. He retrieved a black velvet rope from the upper lobby and used it as a "rope-line" in front of that crowd. Most significantly, he had taken a photo, which showed Hinckley standing among the press moments before he shot the president.

As Hinckley was interviewed, the investigation began to unfold. He did not deny his identity. He did not deny he shot the president. Hinckley told the agents he was staying at the Park Central Hotel (which no longer exists) at 18th and G Street. Special Agent Tom Bush was selected to do the affidavit for the search warrant of the hotel room.

We secured the hotel room. A police officer and an agent were posted outside, so no one could disturb it. Tom Bush was busy all afternoon with the US Attorney's office preparing the affidavit for the search warrant. It was not until that evening that the hotel room was searched.

Data searches in FBI headquarters and elsewhere provided more background about Hinckley. The serial number of his revolver was provided to the Bureau of Alcohol, Tobacco, and Firearms (ATF). They were able to determine where it was purchased.

In the meantime, as we received information about Hinckley, we opened the phone lines from our forward command post at the Hilton. As the afternoon wore on, we opened a line to Dallas. Hinckley had been living there just before coming to Washington DC. We now knew, too, that was where he purchased the firearm.

That afternoon, an agent in the Dallas field division, Rich Garcia, happened to be sitting in his car outside Rocky's Pawn Shop when the call went out for an agent to go to the pawn shop. Special Agent Garcia was able to handle the lead immediately. Hinckley had purchased the firearm, a Rohm RG 22 caliber revolver, for only forty-six dollars the previous October, and Agent Garcia was able to recover all the pertinent records. I learned that immediately on the open line to the ASAC in Dallas, Gary Penrith. The line was left open all afternoon, for there were other leads in Dallas.

The other field office in the investigation was Denver. Hinckley grew up in Colorado and spent time in Denver. His parents lived in Evergreen, Colorado. During the afternoon, a group of FBI agents accompanied by a Secret Service agent, went to the Hinckley's residence. His parents were devastated. They kept a room for him, which Mrs. Hinckley permitted the agents to search.

They found some photographs and other things, but nothing terribly significant. But within a few days, a national newsmagazine published a photo of Hinckley which had been taken from his bedroom. An FBI internal investigation was initiated, called an OPR (Office of Professional Responsibly) in FBI jargon. This was a big distraction and a cause of some concern. As the Office of Origin (OO) in the investigation, WFO had received much of the evidence—or at least copies—from Denver. We were under the microscope as much as them. It turned out the Secret Service agent who accompanied our agents to the Hinckley residence had taken the photo and given it to a journalist. An incredibly stupid move.

Meanwhile, Tom Bush now had a warrant in hand for the search of the hotel room. It was about eleven at night when it was executed. That was when I left the forward command post at the Hilton and rendezvoused at Hinckley's hotel with Bush and the search team.

Before we touched anything, we filmed and photographed the entire room. Then we dusted it for fingerprints in case there was an accomplice. Everything was "by the book." We wanted to have everything covered just in case an additional name came up in connection with the shooting. We also wanted to be prepared for any allegation of involvement by others. We needed a record of the fingerprints in that room.

What we found in Hinckley's room at the Park Central Hotel was bizarre. On the desk, laid out for us to find, was his whole plan. He left a map of where he was going. He had the morning's newspaper open to the president's schedule for the day. He circled that President Reagan was going to be addressing a labor union group in the ballroom at the Washington Hilton Hotel. Strangest of all was a letter to actress Jodie Foster, proclaiming that he would be committing an historical act of presidential assassination to win her heart.

That's it. The motive and the whole story.

Hinckley had a perverse infatuation with Foster. He watched the movie *Taxi Driver*, in which she stars, numerous times. It is an extremely violent film. Robert De Niro's character, Travis Bickle, is obsessed with Jodie Foster's character and then plans an assassination of a presidential candidate. An extreme example of life imitating art. The entire movie was later played for the jury during Hinckley's trial.

THE CRIME

Hinckley had positioned himself next to the press mob behind a simple velvet rope, the very rope Al Fury placed there after being ignored by the Secret Service. Hinckley waited with the press—about a dozen reporters and photographers—for the president to emerge from the ballroom exit door.

Al Fury and Bill Smith were standing right beside the door where Reagan would exit. It is a Hilton Corporation tradition, when the president leaves the property, the hotel's general manager is there to see him off. They can be seen in some of the photos taken immediately after the shooting. Before the president emerged, Al Fury took some photographs of the small group of press people. That is how we have the photograph of Hinckley standing in the waiting crowd. His face is completely passive. There is no emotion on his face whatsoever, whereas the others are smiling.

The president emerged and was waving as he walked towards his limousine when Hinckley started shooting. He fired hollow point bullets with a particularly odd round called "the devastator." It had an explosive mixture of aluminum and lead azide inside the hollow point, designed to explode on contact. In just 1.7 seconds, he was able to get off all six shots. One of them hit the building across the street. Other rounds hit the victims. There were four casualties. Nobody was killed, but four people were shot.

One round hit MPD Officer Thomas K. Delahanty in the back of the neck. He had turned his back to Hinckley and was not looking at the crowd. Instead, he was staring at the president, who was stepping out of the building. Delahanty retired on a disability pension from the MPD. He died several years ago of natural causes.

Secret Service Agent Timothy McCarthy was facing the crowd of people. He was shot in the abdomen. In video of the incident, he can be seen being knocked back off his feet from the round's impact. He eventually recovered and went back to work. McCarthy just retired from his second career as the police chief of a town in Illinois.

James S. Brady, the president's press secretary at the time, was in the line of fire. He was right beside the president and was hit in the side of the head with the only devastator round that exploded. He was seriously injured and suffered a significant degree of debilitation for the rest of his life. Brady died in Virginia on August 4, 2014. It was ruled Brady's death was a result of the injuries he had sustained years earlier in the shooting. The state authorities briefly contemplated charging Hinckley with murder. But neither the state of Virginia nor the federal government ever moved ahead with homicide charges against Hinckley.

The president was not directly shot by Hinckley, but one of Hinckley's rounds hit the side of the limousine. Jerry Parr, a Secret Service agent, was pushing Reagan from behind into the limousine. The limousine door was open. The bullet ricocheted from the side of the limousine and passed through the two or three inch opening between the open door and the body of the car. Only the hinges were in the way. The ricochet hit Reagan in the upper left chest as he was waving. Then he was pushed down into the car. It turned out the bullet lodged less than an inch from his heart. It cut some significant blood vessels and he began to lose a lot of blood.

Jerry Parr and the agent driving the limousine spotted blood when the president coughed, so they decided not to go back to the White House. The nearest hospital was George Washington University Hospital. That turned out to be a lucky break. GW hospital, located in the heart of DC, had an emergency room that frequently treated gunshot wounds.

When they arrived at the hospital, the President got out of the limousine on his own. He tried to walk into the building, but fell to the ground, passing out from the loss of blood. The hospital team put him on a stretcher and wheeled him into the emergency room. There they cut off his clothing, and his garments fell to the emergency room floor. The hospital team immediately took the president into surgery.

As he was being lifted onto the operating table at GW Hospital, Reagan looked up at the medical team and famously cracked, "I hope you're all Republicans." This would be the first of many jokes he would surprise us with in the shooting's aftermath.

The bullet had lodged behind Reagan's heart, and an experienced surgeon was trying to extract it from the president's now open chest. An intern at George Washington Hospital reached into the open chest and cupped the president's beating heart in his hand. He held it back so the main surgeon could find the bullet. It is quite remarkable: a twenty-four-year-old recent medical school graduate literally held the president's beating heart in his hand. To add to the tension, they all knew by now that the devastator bullet could explode.

MISINFORMATION

I arrived at the Hilton knowing the president had been shot, but as so often happens in these crises, especially early on, misinformation was abundant. David P. Prosperi, the Assistant White House Press Secretary, immediately told me at the scene the president was *not* shot.

Prosperi said the president had suffered a heart attack while getting in the limousine.

Erroneous information comes from all directions. Very briefly, it was even reported the president had died. It was also reported, for a longer period, that Press Secretary Brady had died.

The day of the shooting there were four injured people being taken to two different hospitals. Hinckley had been taken to the Washington Metropolitan Police Department. The Secret Service took the limousine to their garage. So, there were several different areas of focus for the investigation just within Washington DC.

WIDENING INVESTIGATION

I gave agents assignments as they arrived, and I used the criminal squad supervisors to help manage the scene. The police had been herding the witnesses into the hotel auditorium where Reagan had so recently given his speech. I had a supervisor go into the auditorium with his agents to begin interviewing the witnesses. There they could do it one by one, in a relatively calm atmosphere. Some of the witnesses saw a lot, and some, like the press people who had been there earlier, had seen Hinckley beforehand. There was a lot of detail to be mined.

Another supervisor was dispatched to Secret Service headquarters to establish liaison. We needed to identify Secret Service agents who were witnesses or who possessed other firsthand information.

I sent a supervisor and agents to George Washington Hospital, where the president had been taken. They were to recover whatever evidence they could and to establish liaison there. They recovered Reagan's blood-soaked suit and shirt. The president was carrying virtually nothing on his person. Like other presidents, he didn't carry a wallet. However, President Reagan did have one particularly important item with him, especially considering the tenor of the times. In his pocket was the nuclear authentication card.

LOST AND FOUND

It is widely known that presidents, throughout the cold war, were always followed by a military officer who carried what was called the nuclear "football." It is actually a big leather bag that would be used in the event of a nuclear war. The card Reagan had in his pocket—which had fallen to the floor when medics cut his clothes off in the emergency room—is the "key" so to speak required to tell command and control to launch nuclear weapons.

The authentication card became a memorable incident in the immediate follow-up to the shooting. This significant little item had been lying on the emergency room floor in Reagan's blood until Special Agent James A. Werth recovered it.

The agents at the hospital also picked up a gold cufflink, which Reagan had been wearing. It was a golden grizzly bear, symbolizing the bear on the state seal of California, where Reagan had been governor. The cufflinks were a gift, and they were dear to him.

But our agents recovered only one gold cufflink. It certainly could have disappeared in a lot of places along the way, but because we recovered only one, there was an insinuation that one of our people took the other one as a souvenir. I resisted opening an OPR inquiry into who "took" the other gold cufflink because I believed then and believe now that the cufflink was simply lost.

In the early morning of March 31, about 2:00 a.m., I finally got back to the office. The SAC, Ted Gardner, had returned. We had to make several decisions. One was to choose the case agent, a key role in the FBI. We saw that as particularly important and picked Frank Waikart. Frank had been a supervisor for a few years and had resumed his role as working level investigator, a "street agent" in Bureau slang. He was an excellent choice. A very polished individual and a bright guy, perfect for a sensitive case such as this one.

The following day, the SAC and I were in my office. Ted and I were looking at the authentication card, which is slightly bigger and thicker than an ATM card, with rectangular holes punched in it.

The SAC asked, "Do you know what you have here?"

"No," I said passing it back.

The White House had just called him. They realized the card was missing and wanted it back. He told me we were going to make a point of this. Make them wait a little bit.

"Tell 'em it's evidence." Therefore, they can't have it.

Two days later, we gave in, breaking with procedure, and had Jim Werth give back that one piece of evidence to Edward V. Hickey Jr., the director of the White House military office. Considering the national security implications, it really needed to be returned. As part of our effort to impress upon the White House and the Secret Service that this was a genuine criminal investigation, we did make a bit of an issue of it though. Years later, former Attorney General Edwin Meese would say Werth "did exactly the right thing" in the handling of the card.

INTERVIEW OF RONALD REAGAN—VICTIM

I knew we would have to interview the president. He was both a victim and a potential witness. We were already getting pushback from the White House and the Secret Service; they did not want this treated as a proper criminal investigation. We did. In part this difference was a matter of culture. The Secret Service was focused on protection, while our focus was investigation. I had another concern: I thought it would be inappropriate for an SAC or ASAC to interview the president. I would have loved to have done the interview, but I knew as a boss it would be disastrous for morale.

I always had Jim Siano's demoralizing experience with the arrest in the Mackle case in mind. The president's interview had to be done by the street agents. We should not usurp the agents' role. I was concerned the SAC would get it in his head to do it, but he didn't. He had the same view as I did. Although the interview would not occur for a few more days, we chose the interviewers that morning, two criminal division agents: John Pavlansky and Robin Montgomery.

Montgomery worked Public Corruption and Pavlansky did accounting cases. Pavlansky had been in the Army, while Montgomery had been in the Marine Corps. Both men were combat veterans and both had suffered gunshot wounds. We thought they could empathize and establish a rapport with the president.

President Reagan had been in the hospital for three days recuperating when it was arranged for the two agents to interview him. Director Webster decided, to his great credit, he wouldn't talk to the president until the agents had completed the interview. Webster waited outside the hospital room with Nancy Reagan, the First Lady.

Edwin Meese, who was then a presidential counselor, was also waiting outside the president's hospital room. (He became the attorney general in Reagan's second term.) So, waiting for our agents to conduct the interview were Mrs. Reagan, Judge Webster, and Ed Meese. No pressure.

The president's famous sense of humor was not interrupted by the shooting. When Nancy Reagan first saw him at the hospital, his first words to her were, "Sorry honey, I forgot to duck." While still wearing an oxygen mask, after his operation, and asked how he felt, he echoed W.C. Fields by scribbling on a pad, "On the whole, I'd rather be in Philadelphia." Later, when talking about Hinckley, the president asked, "Brady, Delahanty, McCarthy, and Reagan; what does this guy have against the Irish?" Reagan's bedside quips continued right on into his interview with our agents, providing a welcomed dose of warmth to the scene.

When Pavlansky and Montgomery entered his room, to their great surprise, a Secret Service agent was on the far side of the bed standing over the president. It had been agreed our agents would be allowed to interview the president alone—with no Secret Service agents. Yet there one was, and he showed no sign of budging. With the wounded president lying in the bed between them, our guys made an on-the-spot decision not to make an issue of it.

After the interview, they remarked that Ronald Reagan was a charming, entertaining, very down-to-earth person—just like his public persona. They did connect: These two ex-military agents certainly understood, as well as laughed, when the President quipped "getting shot hurts." Reagan treated the interview as if he was a host. He reached over to a water pitcher and tried to pour two glasses of water for them, in a gesture of welcome. Montgomery reached over immediately and said, "No, Mr. President, I'll get that."

Referring to his well-publicized wisecracks after the shooting, he said, "Fellas, I just made all those joking remarks to make people feel better."

That was his explanation.

The agents emerged very touched by their meeting.

But the bottom line for us in an investigative sense was the president's comment: "I don't remember a thing; I could never identify the shooter. I have no idea who shot me." When the interview was over, Director Webster went in to deliver a gift for the president. The FBI laboratory had created a cube of Lucite with a devastator bullet, like the bullet that had lodged near Reagan's heart, in its center. The laboratory had created the replica as a potential exhibit, but then Webster had the idea of giving it to the president. Reagan seemed to like it. Webster also wanted this investigation to go meticulously well. He also recalled how the Kennedy assassination investigation had been mishandled.

Over the years, there was a misunderstanding about the bullet. Webster gave the President a *replica* of the bullet that had been removed from his chest. The *actual* bullet was evidence and was held in the FBI laboratory for years. Like much of the other evidence gathered after his shooting, it is now in the National Archives portion of the Ronald Reagan Presidential Library and Museum. I have read accounts by people who visited Reagan when he first retired in California. They saw the plastic cube with a bullet in it in his library, and later claimed they had seen the bullet that was taken out of the President's chest after he was shot. This assumption found its way into their biographies or memoirs. But that's inaccurate; it is not the bullet.

Another example of how something gets out there, gets repeated, and then becomes accepted as common knowledge.

FOLLOW-UP INVESTIGATION

The case agent Frank Waikart and I went to Hinckley's initial hearing. That was the first, and one of the few times, I ever saw Hinckley in person. Again, he was completely passive, displaying no emotion whatsoever.

On the first day after the shooting, we had a conference at WFO concerning the investigation. It had been quickly discovered that the Secret Service was interviewing witnesses—doing in effect a parallel investigation. When confronted, they claimed it was part of their mandate to determine what went wrong. Then the US Attorney, Chuck Ruff, got involved. He laid down the law to the Secret Service and the MPD: the FBI was in charge, and we all needed to work as a team. So we all did.

Tom Bush was now the lead coordinator under the case agent, Frank Waikart. Most of the early leads in the DC area were jointly covered with the MPD and Secret Service. Elsewhere in the nation it was just the Secret Service who occasionally accompanied our agents. We were also, according to our team agreement, providing the Secret Service with the results of our investigation as they came back to our lead coordinator. For example, copies of the form FD-302s on which the agents memorialized their interviews.

About five or six days into the investigation, I received a visit from Robert Snow, a Supervisory Agent in Secret Service headquarters. He asked me—*told* me—we had to change some of our agents' FD-302s because "they make the Service look bad." Before he got much further into his pitch I told him, "Bob, that's something we just don't do." I could never ask an agent to alter his or her FD-302. It just wasn't done. The FD-302 was used to record what the agent heard or observed, i.e., potential testimony for court. Some years later, Frank Waikart and I were chatting about this case. He mentioned Bob Snow had approached him with the same request and that he had given the same response.

The follow-up investigation determined Hinckley had traveled the country, gone to shooting ranges, and indeed had a fixation with Jodie

Foster. He watched *Taxi Driver* a number of times and his obsession with her prompted his desire to impress her, so he planned and committed an assault on the president.

The investigation traced Hinckley's history for months preceding the shooting to see if anyone else was involved with him. We recovered video showing him in a crowd trying to get close to President Carter, but he never got close enough to act. There was no political motivation. It didn't matter if it was Reagan or Carter. Hinckley just wanted to shoot a president. He wanted to do something dramatic. There was never any hint of a political motive. He was a mentally deranged man.

Jodie Foster was then a student at Yale University. On the day after the shooting, agents from our New Haven office went to Yale to see her. She was not at all surprised when they contacted her.

She knew all about Hinckley. He had been calling her at her Yale residence. She had recorded some of his phone calls to her. Our agents recovered the tape of those calls. They made a duplicate immediately, as was the practice. They sent both to WFO that same day, entrusting them to a commercial airline pilot. This was an old FBI method used before FedEx. The tapes arrived within hours. The original was never touched, but the duplicate copy, the "dupe," was played. I remember a couple of us listening to the tape of Jodie Foster answering the phone. Hinckley would go on for a while and we could hear her saying, "You really shouldn't call me." She was so polite. "We can't have these conversations." We could barely hear his hesitant voice in the background, but we heard her voice very clearly.

The room erupted. I was married with two young daughters and the others also had children. We were all yelling at the recording, "Hang up! Hang up!" because that's what we would tell our wives and daughters. Don't stay on the phone with a nut who is bothering you. But Jodie stayed on the phone with Hinckley, trying to explain to him why she could not take his calls. It was remarkable.

THE TRIAL

The US Attorney and his staff thought they could get a conviction.

Chuck Ruff, a holdover from the Carter administration, was the US Attorney. The lead prosecutor was AUSA Roger Adelman. The president did not testify, nor did Brady, who was in no condition to testify. But Tim McCarthy and Tom Delahanty, the two other victims, did.

On June 21, 1982, after an eight-week trial, despite the best efforts of the US Attorney's team, Hinckley was found not guilty by reason of insanity. The widespread reaction in the country was outrage. This led to the Insanity Defense Reform Act of 1984, which shifted the burden of insanity to the defense, greatly limiting the ability to use the insanity defense in federal criminal cases. Most states enacted similar legislation. Three states abolished the insanity defense altogether. The number of insanity defense cases substantially decreased nationwide. That was a significant long-term result of this case.

Another significant change was the passage of the Brady Handgun Violence Prevention Act in 1993. Better known as the Brady Bill, it created the National Instant Criminal Background Check System (NICS), which the FBI manages to this day. The third thing, which has not gotten as much publicity, pertains to the Secret Service. They made a lot of in-house changes. The president's daily schedule is no longer published in newspapers, and they began the use of magnetometers at presidential appearances.

On the day Reagan was shot, the immediate investigation was handled professionally and carried out properly. That success was largely due to the fact everyone knew each other: the FBI, the police, the Secret Service, and the people at the Hilton Hotel. Law enforcement cooperation is always a force multiplier. One and one equals more than two in these instances. We all knew each other and that helped things go so smoothly. The number one lesson of that day for law enforcement leaders is that you must get out of the office and meet your counterparts and the key people in your community.

Fortunately, I was the kind of guy who liked to do that.

We now know on the day of Reagan's attempted assassination the Soviet leadership canceled their planned invasion of Poland.

Later meetings with saints Mother Teresa and Pope John Paul II strengthened Reagan's belief that God spared his life for a greater purpose.

John W. Hinckley Jr. was released from St. Elizabeth's Mental Hospital on September 10, 2016, and in the summer of 2022, began performing as a singer.

Officer Swan rose in the ranks of the MPD, and later became the District of Columbia's Taxi Commissioner. He has since passed away.

Gary Penrith rose in the ranks of the FBI, becoming a deputy assistant director. I count him among my closest friends.

Robert Powis rose in the ranks of the Secret Service, and later became a deputy assistant secretary of the Treasury.

Tom Bush rose in the ranks of the FBI. I was able to work with him again when he was the Assistant Director in Charge of the Criminal Justice Information Services Division (CJIS) and I was a consultant helping the FBI implement Next Generation Identification (NGI).

Al Fury remained at the Washington Hilton. In July 1983, he helped us celebrate the FBI's 75th anniversary with Jimmy Stewart in the same ballroom where Reagan had been on the day of the attack. The photo he took of Hinckley has been donated to the Ronald Reagan Presidential Library and Museum.

Edwin Meese became the Attorney General in Reagan's second term.

Henry Ragle became the head of Attorney General Meese's security detail.

Jim Werth, the agent who recovered the authentication card, also served on Attorney General Edwin Meese's security detail.

Roger Adelman lost his biggest case. But he worked closely with us in successfully prosecuting some of the ABSCAM defendants.

Robert Snow rose in the ranks of the Secret Service, becoming an assistant director. In his second career, he was deeply involved in the National Center for Missing and Exploited Children. We remain friends.

Legal Attaché—Legat

The FBI stations special agents and other personnel overseas to help protect Americans back home by building relationships with law enforcement, intelligence, and security services around the globe. This helps ensure a prompt and continuous exchange of information.

Today, we have 63 Legal Attaché offices—commonly known as Legats—and more than 25 smaller sub-offices in key cities around the globe, providing coverage for more than 180 countries, territories, and islands. Each office is established through mutual agreement with the host country and is situated in the US embassy or consulate in that nation.

The Legal Attaché, as the representative of a federal agency within the American Embassy, is a member of the Country Team, a key cabinet of advisors to the US Ambassador.

from the FBI website

CHAPTER ELEVEN

A TALE OF TWO AMBASSADORS

During my last ten years in the FBI, I had the unique opportunity of dealing with dozens of US ambassadors. I served as the Legal Attaché (Legat in Bureau jargon) at two large US Embassies: Canberra, Australia, and Paris, France. However, for the FBI and the DOJ, our office had wide regional responsibility. From Australia this included New Zealand and nine other South Pacific island nations. From Paris, France, we were also responsible for the business of justice with the principality of Monaco, as well as twenty-six countries in Africa. Consequently, I had to deal with a wide variety of our ambassadors at posts large and small.

In the media, and in many people's minds, "political" ambassadors are dilettantes who "buy" their appointments with large campaign donations. They are often contrasted with "career" ambassadors, who rise through the ranks of the State Department. Based on my own experience, I formed a quite different impression. I found career State Department ambassadors often tended to narrowly protect and represent the interests of the State Department, while the political ambassadors, who came from various niches in American society, saw their mission as representing the United States as a whole.

In the staffing of an embassy there are representatives of a wide variety of federal agencies, such as the FBI, Drug Enforcement Administration (DEA), and departments like Agriculture and Commerce. State Department careerists sometimes regard these other agencies as "the tenants." Hearing them use that term does not engender the idea of one team. The career ambassadors often regard the other agencies as a challenge they couldn't control. In many posts in Africa, we encountered instances where they clearly did not want the DEA or the FBI around. They derided the law enforcement agencies as cowboys who might create an incident and cause problems for them. These careerists wanted to keep everything quiet, while they marked time in a small post, waiting to move to a bigger position as an ambassador.

In contrast, the so-called political ambassadors saw every agency under their roof as having value. As individuals who had lived most of their lives in the USA before becoming an ambassador, they knew what an agency like the FBI does, and in most cases, they appreciated the Bureau. The political appointees understood that we are all Americans and are all on the same team.

Fortunately, I got to work with two political ambassadors who exemplified these qualities. Mel Sembler, a Republican, was President George H.W. Bush's Ambassador to Australia, while Pamela Churchill Harriman, a Democrat, was President William Jefferson Clinton's Ambassador to France. They each had achieved financial success and stature in their own spheres. Yes, they were substantial fundraisers for the presidents who appointed them, but they also continually demonstrated a love for their country, which they served with honor.

THE WAR ON DRUGS

Both Ambassador Sembler and his wife Betty had a great interest in and commitment to helping the cause against drug abuse. They had both been major players in the formation of both drug treatment and drug prevention programs. They first got to know George H.W. Bush when he was Reagan's vice president. Bush had been given responsibility for coordinating the DEA's and FBI's efforts in drug law enforcement. Bush's involvement in the war on drugs was one of the reasons the Semblers were initially attracted to him.

During that same period, Nancy Reagan had undertaken her own anti-drug campaign. The FBI had started a Sports-Drug-Awareness program targeting young people. Working out of the FBI Director's office, I oversaw that program. It was closely coordinated with a similar effort being run out of DEA headquarters. These efforts at demand reduction were meant to compliment the enforcement efforts of the DEA and others against the supply side of the drug problem. Nancy Reagan, with her "Just Say No" program, put a celebrity's face on these combined programs.

The First Lady traveled the country on this campaign, and I was fortunate enough to accompany her on some trips. The combined FBI-DEA program even traveled abroad to reach the far-flung network of American overseas schools. At that point in history, there was a large American presence in Germany. I traveled from Dulles Airport with Mel Kaufman, a star player with the then Washington Redskins, to visit a series of American high schools throughout Germany. There we teamed up with DEA agents, who were accompanying other NFL players on this trip.

Once Mel Sembler learned of my experience in drug demand reduction and our shared familiarity with the issues and some of the personalities involved, we became friends. Ambassador Sembler understood and appreciated the FBI's mission. I probably would have eventually hit it off with him, when he was ambassador to Australia and I was the Legal Attaché, as he was a very warm individual.

Career ambassadors would seldom expend any funds for entertaining on behalf of the FBI or other agencies, but the expectation of entertainment by any diplomatic representative is a reality. Our budget in the FBI is very minimal for representational events. We used it up with one event. Then we must contribute from our own pockets, and most of us don't have very deep pockets. When you have a political ambassador like Sembler who is willing to help, it is a blessing.

First Lady Nancy Reagan's "Just Say No" initiative dove-tailed with the FBI's Sports Drug Awareness Program. I had the great fortune to do some events with her as well as with professional athletes.

As St. Mother Teresa told us, "Just ask." With Mel Sembler, one only had to hint. James Greenleaf, then the FBI's associate deputy director, came to Australia to attend an event on behalf of the National Academy Associates' Asia/Pacific Chapter. I simply told Ambassador Sembler this FBI official was coming. He asked me, "What does this guy like to do?" "Well, I know he plays tennis." Sembler then set up an afternoon of doubles on the tennis court at the ambassador's residence. The Ambassador, Greenleaf, the Minister of Justice, and the Australian Attorney General played together that day. Sembler, in this way, put the FBI's number three executive with two key Australian Cabinet members.

Sembler generously contributed his time as well as his funds. When the eight Australian police commissioners were meeting in Canberra, Anne and I had them to our home for dinner. We invited the Semblers, too. The Australian Commissioners were impressed at meeting Ambassador Sembler. The American ambassador is a big deal in any country. To have him at our home to meet these key contacts was a coup. He made Anne and me, and the FBI, look good.

President George H.W. Bush and First Lady Barbara Bush made a trip to visit Australia, which began on December 31, 1991. Ambassador Sembler had been pushing for this visit for some time. Only once before had a sitting US president visited Australia, and Sembler rightly felt this visit was long overdue. He arranged the schedule so the first couple would have a few hours of downtime to rest in their rooms at the ambassador's residence. He also ensured there would be time for the president and First Lady to meet with embassy staff and their families.

At the reception in the residence's garden, the first couple mingled with the embassy staff and their families, greeting everyone. Ambassador Sembler introduced me to President Bush. Mel was bursting with happiness, as he put his arm around me and put his other arm around President Bush and pulled the three of us together.

"Mr. President, I want you to meet Tom Baker," Sembler said. "He's the Legal Attaché here."

As I was shaking the president's hand, Mel squeezed us tighter together, and semi-whispered in the president's ear:

"Legal Attaché, Mr. President. That means Tom's the FBI man here."

"Mel, I know that!" Bush responded.

"Oh, but Mr. President, he's *my* FBI man," Sembler stressed.

We all laughed.

The visit of President Bush, for which Mel Sembler had pushed so hard, had a long-lasting impact. Every US President now visits Australia.

Later the Semblers visited Paris when I was there as Legat. At the time, our daughter Virginia was staying with us for the summer, while she interned at the embassy. Because she had an event scheduled at our home with other interns, she could not go out to dinner. I mentioned this to Mel, and he volunteered to talk to the interns. He came over early and met with these half dozen college students for more than an hour. He ran an informal seminar and answered their questions. He usually dealt with the titans of European business on these trips, yet he took the time to be encouraging to these young people.

Mel Sembler, George H.W. Bush's Ambassador to Australia and George W. Bush's Ambassador to Italy, was an outstanding example of the virtues of a political envoy. Our shared experience in drug demand reduction led to a close working relationship and ultimately a friendship.

The American Embassy in Paris, France, is a much larger post than Canberra. When we were there it was also led by an ambassador who understood and valued what we could do. Pamela Churchill Harriman, a British-born aristocrat who knew some of the most important figures on both sides of the Atlantic, had become the US ambassador to France just months before our arrival at that post.

As with my shared experience with Mel Sembler in drug demand reduction, I hit on something with Ambassador Harriman on my very first day at post.

Following the usual practice, I had an appointment to present myself to the ambassador on my first day at the embassy. It was early June 1994, and the appointment was in the early afternoon. When I showed up in front of her secretary's desk, I was not directed to go straight back to her office, but instead to the right, into a reception room. It was large, with a fireplace at the far end and easy chairs placed in the corners. Pamela Churchill Harriman, the American Ambassador to France, was sitting rather regally in one of a group of high-back easy chairs. We exchanged greetings as I walked into the grand room and she gestured for me to sit in a chair, at an angle to hers.

THE WINTER OLYMPICS

She began the interview—that is what this was—with the typical questions. Where else have you been assigned? Is your family with you? And then my opinion on very general policy matters. I could see she had a copy of my one-page bio on her lap. Glancing down at it, she said "I see you had some involvement with the Calgary Winter Olympics." This would be, unforeseen by me at the time, a point on which we would make an initial connection.

In February 1988, for the two weeks of the Calgary Winter Olympics, the Bureau assigned me as liaison to the Royal Canadian Mounted Police Command Post in the western Canadian city. There, equipped with a STU II (a secure telephone), I was to coordinate counterterrorist efforts with the Mounties. There were no terrorist incidents at those Olympics. And, as my bio reflected, I was decorated by the government of Canada for this contribution, which seemed to impress the ambassador.

She knew the International Olympic Committee was meeting in Paris, and a group from Salt Lake City were also present to lobby for the 2002 Winter Olympics. She decided to host a reception at her residence that evening for "some Olympic people" and asked if I—she glanced again at the bio on her lap—and Anne could possibly make it. I responded I was sure we could. I called Anne and as I knew, even at such short notice, she was more than up for the reception at the residence.

The reception for "some Olympic people" involved nearly a hundred individuals—a testament to the ability of her household staff to put something like that together on short notice. The delegation from Salt Lake City was led by Deedee Corradini, the city's mayor. Accompanying them were sponsors, most noticeably Cola-Cola executives. American officials of the various sport federations were also present, and from the International Olympic Committee, a variety of European notables, including Princess Anne of Great Britain.

My Anne and I thoroughly enjoyed this event. Like many of Pamela Harriman's efforts, this reception led to a success: One year later, on June 16, 1995, Salt Lake City was chosen as the host for the XIX Winter Olympic Games, to be held in 2002. We had observed, other than the ambassador herself, we were perhaps the only embassy people present. I came to realize an invitation to the ambassador's residence was not a common event. To be there on one's first night at post was truly exceptional.

Again, it is a great benefit to have a political ambassador who is willing to help with representational-type events. As with Mel Sembler, you seldom had to ask Pamela Harriman for help. Again, a hint would do. I would just inform her of upcoming visitors or events, and she would respond, "Well, Tom, what do you think I should do?" We would look at the schedule and decide on a cocktail party, a luncheon, or something else. That is how we happened to set up a luncheon for a group of US Attorneys and federal judges who were in Paris for an event at the *École Nationale de la Magistrature*, a training school for judges and prosecutors.

At that luncheon, along with the ambassador, I was seated at a table with Thomas S. Ellis III, a federal district judge from the Eastern District of Virginia. The discussion turned to the World War II Normandy landings, which were then being commemorated in France.

Tom Ellis was recommending a new book, which touched on the subject. He then mentioned a specific finding by the author, concerning a key allied decision.

Ambassador Harriman responded, "No, that was Ike's call."

Judge Ellis persisted. "This author says..."

The Ambassador: "Oh, no. Omar Bradley told me it was Ike's call."

A look of recognition came over Judge Ellis's face: He realized he was in the presence of someone with firsthand knowledge of World War II.

Pamela Churchill Harriman was truly a remarkable woman. Once married to Winston Churchill's only son and the mother of Churchill's namesake grandson, she was in the room when many of the key decisions of World War II were made. And for the next half century after the war, she would continue to meet influential men, be they from London, Washington, or Hollywood.

THE MAN FROM ALABAMA

The increasingly comfortable relationship with the ambassador included Anne as well as me. In addition to her volunteer service on the embassy's commissary board and as a docent with the impressive art collection at the residence, Anne worked as the "American" nurse in the embassy's health unit, which was staffed by her, a French nurse, and a secretary. They were responsible for routine health care and vaccinations of all embassy personnel. In that capacity, Anne received a summons to the ambassador's office. Pamela Harriman had a favor to ask. Part of the request was for it to be kept a secret: The ambassador had a "special guest" staying at the residence.

Gregory Peck and his wife, Veronique, were traveling in Eastern Europe when he developed an acute medical problem that required surgery. The surgery was successful, but he could not travel back to California. He could, however, make it to Paris, where his good friend, Pamela Harriman had a room—the Thomas Jefferson suite—for him in her official residence.

Anne committed herself to this special mission. For a week she checked in on Gregory Peck each morning and, in consultation with a French doctor, provided whatever medical care he needed. She was warned Veronique Peck could be exceedingly difficult. On her first day, Anne discovered Veronique was not difficult at all, but genuinely concerned for her husband. Anne asked Gregory Peck if his wife could stay while Anne took his vital signs, changed his dressing, and did a short medical history. Veronique was satisfied Anne was taking good care of her husband and was not there each morning thereafter.

For her part, Anne was impressed by eighty-year-old Peck's general good health and stamina. When she said as much, Peck responded "I thank God and His Blessed Mother." This was very touching to her and to me, as this one of my mother's favorite prayers.

The Residence at 41 *Rue du Faubourg St. Honoré* had guest suites furnished to evoke a personage who had an historical connection to the American Embassy in Paris. Thus, the Lindbergh room had the original map the famous aviator used flying from America across Ireland and onto France. On the map, Lindbergh drew Irish fishermen in their small boats waving up at him. The Franklin bedroom has a bust of the history-shaping politician, scientist, writer, and inventor. Peck's room was named after Thomas Jefferson, an early ambassador to France. It was furnished with replicas of furniture Jefferson had designed, including a reading table that could hold numerous open books and rotated so that the reader could easily access the books. The framed letters on the walls were all Jefferson originals—written in his own hand. These were Peck's favorite part of the room. Anne walked around the room with Gregory Peck as they discussed each item.

Also as expected, Anne asked him about the man from Alabama, Atticus Finch. Gregory Peck said it was his favorite role and that he had stayed in touch with the children in the movie. Atticus Finch was named "the greatest hero in motion picture history by the American Film Institute." Gregory Peck also won an Oscar for his role, and in 2010, the US Postal Service issued a stamp portraying Gregory Peck as Atticus Finch.

While Anne was getting to know this interesting man, I was sworn to secrecy. I endeavored to keep that secret.

During that same week Attorney General Janet Reno made one of her several visits to Paris. This was a one-day stop at an anti-terrorism conference at *Le Place Kléber* with her European counterparts. Because of other pressing matters that week, most of the heavy work in managing the visit and our role in the conference was delegated to Allyson Gilliland, an assistant Legal Attaché. At the end of the conference, I showed up to accompany the Attorney General to the airport. At almost the same moment, the ambassador arrived on the scene. She wanted to pay her respects to the cabinet member before her departure.

As several of us were standing in a circle, exchanging pleasantries, Ambassador Harriman uttered, "Tom, Anne is doing a wonderful job with my special guest." In a minute or two, as we made our way to the cars, Allyson urgently asked me, "Who's the special guest?" I told her—and I told her it was a secret. There was no way I could not; she had worked so hard that day, and besides, the ambassador herself had babbled it out. Allyson promised to keep it to herself.

I proceeded with Attorney General Reno to Charles de Gaulle Airport. It would be nearly two hours before I got home. Allyson returned to the embassy in minutes. As the elevator was taking her to our office on the third floor, the door opened on the second floor. Standing there, waiting to go down, were Anne and the French nurse. As the elevator doors started to close, Allyson quickly remarked to Anne, "Tom told me you're taking care of Gregory Peck."

I had a lot of explaining to do when I got home.

CAN YOU MAKE THIS GO AWAY?

Not all the celebrities in Paris who crossed the ambassador's trail—or ours—were as endearing as Gregory Peck. One was Régine Zylberberg, who ran Régine's nightclub on East 54th Street in New York City and similar establishments in Paris. On April 17, 1996, Régine and her son, Lionel Rotcage, were on American Airlines Flight 63 from Paris enroute to Miami, where they were opening an additional nightclub. Midway across the Atlantic, Rotcage lit up a cigarette. He was asked to stop smoking by the cabin crew, but he refused, and one thing led to another. The aircraft's pilot diverted the flight to Boston, where Régine and Lionel were arrested by the FBI and charged with interfering with a flight crew,[13] a felony which could lead to up to twenty years imprisonment.

The French media, particularly the tabloids, had a field day making fun of the puritanical Americans, who were so against expressions of individual liberty, such as smoking. Even the serious press and Sunday TV talk shows questioned the wisdom of diverting an aircraft for "one lit cigarette." Ambassador Harriman did not like this mockery of her adopted country. I was asked the status of the Boston case several times and furnished her regular updates.

At the end of April 1996, Attorney General Janet Reno again returned to France, this time for several days. Early in the morning, I met the ambassador at her residence and rode with her to Charles de Gaulle Airport, where we would welcome the attorney general back to France. Sitting together in the back seat of her limo, Ambassador Harriman again asked about Régine's case in Boston. I told her that Régine was constantly invoking the ambassador's name. She leaned over towards me and said, "Tom, she is, what we used to call, a cheap broad." I turned and responded, "Madame Ambassador, we still call them that." She let out a loud, throaty laugh.

Three days later, I accompanied Janet Reno to Paris' Orly Airport. We had grown comfortable with each other, as I had accompanied her to meetings and meals over the past few days. Ambassador Harriman joined us in a VIP lounge at the airport. The conversation was friendly and somewhat jovial, as these two remarkable women jokingly critiqued the ministers and other personalities the AG had met during the previous days. When we stood and said our goodbyes, the ambassador,

---

[13] Title 49, U.S. Code, § 46504.

directly facing the AG, asked, "Can you can make Régine's case in Boston go away?"

AG Reno, until now relaxed and chatty, just stared straight ahead, not uttering a word. The silence was palpable. After a minute, I spoke up. "Madame Ambassador, the attorney general can't comment on that." The ambassador responded, "Oh, I see," and we said our final goodbyes as we all walked out the door. The AG could not and would not interfere in what was a decision for the US Attorney in Boston. The ambassador, not being an attorney and having no previous experience in government, did not initially grasp that concept, but she meant no harm. I would recall this exchange twenty years later, when it was reported that President Trump posed a similar hopeful question to FBI Director Comey.

In the final days of January 1997, I received an invitation to lunch at the ambassador's residence for the following day. I had received a few of these summonses in the past, and each time it was followed by an actual seating plan and sometimes even issues and suggested talking points. Good planning whenever we would be lunching with an important French official or journalist. Mid-morning, before the late January lunch, I had not yet received this usual "cheat sheet." I phoned the ambassador's secretary to at least learn the name of the VIP guest. I was surprised to learn there was none. This was to be a private lunch.

On what was a cold wet day in Paris, I arrived a few minutes early. At almost the same moment, the head of the US Information Agency arrived. He was the embassy's press officer. We were directed upstairs to the ambassador's quarters. There we stood in a small room, with a fire blazing in the fireplace. "Joseph" (Giuseppe Santos), the head butler, a loyal employee of Pamela Harriman, asked us what we would like to drink. It still being a few minutes before noon, we both cautiously asked for a Perrier. A minute or so later, the ambassador appeared. She had obviously just come in from the chilly weather. She stood with her back to the fire, warming her hands behind her back, and asked us if Joseph had taken our drink orders. As we responded positively, she added, "I hope you didn't order anything sissy, like a Perrier."

At that very moment Joseph, a very self-assured individual, reappeared with three Bloody Marys on a silver tray and a sly smile on his face. Saved by the butler! As we enjoyed our drinks, Pamela Harriman explained she had been out shopping for an apartment that morning. She had expressed an interest in buying a French apartment since her arrival in Paris. She told us her plans were to divide her time between a home in Middleburg, Virginia, and Paris, when her term as ambassador ended in a few months. We were joined by another officer from the embassy and then shown into an adjoining room where the four of us sat at a small round table. It was a private lunch. Pamela Harriman was very cheerful and relaxed, making plans for the next stage of life.

In a week she would be dead.

DEATH AT THE RITZ

Just as I was leaving our Paris apartment on the morning of February 5, 1997, the phone that was an extension off the embassy switchboard rang—usually not good news. I was quickly told there was an emergency Country Team meeting at 9 a.m. and I was to be there.

The deputy chief of mission, the number two in the Embassy, Don Bandler, had called the meeting. Once we were in the secured conference room with the doors locked behind us, he got right to the point. Ambassador Harriman had suffered a stroke hours ago, while swimming in the pool at the Ritz Hotel. She was on life support and not expected to live. We would be facing several stressful days surrounding the death of this major personality. Don Bandler—now the *chargé d'affaires*—asked for all our help as both Washington and Paris would want to honor her. He was right.

The following day, February 6, 1997, Pamela Churchill Harriman, aged seventy-six, died at the American Hospital in suburban Neuilly. On the day following her death there was a solemn service in the back garden of the residence. An honor guard of US Marines, coordinating with the French *Garde Républicaine* and their marching band, accompanied the casket with the traditional slow dirge march. Cardinal Jean-Marie

Lustiger, the Archbishop of Paris, presided. It was not widely known that Harriman was a Catholic who had converted at age thirty, when she got her earlier marriage annulled. The President of the French Republic, Jacques Chirac, placed the Grand Cross of the *Légion d' Honneur* on Harriman's flag-draped coffin.

President Bill Clinton sent the aircraft usually used as Air Force One to Paris to carry Harriman's casket back to the United States. There she was again honored, on February 13, 1997, in a televised service from the National Cathedral in Washington, DC. Among the political and diplomatic personalities in the large crowd was Gregory Peck. How ironic, given six months earlier, she was concerned about *his* health. Now he looked perfectly robust at her funeral.

It would not be until mid-September—a full six months later— before we would get a new ambassador to Paris. In the meantime, my office and the embassy would continue to face crises as we had before.

CHAPTER TWELVE

LIES, LIES, AND MORE LIES

O n the afternoon of February 10, 1995, as I walked towards the door of Ambassador Harriman's office, I passed Richard L. Holm, the CIA's Paris chief of station, walking out. His body language was unmistakable. Head down and shoulders slumped, he said to me as we passed, "This is the worst day of my life."

A remarkable statement from Dick Holm. A genuine hero of the CIA, he had escaped across the green line at night in Beirut, been under fire in Southeast Asia, and crashed and burned in Africa, resulting in the loss of an eye and a face scarred for life. What could have possibly transpired in the ambassador's ornate offices to rival his lifetime of danger and pain?

The relationship between a Legal Attaché and a Chief of Station (COS) can be a difficult one, reflecting the difference in mission and consequently culture between the FBI and the CIA. The most basic difference is that the Bureau mission leads to an agent raising the right hand and swearing to tell the truth, the whole truth, and nothing but the truth, while the CIA's covert mission requires the use of deception and deceit. Nonetheless, both organizations are staffed with patriots, and cooperation between the two is in our nation's best interest.

In Australia, I worked beside a brilliant chief of station. She was in her last post before retirement and accompanied by her husband, who was a CIA retiree from the agency's earliest days. We all got along quite well, and I learned a lot from them. They frankly discussed the extra strain that constant deception places on lives and marriages. One afternoon in Canberra, her deputy provided me with a surprisingly clear example of that dynamic.

The Australian Security Intelligence Organization (ASIO) had uncovered a KGB mole. As the US is a close partner with Australia, both the CIA and FBI had an interest in the details of the spy's damage. ASIO headquarters had promised us a detailed report by a certain hour on a given afternoon. When the time came, it had not arrived, nor were we summoned to pick it up at their headquarters. So, close to closing time, I called our contact at ASIO, who said the CIA's deputy chief of station had been there and ASIO had entrusted our copy for him to bring back to the embassy.

I called the deputy and he flatly denied to me he had the copy for us. Strange. I immediately called ASIO and confirmed my original understanding; our copy was given to the CIA's Deputy COS.

I walked over to the station. Upon admission, the deputy immediately, and in a surprisingly sorrowful tone, told me he was sorry; he didn't know why he had denied he had our copy of the report. He said he operates so much he did not know how to stop operating. I came to learn "operates" and "operating" are CIA euphemisms for lies and lying. This man seemed genuinely contrite. He explained falling into the habit of lying was an actual occupational hazard for CIA officers.

The instructions from FBIHQ to the Legats was we could be "joined at the hip" with the CIA inside the embassy. But we should stand apart from them outside the embassy, since in most countries, even with our closest allies, the CIA was viewed with suspicion. A tricky situation.

In Paris, my predecessor and the COS had instituted a very sound practice to help avoid any misunderstandings. Immediately after the weekly Country Team meeting, I had a one-on-one meeting with the COS, and we briefed each other on any matters that might touch on the other's area of interest. Simple, yet usually effective. But sometimes, even when dealing with a pro like Dick Holm, their habit of "operating" got in the way of a more mutually trusting relationship.

At that time the FBI was attempting to create an international police training academy in Budapest, Hungary, to train the police of newly emerging democracies in Eastern Europe. At its initiation, it was proposed as the "FBI Academy in Europe." That name was eventually dropped in the interest of getting broader support. FBI headquarters tasked me to persuade our French colleagues to join this project. I was approached by an officer from the embassy's political section, who told me his portfolio included justice and police issues. He asked if he could attend the meetings I had with the French about the Budapest initiative in order to enhance his reporting to state. I agreed in the interest of comity with other entities in the embassy.

After having taken this person to several meetings with high-ranking officials in the French National Police and Interior Ministry, and having introduced him as a State Department officer, he very casually mentioned to me that he was in fact CIA, undeclared to the French. This was genuinely concerning. In fact it was just what we had been warned against, and it also put me in the position of having introduced an undeclared CIA operative to our police contacts—which could adversely affect my credibility and do long-term damage to the FBI's relationship with our key police contacts.

I brought this up with Dick Holm. He denied the individual in question was CIA. Had I misunderstood? Not likely, but I checked again. And again, I asked Dick. "Well, he does not work for me," Holm qualified. Turns out, the individual in question was from the analytical side of the CIA, while the station is part of the operational side. As I would come to learn again, this is a big distinction inside the agency, but it's a distinction without a difference to anybody else.

Russian organized crime was then emerging as a bigger issue for the FBI, as well as for our French counterparts. Russian oligarchs and even less savory figures were taking up residence in Paris and on the Riviera. The CIA, having a wealth of data on Russians and now being slightly less concerned with Russian intelligence, turned some of their considerable resources towards this new target, and so in the fall of 1994, a team from the new Russian Organized Crime Unit at CIA Headquarters paid a visit to Paris.

During the visit, we gathered in Dick Holm's large office. From CIA headquarters was Anne Jablonski, their lead Russian OC Analyst, who would later be involved in Bob Levinson's tragic mission to Iran. With her was Bill Tucker, a friend and fellow FBI agent, who had been detailed from the Organized Crime Section at FBIHQ to this new CIA Unit. Dick Holm was behind his desk; his deputy was at the far end of the room facing him. Anne and Bob were sitting on a couch facing me. Between them sat a woman, who I knew as the wife of one of the political officers in the embassy. We had visited their home for a social event, where she confided she was agency. So, I was not at all surprised seeing her there.

As part of our discussion, she was given the assignment by Holm to begin a search of all French language newspapers and magazines for any mention of Russian Organized Crime or of several specific individuals. Sometime later, for whatever reason, I mentioned her by name to Dick as someone with his agency. He said to me she was not CIA. I was so surprised by this response I am sure I paused for several seconds before reminding him I was in his office when he gave her a specific assignment. He said nothing more. I was astounded someone whom I considered a friend could lie to me so easily. But for him it was just knee-jerk "operating."

The news Richard L. Holm received that February afternoon from a furious Ambassador Harriman was shocking. Earlier that day, she had been summoned to the office of French Interior Minister, Charles Pasqua. There she received a stern official complaint about CIA spying in France. Pasqua detailed—with photographs—an agency operation, busted by the DST—*Direction de la Surveillance du Territoire*, French counterintelligence. Pasqua named several CIA officers caught up in it, whom he said must leave the country. I now realized why Dick's head was down and his shoulders slumped. Not only was his time in France at an end, but his CIA career was effectively over.

We already knew something about this simmering problem. Earlier, on January 26, 1995, Interior Minister Charles Pasqua had issued a warning to the ambassador about the CIA spying and demanded it stop. She passed that warning on to Dick Holm and a small number of us were read into the situation. In our weekly meeting, Dick told me, in a rather angry tone, that he was not going to stop, that he got his "marching orders from headquarters, not her." And he was not going to tell the ambassador what they were doing. Effectively, he was saying he would be deceiving her. It surprised me. The ambassador is the representative of the US President.

Two weeks later, when the ambassador was summoned to a second session with Pasqua, where the whole case was presented, as well as the fact that the agency did not stop after being warned, her embarrassment and anger was more than understandable. It would be almost another two weeks before the matter became public in a February 22 leak to the French newspaper *Le Monde*, which was then picked up by the world media. We eventually learned more details.

The operation was aimed at gathering information about the French position on certain trade negotiations. At least five operatives, four officers who were diplomats and a woman posing as the Paris representative of a private American foundation, were assigned to the operation. The woman began a sexual affair with the French official they were targeting. Dick Holm found out about the affair. It should have been clear the romance could compromise the operation, but Holm wanted to continue, and he convinced his headquarters to let him march on.

The CIA as an institution pushes back at allegations, and it did in this instance. First, it belittled the importance of the matter by simply—and consistently—calling it a mere "flap." Then they tried to counterattack. I received a secure phone call from the Assistant Director in Charge of the FBI's Intelligence Division, Robert "Bear" Bryant. He related that the agency was pushing the Bureau to go public about any economic espionage cases we had on the French. The fact was, we had no such cases. More importantly,

Bear Bryant stressed to me, we didn't want to do anything to damage the Bureau's valuable relationship with the French DST. I understood the message. I let him know the Director of the DST had personally contacted me to tell me they understood we were separate from our "cousins." They too wanted to maintain the excellent relationship.

At the same time this imbroglio was unwinding, Anne and I accompanied Ambassador Harriman on a visit to the Pernod-Ricard plant and headquarters on the south side of Paris' périphérique in Créteil. The firm's public relations director, Daniel Bridoux, a friend of long standing, had arranged the visit. The giant international firm's CEO and chairman had long wanted to meet the ambassador, and Pamela Harriman saw these visits as part of her job. Riding out and back in the security of the ambassador's limo, the CIA crisis came up more than once. Now knowing the object of the operation only added to her annoyance. "Wanted to know the French position on a trade issue, did they?" I could invite someone from the Trade Ministry in for coffee or a cocktail and just ask them," the ambassador asserted.

We toured the Pernod-Ricard plant and then had an enjoyable lunch, during which French and American leadership and issues were discussed. Ambassador Harriman seemed unrushed and focused on the conversation with these French business leaders. As soon as we got into the limo, however, she let the driver know she was in a hurry to return to the embassy. She had a secure phone call scheduled with President Bill Clinton at 3 p.m. He wanted a direct conversation about the CIA's Paris fiasco, without any filters.

After the demand from the interior minister for the ousting of the CIA officers, but before the matter went public, FBI Director Louis Freeh made a long-planned visit to Paris. When I sat down with him for a discussion with the ambassador and the deputy chief of mission, the current diplomatic crisis immediately came up. The ambassador repeated her assertion that for the price of a cup of coffee or a cocktail, she could find the information these operatives were chasing. Director Freeh assured her that the FBI's relationship with the DST remained secure.

Anne and I accompanied Ambassador Pamela Harriman on a visit and lunch with French business leaders at Pernod-Ricard, the international liquor company. In less than an hour of smiling with this group, the Ambassador would be on a secure phone call with President Clinton to discuss the CIA's Paris debacle.

That evening, Anne and I hosted a reception at our home for Director Freeh to meet the French graduates of the FBI National Academy. We also included a few colleagues from the embassy, significantly Dick Holm. As he was pulling on his topcoat, and after Louie and I had walked him to the door, Holm brought up the elephant in the room:

"I guess you heard about the flap."

"Yes," said Louie with a nod.

"It would have gone the same with you guys in the states," Holm continued.

"Oh, no," Louie immediately responded. "We would have had 'em in handcuffs."

This wasn't joking; Louie was serious, and Holm took it that way.

The message was clear: *There is a big difference between us.*

None of the CIA officers were arrested by the French, nor were they officially declared persona non grata. After the publicity surrounding the case started to die down, they simply quietly left France.

With Director Louis Freeh in our Paris apartment. Later that evening, he would tell the CIA's Chief of Station, "we would have had 'em in handcuffs."

But the incident led to an investigation by the CIA's own inspector general, Fred Hitz. His report found that Dick Holm had kept the United States Ambassador in the dark about important aspects of his work. It said Holm allowed an operative to carry on an affair with a French official that the operative was targeting, a decision that may have doomed the operation. The IG report also showed that the basic facts of the case as first disclosed by Charles Pasqua, France's Interior Minister, in February 1995, were accurate.

Richard L. Holm retired from the CIA before the IG report was completed.

CHAPTER THIRTEEN

"BRING ME GOOD NEWS"

Father Lucien Ripoche, parish priest of the 11th century Church of the Holy Cross in Aubusson, France, entered his church through the massive, solid-oak door as he had every morning for years. That morning, September 29, 1989, the oak door was off its hinges. He looked over to a side altar where a 17th century tapestry hung. The tapestry was gone. *La Pêche Miraculeuse*, representing Christ and the miracle of the fishes, had been stolen.

A big part of the globalization of crime involves art theft. Art stolen in one country often ends up in another after passing through numerous hands. In this form of criminality, illicit dealers—in police jargon, "fences"—are often more important targets for investigators than are the original thieves. The dealers in stolen art create demand and provide the market for the thieves. The loot from many thieves will pass through the same fence. Often, after passing though the hands of criminal fences, stolen art finds its way into the legitimate market, where it passes though the hands of unwitting dealers. This type of crime calls for a multi-agency and multijurisdictional approach.

The FBI usually becomes involved in art theft investigations via the National Stolen Property Act, which forbids the transportation of stolen property in interstate or foreign commerce.[14] Labeled ITSP (Interstate Transportation Stolen Property) in Bureau casefiles, it is simply called "ITSP" by the agents. The interstate—or foreign—transportation element of the crime will have to be proven at trial. But the FBI often opens an initial investigation on the assumption that stolen property of great value will move interstate.

A significant portion of the criminal portfolio in the Paris Legal Attaché's office involved art theft investigations. Although stolen art can flow in any direction, most fine art moves from Europe to the United States. This is following the economic law of supply and demand. Europe has been producing great art for more than 2,000 years. The old continent is a storehouse of treasures. This art exists in many forms— paintings, sculptures, tapestries, rare documents, and religious relics. The United States, while having produced some great art and artists in little more than two hundred years, can't match the head start Europe has had in production. What we do have in America is a great number of people with the interest and resources to purchase fine art.

One of the nations most affected by art theft is France. Not surprisingly, the French National Police have developed significant expertise in art theft investigations and recovery. They established the *L'Office Central pour la Répression du Vol d'Oeuvres et Objets d'Art*—The Central Office for the repression of the theft of art works and objects—which we simply called the French Art Theft Squad. These detectives developed great expertise in fine art matters, which came from their commitment to training. The opportunities for such training were certainly available in France. The squad had a close working relationship with the leading art museums, including the Louvre and the Musée d'Orsay, as well as with church officials, art historians, curators, dealers, and the French Ministry of Culture.

---

[14] Title 18, U.S. Code, §§ 1314–1315.

The FBI benefited from this expertise by the close working relationship between the French Art Theft Squad and the Legat Office in Paris. Along with other agents from the Legat office, I attended art training sessions conducted by the French National Police. Eventually, we secured places in these classes for agents from key domestic field offices.

In December 1995, we jointly organized an international conference on art theft cooperation. During an intensive week-long session, the conference brought together investigators from the French National Police, French Customs, and Gendarmes to meet with representatives of the US Customs Service and the FBI. The Customs delegation included representatives from the Service's New York and Paris offices. The FBI was represented by field investigatory and supervisory personnel from Chicago, New York, and Paris. An FBI Supervisor from the Interstate Theft Unit at FBI Headquarters in Washington, DC, attended.

The relationship between investigators and prosecutors is key to fruitful outcomes in criminal matters. We must be singing from the same sheet of music. Thus, conference participants included representatives of the French Prosecutorial Services (known in France as *Magistrates*) and an experienced assistant US attorney from the Southern District of New York, as well as representatives of the Office of International Affairs at the US Department of Justice.

The conference participants visited Bernheim-Jeune, one of Paris' most storied art brokers, where a member of the founding family explained the intricacies of the fine art market. The group also had the opportunity for a behind-the-scenes tour of art maintenance and cataloguing at the Musée d'Orsay.

My wife Anne organized an exclusive tour for the conference participants of the US Ambassador's residence, where she was a docent. Located on the *Rue du Faubourg Saint-Honoré*, the mansion formerly known as the *Hôtel Pontalba* held a world-class art collection. The permanent residence collection included paintings by the early American artists Gilbert Stuart and Charles and Rembrandt Willson Peale, as well as Houdon sculptures of Benjamin Franklin and Thomas Jefferson. Added to that was Ambassador's Harriman's personal collection, which

included Cézanne, Picasso, Renoir, and Matisse. There were small draw-
ings by Winston Churchill—Pamela Harriman's father-in-law—as well
as Vincent van Gogh's *White Roses*. Now in the National Gallery of Art
in Washington, DC, it was estimated at the time to be worth fifty million dollars.

Anne led a tour of the Ambassador's residence for a team of visiting prosecutors
and agents. They are seen here in front of van Gogh's fabulous *White Roses*

As a result of the conference, cooperation between the FBI and
the French Art Theft Squad continued to grow and become even more
productive. The French investigators would continue to focus on the
thieves, while the FBI focused on the fences and other resellers. A specific
commitment was made for the exchange of information between the
FBI's computerized National Stolen Art File in Washington, DC, and
the French National Police Art Theft Data Base *Trema*, which is maintained at its Paris headquarters. At FBI headquarters, the supervisory

special agent in the Interstate Theft Unit assigned art theft matters now had it as a full-time job. That task would continue to grow to such an extent that in 2004, FBI headquarters established an Art Crimes Team, which now numbers over twenty special agents.

The American Embassy in Paris has a long tradition of holding its own art show. This was a fun occasion to showcase the artwork of embassy employees, their families, and friends. It has grown over the years and occasionally features guest artists. My mother had taken up painting in her retirement on the New Jersey shore. She sent a few of her pieces to be displayed.

The show was held in the former home of the famous French diplomat Talleyrand. The eponymous Building, an ornate 18th century mansion at 2 *Rue Saint-Florentine*, just off a corner of the Place de La Concorde, is now the property of the US government. My office invited a half dozen members of the French Art Theft Squad to be our guests at the opening evening. An invitation to any event at the American Embassy is universally appreciated. The opening of an art exhibition often begins with a private showing—called a "vernissage"—for key guests.

As we were entering the Talleyrand Building's courtyard with our guests, Ambassador Harriman was just exiting. As we passed each other, she exclaimed "Oh, Tom, I just saw your mother's paintings and they are the best in the show!" Her remark to me was typical of her manner. But to these French police detectives, Pamela Harriman was a celebrity and her recognition of me clearly impressed them. I then paused to introduce them to the ambassador, explaining their important work. They were completely charmed by her.

Numerous items of valuable art were returned to France during our assignment there. Primarily paintings, but other objects as well. An extremely valuable Beauvais tapestry from the 18th century was recovered by the FBI in New York. Some items, however, have a value that can't be calculated in monetary terms alone.

The French National Archives had discovered the April 11, 1814 Treaty of Fontainebleau was missing. This was the document by which

Napoleon had renounced all claims to his empire as he went into exile on the island of Elba. In May 1996, the New York Office of the FBI located the nine-page treaty just before it was to go on the auction block at Sotheby's, with an estimated dollar value at between $50,000 and $75,000—and an even greater historic value to France.

Although the priceless document had been recovered, the question of how it had disappeared remained. The French National Archives are housed in a massive building on the *Rue Frances-Bourgeois* in Paris, which welcomes thousands of researchers to its reading rooms each year. Officials there simply said that some scholars might stuff the papers into their shirt and walk out. Sotheby's was not much more helpful. The New York auction house simply said they had received the document in the mail and further indicated that this "blind" offering for sale was not all that unusual.

Thus began a long investigative trail. Ultimately, two Americans were identified as the culprits. They were a college professor and a graduate student. And they admitted they did it just as those at the Archives had supposed: stuffing the treaty and other valuable documents into their shirts and walking out the door. The two suspects were arrested by the FBI in Tennessee on March 28, 2001, for interstate transportation of stolen property. In 2002 they were convicted of the charge in the Southern District of New York.

The art recoveries often generated positive coverage in the French media. At a Country Team meeting, just after the negative publicity of the CIA spying debacle, Ambassador Harriman arrived with a folded newspaper in her hand. After taking her place at the head of the long conference table, she unfolded the morning's paper, *Le Figaro*, to a front-page story with photos of our recoveries. Pointedly looking down the table at the CIA's chief of station, she exclaimed, "I wish everyone, like Tom Baker and his team, would 'bring me good news'!"

After years passing through many hands, the tapestry of *La Pêche Miraculeuse* was recovered, thanks to the efforts of the FBI's Chicago and New York field offices. On March 19, 1996, a celebration took place in the small French town of Aubusson, to mark the tapestry's return. I was there as an invited guest, representing the FBI. Seeing how grateful the people were by the return of this piece of their patrimony made it a memorable day. Among the throng of police, civic leaders, and media was Father Lucien Ripoche, delighted to see "his" tapestry back home.

The tapestry of *Le Pêche Miraculeuse, The Miracle of the Fishes*, was recovered by the FBI in New York after having been stolen in France years earlier. Anne and I participated in its repatriation to the town of Aubusson. The resulting positive publicity in France led Ambassador Harriman to ask others in the embassy to "bring me good news, like Tom Baker and his team.">

CHAPTER FOURTEEN

DEATH OVER WATER

TWA Flight 800 was only twenty minutes out of JFK Airport enroute to Paris, flying at 14,000 feet above the Atlantic, when it exploded and crashed into the water still within sight of New York's Long Island. All 230 people—eighteen crew members and 212 passengers—were killed. It was shortly after 8 p.m. on July16, 1996.

PARIS

In Paris it was 2:30 a.m. when the phone began to ring in our Paris apartment. The FBI's New York Office, the NYO, heard the news first naturally, then the Assistant Director-in-Charge of the New York FBI office, James K. Kallstrom, called me to start the French end of the investigation. In quick succession I heard from FBIHQ and the embassy. At headquarters, the SIOC (Strategic Information and Operations Center) was activated. On the fifth floor of the Hoover Building in DC, the SIOC is a state-of-the-art command post, which was created to help manage crises. The message from the embassy was that the ambassador wanted to be briefed as soon as possible.

So began one of the largest investigations in FBI history and a case that would stay a priority for our Legat office for over a year. Fortunately, in the NYO we were blessed with great leadership and longstanding support and partnerships with other law enforcement agencies.

In the first months of the investigation, nobody seriously questioned the assumption that this had been the work of terrorists. The FBI, French police and intelligence, as well as most of those of Western Europe, proceeded on that assumption. This was, after all, a period that had seen Algerian terrorist bombings in France and the destruction of the federal building in Oklahoma City. It was only a month after the Khobar Towers bombing in Saudi Arabia.

In just two days, on July 19, the Summer Olympics would open in Atlanta, Georgia, where the FBI and others were already in a heightened state of alert about terrorist threats to that event.

In the last two days of July, Attorney General Janet Reno again came to France on a long-planned return visit to her counterparts in the ministry of the interior and justice. It was to be a short, two-day stop. By this time, the AG's security detail had become a bit more sophisticated. They now had an "advance detail," which arrived four days ahead of her. Despite her important position, Reno was an easy guest—her advance detail, not so much. They demanded a lot of our time and attention, when our focus needed to be on the diplomatic, legal, and investigative hurdles of getting the TWA 800 case moving forward on the French side. Ten days had already gone by.

And much of the AG's focus, I would quickly learn, was back home. Just after midnight in Atlanta, on the morning of July 27, a bomb had detonated at the Summer Olympic site. The investigation of that attack immediately targeted Richard Jewell, a security guard who had first spotted the device, as the prime suspect. In Paris we had received an investigative summary of the bombing to furnish to our counterparts. The news of the suspect's identity was leaked to the press while the attorney general was with us in Paris. The *Atlanta Journal-Constitution* first broke the story on Monday, July 29.

By Tuesday, the story was everywhere.

Before the leaks, Janet Reno had obviously been reading the same summaries I had, and likely a lot more. When we were alone in the car between visits, she startled me by turning towards me and asking what I thought of Richard Jewell as a suspect. I really had not thought about it much at all. Like many, I just assumed—consciously or not—that the accused was likely guilty. Then this imposing woman bent her head sideways to answer her own question with, "I'm not so sure." Her dubious response surprised me even more than her initial question.

Turns out, she had reason to be skeptical. Jewell was not the bomber. An injustice was done to him. By October, the FBI would rule him out as a suspect. AG Reno would take it upon herself to publicly apologize for what he had endured. Clint Eastwood would dramatize the injustice done to Richard Jewell in the eponymous film.

There were no complaints from the Attorney General's counterparts concerning our response to TWA 800. But there was overwhelming interest. Forty-five French citizens perished in the plane's explosion. The French public, press, and government authorities were every bit as anxious to know the cause of the catastrophic event as we were. The US Embassy in Paris had to provide the French government with information concerning the direction of the investigation affecting their citizens. As the senior FBI and Justice official at the embassy, I became a key point in this liaison. Daily summary reports to the judicial police, who would be handling leads in France, began on the first day. The timely, detailed, and objective reports we received from the scene were greatly appreciated by our French colleagues. Similar summaries were regularly provided to Ambassador Harriman and key embassy officials.

FALSE LEADS

The loss of TWA 800 was very emotional on several levels.

Pierre Salinger, the former press secretary to Presidents John F. Kennedy and Lyndon B. Johnson, was then living in France. He spoke fluent French, was then a very well-known personality, and still had a great deal of cachet from his Camelot days in Kennedy's White House. He put forth the theory that a US Navy missile brought down the plane.

He said he had facts to back up his assertion. Two assistant Legats located Pierre Salinger in a matter of hours and interviewed him about his "facts."

He could not provide any information of value; he said he was merely asserting what he believed to be true, but would not say more. In the country team meeting where the case was first discussed, Ambassador Harriman, who personally knew Salinger, used the word "traitor" for his charges against the US Navy. Emotions ran high. Despite our best efforts to get at whatever information he had and resolve his allegations, we couldn't get anything concrete and he would continue to air his opinions over the coming months.

Others airing their opinions, while not as malign as Salinger, were every bit as distracting. Jean-Charles Marchiani, for example, a French politician and businessman, was a key advisor to Interior Minister Charles Pasqua. In the months before the TWA crash, he received a great deal of recognition for leading the attempt to free seven Trappist monks kidnapped in Algeria, but a year earlier, he had contacted our office claiming he "knew" Iran was responsible for the Oklahoma City Bombing. (Fortunately, the investigation in Oklahoma quickly determined the real culprits.)

Now Marchiani was again proclaiming Iranian responsibility, this time for TWA 800. French police interviewed him a number of times but couldn't get any details, other than an avowal that he "knew" Iran was behind it. Then Marchiani began calling American businessmen and politicians of his acquaintance. Receiving this "fabulous" tip, they in turn called FBIHQ, which then contacted us with this "great new lead." The director of the Judicial Police personally assured me that Marchiani had nothing to provide, but he also admitted he was "untouchable" and would continue to be a headache.

The National Transportation Safety Board (NTSB) has responsibility for aircraft accidents. The FBI had jurisdiction for the criminal destruction of aircraft.[15] Some commentators, in hindsight, would later question the FBI's role. Aside from everybody's initial belief this was a terrorist incident, i.e., a crime, the NTSB just did not have the manpower available to the FBI. When I received the early morning call from Kallstrom, he already had over 200 agents on Long Island. They had been there all night, trying to locate witnesses. By dawn, they were already out in boats searching the Atlantic. The NTSB team did not arrive from Washington until the next day.

The manpower of the NYO, the FBI's largest office, was significantly augmented by its state and local partners. For years, the NYO had been developing deep relationships with these partners, the heart of which was the JTTF (Joint Terrorism Task Force). Since the explosion of TWA 800 was considered a terrorist act, the NYPD, Nassau County, Suffolk County, and other police agencies were fully committed under the rubric of the JTTF. The US Navy and Coast Guard were also committed to the recovery of the victims' bodies, aircraft debris, and any other potential evidence.

For years TWA's Flight 800 was a routine, nightly flight from JFK to Paris. We learned it carried the mail from the APO (Army Post Office) depot in Brooklyn to Paris. In the weeks and months following the crash, envelopes and credit card bills would keep arriving in clear plastic at the embassy's APO. Some were damaged, some water soaked and now dried out—a continuing reminder of the tragedy.

FRANCE

Assistant Legat Becky Bosley, one of the agents who interviewed Salinger, became our case agent for TWA # 800, a key role in the FBI. The French legal system being so inherently different from ours presented challenges. International Letters Rogatory (ILR) were required to collect evidence in France—a complex and cumbersome diplomatic process requiring delegation of the ILR first to a judge and then to the

---

[15] Title 18, U.S. Code, § 32 (a).

judicial police. Through her contacts at the French Justice Ministry and the Paris prosecutor's office, Becky significantly expedited the process. Her French language skills and knowledge of the French legal system were invaluable. What would normally take a year took months, what had taken months now took weeks, and what took weeks was done in days.

Once diplomatic and legal paths were cleared, three teams of investigators came from New York. The first team focused on the immediate families of the forty-five French victims. The same approach had already started in the US with the American victims. Sensitive but probing, interviews had to be conducted to find anyone with an ideological, psychological, or other reasons for wanting to harm themselves or bring down the plane. Most of the investigators were, as I expected, FBI Special Agents from the NYO. But I was surprised—and ultimately impressed—that some were NYPD detectives who were long-time members of the JTTF. I reviewed much of the outgoing communications after their interviews. These detectives were preparing their interviews on FD-302s, as any FBI Special Agent would. They were excellent.

The New York investigators were paired with French police. As only some of the French police spoke English and only a couple of the agents from New York spoke French, the agents in our office were kept busy. The travels of the New York team with French police throughout France required constant troubleshooting beyond help with interpreting.

All of these sessions with French families were very emotional. In some cases, the agent interviewing victims' families had photos of jewelry or other valuables recovered from the crash site. The display of this material often led to outbursts of tears. The agents and police returning to the office after these sessions freely admitted their interviews often ended in much hugging and crying with people they had never met until that day. In a strange way, much good will was generated by the demonstrated humanity of the New York investigators.

CARGO

One of the later teams of investigators dealt with the plane's cargo. The interviews of French companies and individuals who had cargo aboard the flight were very revealing. Avoiding taxes was a way of life for French people because of the country's onerous taxes and import duties. Time and again our agents discovered what was listed on the cargo manifests was not actually what had been shipped. French small businesspeople made these admissions with a French police officer sitting in the room. The officer often promised or implied he would not share this information with *le fisc*–the dreaded tax man. Fax machines, copiers, and similar office equipment were expensive in France and heavily taxed. Orders for these items were placed by phone or fax to discounters in lower Manhattan, with a request to have the contents of a shipment identified as a low-tax item. The purchasers when interviewed were often surprised. They did not know their package was on TWA 800. They just knew there was a delay.

One French entrepreneur, who owned a chain of garden supply stores in the suburbs, was contacted some weeks after the crash. A shipment of several thousand small green turtles, consigned to him, was among the cargo on TWA 800. The turtles originated on a turtle farm in Louisiana. He expected them over a month prior and was demanding the seller in Louisiana refund his deposit. The man in Louisiana insisted the turtles were shipped, and he was demanding full payment. The Louisianan of course had no way of knowing the turtles were transferred to Flight 800 in NY. Neither did the French buyer. They continued a heated exchange of faxes over the turtles.

The turtles themselves survived the crash. A dozen or more of them were in clear plastic bags half filled with water. Dozens of these bags in turn filled a Styrofoam box. Dozens of these boxes in turn filled a large cardboard and wooden shipping container. These large containers filled one of the metal cargo compartments in the belly of the 747. Evidently, the metal section of the cargo compartments fell out of the belly of the plane. When it hit the Atlantic, with tremendous impact, the metal compartment split open, then the large shipping container split open, then the Styrofoam boxes. By then all the energy was spent and the bags with the turtles were left floating on the surface. Many were scooped up by the first boats collecting debris.

BUILDING GOOD WILL

Some witnesses to the accident had seen a "streak of light," which they described as ascending to a point where a large fireball appeared. Several of these witnesses reported that when the "streak of light" reached its apex, it gave out a loud boom. Some said the fireball split in two as it descended toward the water. There was intense public interest in these witness reports. Some speculated the reported streak of light was consistent with the theory that a missile had struck TWA 800, causing the aircraft to explode. These witness accounts were a challenge as the case moved forward.

Two months into the investigation, the Assistant Director in Charge of the New York FBI office, James K. Kallstrom, made a short visit to France. In one busy day he did a lot of good.

That morning, sitting in a circle in the ambassador's office, Kallstrom briefed a small gathering of key officers. He took questions; the big one was about the streak of light. Sitting like the rest of us, he started by pointing out the significant difference between the speed of light and the speed of sound. The aircraft was flying at 14,000 feet and about nine miles from land. The fuel coming down from the stricken aircraft was burning, the flames ascending, i.e., the streak of light. Then he stood up and dramatically explained the sightings of "missiles" as he walked across the room, counting off the seconds with a clap of his hands: "One, two, three, four, and boom!"—the explosion they had heard happened seconds before the light they saw. Our small group was spellbound by Jim Kallstrom's animated explanation.

That afternoon he made a presentation, using slides and video, at an auditorium for the victims' families and French media. A tough audience of several hundred people attended. The scope of the recovery effort off

Long Island was evident, as was Kallstrom's genuine concern. In the videos we spotted both our mail bags and the bags of turtles as they were scooped up from the surface of the Atlantic. Kallstrom pledged to the emotional assembly they would find out what happened to Flight 800. He was very believable. As with the investigators' experience, there was a lot of crying as the meeting broke up. I spied Jim Kallstrom hugging many of the victims' relatives.

That evening at our home, Anne and I had a reception with our Legat team and the French police who had worked on the case. Jim Kallstrom, the guest of honor, presented certificates of appreciation to a dozen French police officers. Kallstrom had a commanding presence, and at the same time was a very warm and physical person. He patted agents and police on their arm or shoulder just as he had, earlier that day, hugged the victims' relatives. Some of the French police spoke out emotionally that evening, proclaiming that working with the FBI was the highlight of their career.

PIERRE SALINGER REDUX

Meanwhile, Pierre Salinger continued to be a distraction with his insistence that the TWA plane was downed by a US Navy missile. He already had been interviewed that summer. But later, on Friday, November 8, he gave a press conference at an aviation industry meeting on the Riviera, where he again persisted in his missile theory. The day before, sitting in the lobby of the Carlton Hotel in Cannes, he waved a paper in front of a reporter claiming it as proof. Most concerning, he asserted the "FBI has yet to contact me." This was simply not true.

Salinger claimed the paper he was waving came from the *Services Secret*, confusing matters even more. American journalists reported the story as if he were claiming the information originated with the US Secret Service. The French media translated *Services Secret* as Intelligence Services. So, in addition to going back to our French intelligence contacts to again receive assurance they weren't sitting on anything, we had to ask the US Secret Service representative at the embassy. He thought it a joke. The FBI in New York and at headquarters in DC were asking the same, not-so-funny question of Secret Service leadership.

In the middle of this imbroglio, I received an invitation to lunch at the ambassador's residence. There was a seating plan with the names and titles of every guest. We would be lunching with two important French officials from the Transportation Ministry and the Aviation agency, both women. Also on the luncheon seating plan was the name Nicole Helene Gillman, which meant nothing to me at the time. As I was entering the residence for the lunch, Joseph, the ambassador's butler, told me sotto voce that Nicole Gillman was a former wife of Pierre Salinger and a good friend of the ambassador.

I was seated between two women at lunch, as usual. But at this luncheon of five, I was the only man. Although the conversation focused on the actual TWA 800 case, there was a good bit of chatter about Pierre Salinger. Suffice it to say, he was not liked by anyone at that table. All the guests had seen Jim Kallstrom on CNN that morning; his typically pithy retorts to Salinger's latest broadside—"that's crazy" and "he's crazy"—were loved by the media and eaten up by the women at this lunch.

Nicole Gillman joked about the confusion Salinger created with his Secret Service/*services secret* assertions. Salinger had "replaced" her with another Nicole, she said with a smile and a shrug, so maybe he was getting old and simply needed help remembering names. But after a few years, he left the second Nicole, too. So now there were two former Madames Nicole Salinger. "Pierre always leaves confusion in his wake," she concluded with a sigh.

There have been numerous books, journal articles, and TV specials about the crash of TWA Flight 800. Many of these were built on the discredited conspiracy theories of Pierre Salinger. Most successful among the books is Nelson DeMille's 2004 novel *Night Fall*, built around witness statements claiming the fatal explosion was caused by a missile and not by mechanical failure. Although a novel, his introduction opens the way for a conspiracy and the book is cited by many as support for Salinger's missile theory. John F. Picciano's 2012 *Liam's Promise* also uses the explosion of TWA 800, but this time as a backdrop for his novel about a father-son relationship. Picciano makes clear in his introduction that his scenario is a fabrication. Clearly, *Liam's Promise* is not ammunition to support any conspiracy theory.

ANOTHER VISITOR FROM NEW YORK

Six months into the investigation, in early 1997, John Patrick O'Neill came to Paris on this case. He had just transferred from FBIHQ to be a SAC in the NYO. He oversaw that office's National Security Division. His very first trip in his new role was to visit Paris. He had visited us before and would be back again. He liked Paris, and who could blame him?

Back in 1995, when John P. O'Neill became the chief of the counterterrorism section at FBI's headquarters, he made a working trip to Paris. I accompanied him to meetings with our key French counterparts. He was pointed, yet charming, in all these meetings. O'Neill was already warning of the threat from the *mujahideen*, veterans of the Afghan fighting of the 1980s. He demonstrated specific knowledge of Osama bin Laden and Al-Qaeda, which he called "the base." In 1995, most of us hadn't heard of either.

At the DST, *Direction de la Surveillance du Territoire*, the branch of the French National Police charged with national security matters, we met with Jean-François Claire, then their assistant director in charge of counterterrorism, and someone widely respected throughout western intelligence services. After some discussion of Al-Qaeda, John O'Neill impressed Claire when he casually mentioned a sister of Osama bin Laden who was living in the south of France. Bin Laden had many siblings and dozens of half-siblings. O'Neill said he hoped if the DST learned anything useful from her, they would share it. O'Neill did not ask—he did not have to—if this very westernized sister was a DST source.

Jean-François Claire was not just impressed by O'Neill, he was charmed by him. O'Neill was like his boss Kallstrom, a very warm and physical person. When we stood up to leave, as Claire and O'Neill started to shake hands, John leaned in and kissed Claire on the cheek. He was the kind of person who could do that in a very natural way. I could not. When I next met Jean-François Claire he told me when he was growing up as a boy in rural France, it was usual for boys to kiss upon meeting and parting. Nothing sexual about it. It is hardly done today. Claire told me he was incredibly touched by O'Neill's gesture.

The TWA case—still being worked as a terrorist incident—was now part of John O'Neill's portfolio in the NYO. By this point, in early 1997, the French judicial system had opened an inquiry into the death of forty-five French citizens in the crash. That case was assigned to an Investigating Magistrate. In the French system, these individuals are a hybrid between a prosecutor and a judge.

John and I went together across one of the Seine River bridges to the old center of Paris, the *Ile de la Cité*, where the massive Notre Dame Cathedral famously sits. We headed to the opposite end of the island, where behind high spiked gates stood the *Sainte-Chappelle* with its magnificent stained glass. Surrounding this masterpiece of medieval beauty was the equally ornate *Palais de Justice*. There we met the Investigating Magistrate in her chambers.

It was just the three of us, and I did the interpreting—not word for word but summarizing one party's remarks for the other. The Investigating Magistrate, addressed as *juge*, an attractive, well-dressed woman, explained that her task would involve both civil and criminal law. John went back and forth with some brief general remarks until the judge turned slightly to face me and gave a clear and somewhat lengthy discourse in French. She wanted "Monsieur O'Neill" to understand she did not want to interfere with his investigation. But, at the end of the day, she would have to present a written report.

After her minute or two non-stop oration in French, I turned to John. "She doesn't want to interfere in your case, but you have to "throw her a bone."

Then immediately the Investigating Magistrate said—in perfectly clear English—"Yes, that's it!"

John started to make the arrangements right there—as Kallstrom had done for others—for her to visit the crash site on Long Island.

The NYO did these visits right. Their tours of the crash site centered on a former US Coast Guard Station in East Moriches, Suffolk County, Long Island. It was at the Coast Guard Station where the victims' bodies and plane debris were initially kept. And it was there that the Boeing 747 was being reconstructed.

In the end, they accounted for all but 5 percent of the aircraft.

The NYO usually provided a helicopter ride from Manhattan, but for our French visitors they added a slight detour for an "up close and personal" visit with Lady Liberty. I have been in a helicopter with French visitors when they flew around the Statue of Liberty and then hovered yards from the front of her face. More than one Frenchman was brought to tears.

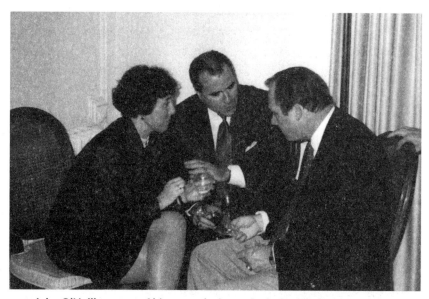

John O'Neill, on one of his several trips to Paris, huddled with me and a French police official in our apartment about the parameters of the TWA 800 investigation. O'Neill was killed in the World Trade Tower on 9/11.

Eventually the case wound down. Numerous terrorist leads were explored and exhausted. With input from the NSTB, Boeing, and

TWA, it looked most likely to have been an accident, an explosion of vapors in the central fuel tank. That was the conclusion announced on November 18, 1997. Both O'Neill and Kallstrom would again come to Paris. The case was a model of cooperation, both domestically and internationally. The FBI and its law enforcement partners had reconstructed the plane's fuselage and bequeathed it to the NTSB. James K. Kallstrom retired from the FBI on December 31, 1997.

Still, 230 people lay dead.

MORE DEATH OVER WATER

John O'Neill would go on to lead the investigation of the attack on the USS *Cole*, the destroyer that was bombed while docked in Yemen's port city of Aden on October 12, 2000. Seventeen sailors were killed, and many others were wounded in the suicide bombing which was eventually traced back to Osama bin Laden, as O'Neill had said from the beginning.

FBI agents arrived on the scene in Aden two days after the attack. From the outset, the US ambassador to Yemen, Barbara K. Bodine, proved difficult to deal with and opposed O'Neill and the FBI every step of the way. She was a career state department employee in her first post as ambassador. She disagreed with O'Neill on how to handle crime scene searches and interviews with citizens and government officials, and above all, she objected to the number of FBI personnel. I had run into this before in other posts. First-time career ambassadors are often afraid that US law enforcement—"cowboys" to them—will "rock the boat." But this was far worse: a ship had been bombed and seventeen Americans killed.

After two months in Yemen, O'Neill returned to New York for what was to be a brief stay between the Thanksgiving and Christmas holidays. I met him in New York City a week before Christmas 2000 at a Law Enforcement Foundation luncheon. We chatted, and although I had heard about the difficult Ambassador Bodine, he just shrugged and smiled at the mention of her name. He clearly hoped and expected to go back to Yemen to continue the investigation. But she blocked his return, something a US ambassador can do to any US government employee, by denying "Country Clearance."

The situation with O'Neill and Bodine was hard for me to comprehend. I had seen John O'Neill up close and personal dealing with all sorts of officials, men and women, including ambassadors. He so easily charmed them and gained their cooperation. Bodine left the post less than a year later, in August 2001, and never served as an ambassador again. Director Louis Freeh withdrew the remaining members of the FBI team from Yemen in June 2001.

John O'Neill was what some used to call a "man about town." When in New York City, he was a regular at Régine's on East 54th Street. (Yes, Régine's own by Régine Zylberberg, who had caused Ambassador Harriman so much heartburn.)

But John could stay out all night schmoozing with friends and still be alert at early morning meetings. I once asked—not really expecting a response—how he did it. The unexpected answer came back: "Visine, tons of the stuff."

Still, O'Neill's habits and lifestyle led to several OPR (Office of Professional Responsibility) inquiries, the FBI's version of an internal affairs investigation. Most significantly was one focusing on the loss of a briefcase containing highly classified information. An August 19, 2001, a *New York Times* report disclosed the entire ongoing investigation of the lost briefcase. O'Neill then decided to retire from the Bureau. He started a new job as chief of security at the World Trade Towers, on August 23, 2001.

On September 11, 2001, John O'Neill was killed in the World Trade Towers.

CHAPTER FIFTEEN

"TURN OVER EVERY STONE"

A phone was ringing in our Paris apartment. The phone was an extension of the embassy switchboard, so its ringing was seldom, if ever, announcing good news. But it had to be answered—even after one o'clock in the morning, on the last day of August in 1997.

THE WHITE HOUSE CALLING

The operator—stress in his voice—told me the White House was on the line with a request from President Clinton, who was vacationing on Martha's Vineyard. The president wanted to know the details of Princess Diana's auto accident, which he had just learned from a brief CNN newsflash. The harassed operator did not know where else to go for an answer. There was no ambassador in Paris at that moment, as Ambassador Pamela Harriman had died of a sudden stroke in February and there was not yet a replacement.

Leaving the phone line open, I used my cell phone to call the command post—*La Permanence*—for the Paris Police. I identified myself to the French police officer who answered. He was suspicious. I heard him repeating my urgent request into what I imagined was a busy and crowded command post. Fortunately, there was someone there who knew me and told me that told Diana, Princess of Wales, had been in an auto accident and two of her companions had been killed. The Princess was being taken to Paris' *Hôpital La Pitie Salpetriere*, after having been treated extensively at the scene, and was, he said, still alive.

I relayed this information to the embassy switchboard promptly and hence to the White House operator, who had been "on hold" the entire time. I was immediately told that was exactly what the President wanted to know: where the Princess was now. The next morning, I was thanked profusely by the *chargé d'affaires*, i.e., the acting ambassador, for promptly handling this presidential request. Sadly, I also learned Princess Diana had died just after my call. A pulmonary vein had been severed in the accident. She was only thirty-six years old.

In France at that time there was a general awareness that "Princess Di," as the popular media called her, was in the country. For more than a week proceeding her death, the French newspapers, and certainly the tabloids, were full of reports accompanied by paparazzi's photos of her and Dodi Al-Fayed enjoying themselves on Al-Fayed's $20 million yacht, *Jonikal*, and at his massive estate in Saint-Tropez on the Riviera. It was clear to even the most casual observers, this was certainly a romance. Dodi's father, Mohamed Al-Fayed, an extremely wealthy individual deeply invested in his oldest son's future, would insist the couple was engaged and planning on marriage. The British Royal Family and their allies strongly pushed back against that idea.

HOUSE HUNTING?

On Saturday, August 30, 1997, Diana and Dodi arrived in Paris. That afternoon they spent an hour inspecting the Villa Windsor, the former residence of the Duke and Duchess of Windsor at 4 *Route du Champ d'Entraînement*. The duke was the former King Edward VII, who famously abdicated to marry the woman he loved, an unpleasant issue for the Royal Family to this day. Mohamed Al-Fayed had secured a fifty-year lease on the property and spent millions restoring the home.

That evening they had dinner at the Ritz Hotel, which was also owned by Mohamed Al-Fayed. Earlier in the day Dodi had purchased a six-figure diamond ring at an upscale jeweler only steps from the Ritz on the Place Vendôme. An engagement ring, in Mohamed Al-Fayed's telling.

About twenty minutes after midnight, the couple left the hotel to return to Al-Fayed's Paris apartment on *Rue Arsène Houssaye*, near the top of the Champs-Élysées. They were hounded by paparazzi. Henri Paul, the hotel's chief of security, had been called in to drive the couple. He had already been off duty for several hours. To evade the paparazzi, they left the hotel from the rear entrance on Rue Cambon along with a bodyguard, Trevor Rees-Jones.

Driving a Mercedes S-280 Sedan, Henri Paul sped them through Paris' streets trying to avoid the paparazzi. Paul took them along the Cours la Reine and the Cours Albert I, which together form the embankment road along the right bank of the Seine. Some commentators have darkly questioned his choice of this route, rather than the more direct run, straight up the avenue des Champs-Élysées. Anyone who has seen the Champs-Élysées at midnight on a Saturday, particularly in the summer, knows why he chose that route. Even at midnight, it is a crawl with bumper-to-bumper traffic and mobs of pedestrians.

DEATH IN THE STREET

His chosen route led them into the Pont de l'Alma underpass. Paul was clearly speeding, perhaps urged on by his passengers, in an apparent effort to lose the paparazzi, who were on their tail. And then, the crash. The police arrived within minutes. Ambulances began arriving within five minutes. Dodi and Paul were pronounced dead on the scene and their bodies were taken to the *Institut Médico-Légal* (IML), the Paris Medical Examiner's office. Diana was treated in an ambulance on the scene for about half an hour.

Much criticism from outside France, particularly from the United States, was directed at this "delay" in getting Diana to a hospital. In the United States, standard operating procedure is to get the injured to a hospital as fast as possible. American medical personnel and EMTs call these first minutes after an accident the "golden hour," where lives can still be saved by the personnel and equipment available in a hospital. The French approach is to bring the personnel and equipment to the injured. Hence, the various French ambulance services not only carry sophisticated equipment but are staffed by nurses and emergency doctors as well. One system is not necessarily better than the other: just two different approaches. Considering the possible delays in Parisian traffic, when getting the injured back to a hospital, their system makes sense in their circumstances.

The death of Diana, "the People's Princess," captured the world's attention. Philippe Massoni, *Prefect de Police de Paris*, the Paris police chief, was himself on the scene within an hour of the accident. Shortly after dawn, the French Interior Minister and the Prime Minister visited the hospital. Later in the day, Diana's former husband, Prince Charles, arrived in Paris. He was accompanied to the hospital by the President of the French Republic, Jacques Chirac.

People at every level of society and from every corner of the world were moved by Diana's tragic death. Within hours of the news of her passing, Mother Teresa issued a statement from Calcutta honoring the Princess. Some might consider them an odd pair, but the two had formed a deep bond. Their last meeting was earlier that summer, when, on June 18, 1997, they toured the streets of the Bronx together. Sadly, Mother Teresa of Calcutta's passing on September 5, 1997, just days after Diana's death, was completely overshadowed by the ongoing mourning and turmoil surrounding the Princess' tragedy.

The ultimate indication of the emotional frenzy affecting so many was a phone call I received on Monday morning, September 1, 1997. A senior official from FBIHQ asked how many agents I needed on temporary (TDY) assignment in Paris to help work the case. I was initially baffled by this unusually generous offer, but quickly realized even those at their desks in Washington were taking this loss personally. As much as we all wanted to "do something" there was no case for us. This was a truly tragic traffic accident in France which killed a British Princess. The FBI had no official role to play.

But I would eventually be given a role to play.

After my retirement from the FBI, I had started working as a consultant when I was contacted by John Hotis. We first met when we both worked in FBI Director William Webster's office. A graduate of Yale Law School, Hotis had been a special assistant to Webster at the FBI and moved with him to the CIA, where Webster served as director until they both left on August 31, 1991.

In a series of meetings in Northern Virginia, Hotis, who was now in private practice, explained he wanted me to work with him on a "very sensitive" case. He needed someone with a knowledge of both the French and British police systems.

FRAUD AGAINST A FATHER IN MOURNING

Hotis was involved in an investigation related to the Princess' death.

Mohamed Al-Fayed, a grieving and angry father, had been contacted eight months after the crash, in April 1998, by a go-between representing "former CIA officers." They claimed to have documents showing Dodi and Diana were murdered in a joint CIA/MI6 operation. The alleged former CIA people demanded millions from Al-Fayed in exchange for the documents. A Washington area law firm, then representing Al-Fayed's interests, brought John Hotis into the picture. Hotis knew the key people to contact at both the CIA and the FBI, and he quickly became Al-Fayed's face to those agencies in this fraud case.

Samples of some of the alleged CIA documents were obtained and it was obvious they were fakes. The investigation by the US Attorney's office in Washington, DC and the FBI's Washington Field Office became wide-ranging. Three subjects were identified, all Americans, but scattered around the world. Numerous Legat offices became involved.

On April 28, 1998, the Legat in Vienna led Austrian police to the ringleader, Oswald LeWinter, who was negotiating with Mohamed Al-Fayed's representative in a Vienna Hotel. They arrested LeWinter and the plot to defraud Al-Fayed began to unravel. LeWinter would serve years in an Austrian prison for his attempted extortion. On August 6, 1999, Al-Fayed initiated a civil suit in US federal court against all the Americans who were involved in the attempt to sell him fake CIA documents.

John Hotis, by getting the case against these extortionists rolling, established his credibility in the eyes of Mohamed Al-Fayed and his DC-area law firm. They now wanted to engage him further in undertaking a mission to Britain and France addressing their other concerns with the deaths of Al-Fayed's son and the Princess. That's why Hotis contacted me.

VOICE OF A FATHER

I had indirectly heard something of Mohamed Al-Fayed's questions and concerns about the deaths of Dodi and Diana. During the preceding year, and since my retirement from the Bureau, I had made numerous trips to France for various clients. During many of these visits I met with Michel Kerbois, a retired French police inspector now working in the private sector. Michel, a highly skilled investigator, had a range of contacts at every level of Parisian society and knew the tricks to cross-matching data sources. We had come to know and trust one another.

I recall during one visit, sitting in my hotel lobby, as Michel Kerbois paged though the flimsy sheets of paper spilling from the hotel's *Minitel* (a French internet predecessor). He mentioned the information on those sheets pointed to the identity of the owner of a white Fiat Uno, which may have been involved in the accident that killed Diana. Michel, not surprisingly, had known Henri Paul, the Ritz Hotel's director of security, who was also killed in the incident.

On another occasion, Michel mentioned he had obtained access to a copy of a forensic report showing Henri Paul had a large amount of carbon monoxide in his blood at the time of the post-mortem, which Michel thought significant. John MacNamara, an Englishman, who was Mohamed Al-Fayed's principal investigator, had commissioned him to undertake this research in France. Michel used the colorful colloquial French expression *nul*—meaning useless, hopeless, worth nothing— to describe MacNamara. I would come to use other descriptions for John MacNamara.

The French judicial investigation was just wrapping up when Hotis contacted me. Their six-thousand-page report was not yet publicly available. But its bottom line was clear: Princess Diana's death was a result of an accident, which was caused by Henri Paul, driving at high speed while intoxicated. Nine photographers, who had been following the Mercedes on August 31, 1997, were charged with contributing to the deaths. A French appellate court dismissed those charges in 2002. Three of the photographers were tried for taking pictures through the open door of the wrecked Mercedes, a gross violation of the victims' privacy. The three paparazzi were acquitted in 2003.

It would be an understatement to say Mohamed Al-Fayed was unsatisfied with these results.

A conference was arranged in the suburban Virginia office of Al-Fayed's law firm to discuss the case and what Hotis and I could bring to the effort. John MacNamara was on the speakerphone from London, while Hotis and I were sitting around the conference table with two of the firm's attorneys. MacNamara was a retired detective chief superintendent from the London Metropolitan Police. Now, he occupied the post of chief of security at Harrods, the upscale London department store owned by Mohamed Al-Fayed. MacNamara was Al-Fayed's right-hand man and was running Al-Fayed's own investigation into the deaths of Dodi and Diana.

Along with numerous specific criticisms of the French judicial system and their conduct of the investigation, MacNamara outlined Mohamed Al-Fayed's belief: The crash was orchestrated by MI6 on the instructions of the Royal Family. Further, he strongly put forth the theory the CIA aided and abated their colleagues in MI6 in this murderous undertaking. The original fraud case, which Hotis had helped resolve, came up in the discussion. MacNamara continued to push the line, "We are convinced these people were connected to the CIA." He continued. "The documents they tried to sell Mr. Al-Fayed may have been fraudulent, but it's still possible they were based on real documents."

Throughout this discussion, both Hotis and I pushed back at various points. It was our view that the CIA had nothing to gain by this undertaking. There was no rational reason, nor national interest, for them to want Diana dead. And, on a practical level, the Brits would not need the agency to carry out an assassination. MacNamara did not like our pushback. I spoke up, promising, even though we did not believe there was a conspiracy, that we would "turn over every stone" to see if there was collusion with French, British, or American services.

Suddenly, without any introduction, a different voice came out of the speakerphone "I like what Mr. Baker promises," said Mohamed Al-Fayed, who also told us, "Yes, turn over every stone."

PARIS VIA LONDON

A few days later, I met John Hotis at Washington's Dulles Airport for the late flight on British Airways to Heathrow. The law firm, on Al-Fayed's orders, had issued us a pair of round-trip business class tickets to London. Once there, I was to get tickets on the Eurostar train for the continuing trip to Paris. We arrived at Heathrow the following day and, as instructed, traveled to an address on London's luxurious Park Lane. The concierge there was expecting us. We were given Dodi Al-Fayed's apartment to use during our time in London. Mohamed Al-Fayed had kept his son's London flat as a shrine. For years, he had refused to sell the Park Lane apartment, one of the sites where his son romanced Princess Diana in the summer of 1997.

The next morning, we had scheduled an early morning conference at Harrods with MacNamara and his team. The concierge had been in the apartment and made us coffee and left out orange juice and pastries. Nice, but an indication that there was not much privacy when working with this crowd. We planned to take a lunchtime train, for which I had gotten tickets, through the Channel Tunnel to Paris. We walked across Hyde Park to our scheduled meeting at Harrods department store, leaving our packed bags in the apartment.

The meeting took place in a green and beige conference room on the fifth floor of Harrods, where Al-Fayed had his executive offices. The others in the room were for the most part members of MacNamara's security team, former members of Britain's fabled SAS. The Special Air Service, paratroopers, whose veterans had had often served as mercenaries in many African conflicts. MacNamara slyly referred to them as his "killers." We settled down around the large mahogany conference table and the usual "Who do you know?" banter began. The name of Ian Quinn, a current commander in the Met police, was dropped into the conversation. Quinn was someone whom I had come to know when we were both at the British Police College in Bramshill a decade earlier. I said something pleasant about him, which really set MacNamara off.

Turns out, Ian Quinn had led an investigation of MacNamara—and Al-Fayed—for burglarizing a safe deposit box in Harrods' basement. A truly bizarre episode. Mohamed Al-Fayed and his former business partner Roland "Tiny" Rowland had a falling out. Finding his safe deposit box burgled, Tiny Rowland complained to the police, claiming valuable gems as well as business papers were stolen. Scotland Yard's ensuing investigation led to the arrests of MacNamara and Al-Fayed, among others. The case never made it to trial, but it was an indication of the strange ways of Al-Fayed and his team.

John MacNamara then asked me if I know Michel Kerbois. I answered yes. MacNamara responded, "We checked you out with him." He said Michel had told them I was "all right." I started to make some sort of lighthearted rejoinder, when MacNamara talked over me, disparaging Michel's findings during the current investigation. I quickly realized MacNamara, and his team, wouldn't be satisfied with anyone who did not completely buy into their conspiratorial theories of this case.

Apparently speaking for Al-Fayed as well as himself, MacNamara told us in an almost argumentative tone, "We have absolutely no doubt

Dodi and Princess Diana were murdered." They were not at all satisfied with the French investigation; what happened in the Pont de l'Alma underpass was to them much more than an auto accident. Henri Paul, they were certain, was some sort of informant for one or another security or intelligence service. I somewhat surprised him by agreeing to that last assertion. A security manager at a large international hotel would likely be carried as an informant on the books of at least one law enforcement or intelligence agency, even if he never considered himself to be an informant.

John MacNamara did not seem to like Hotis or me, and most of all, he was upset we were not buying into to his theory of the case. But what was agreed on was the key focus of our investigation in France: Who was Henri Paul involved with? Was Henri Paul an informant for any agency? We let them know—we could not finesse it—we did not believe there was a conspiracy, certainly not one involving the CIA. Again, I gave my "but we will turn over every stone" speech.

At that moment, Mohamed Al-Fayed stepped into the room. Clearly, he had been listening. Again, he said, "I like what Mr. Baker says," gesturing with two hands cupped together, turning the one palm up as he spoke, "Turn over every stone." He then declared, "Prince Philip, the Duke of Edinburgh, is the one responsible for giving the orders." According to Al-Fayed, the Queen's husband was racist, was German, and was a Nazi. As for the Fiat Uno, according to Al-Fayed, it was built by the CIA on orders from MI6. We just listened. Then the truly grieving father, who had a surprisingly pleasant face, explained why it was his strong belief the Princess and his son were planning to marry. He was sympathetic, and on this last point only, very believable.

Then, as we were all standing and about to leave, he handed Hotis and me each a roll of ten one-hundred-dollar bills, "some pocket money." I had not gotten a tip since I was a teenager. It felt odd. I did not like it.

STRANGE AND CONTROLLING

We all—except for Mohamed Al-Fayed—started to make our way out. MacNamara declared, "You're coming with us." But our luggage was back at the Park Lane apartment. "We've taken care of that" he told us. The two of us, along with MacNamara and a few of his SAS "killers," got into a couple of black Daimler limousines. In minutes we were at a heliport alongside the Thames. There was a magnificently large helicopter gleaming in the green and beige livery of Harrods, the name stylized on the aircraft's side. Its rotors were already revving up. We all got in and it quickly took off. It was surprisingly spacious and luxurious inside.

We were sitting at facing tables, John Hotis beside me. MacNamara and one of his men were facing us, and at least four others were in the passage cabin with us. There were two pilots up front. As comfortable as it was, it had the disadvantage of all helicopters; one could not talk above the roar of the engines. Not that it mattered. Since we left the conference room back at Harrods, MacNamara had hardly said a word to us. His men said nothing. The hostility was palpable.

I am not sure if John MacNamara's hostile attitude towards us was caused by a sense of professional jealousy—why are they bringing these two former FBI men into "my case"—or was it just a manifestation of his own difficult personality. Of course, one explanation does not necessarily preclude the other.

We were soon at a high altitude. It was a crystal-clear day. I could make out the battlefield at Hastings just before we left the English countryside behind and started to cross over water. Bright dark-blue water shimmering in the sunlight far below. The tickets for the channel train, which we had planned to be on about now, were still in my breast pocket. Sitting there in this very uncommunicative atmosphere, I began to experience a sense of dread. Nobody knew we were over the English Channel. They could toss us out over the water, and no one would be any the wiser. None of these guys had made, or were making, eye contact with us. A very worrisome "tell" under the circumstances. I looked around and started to make defensive plans in my head, but quickly come to the fatalistic realization we were no match for these guys. It was foreboding. Later, Hotis acknowledged he shared these same fears.

We landed at a heliport on the south side of Paris' périphérique. This time in in black Mercedes limousines, we were taken straight to Paris' Ritz Hotel. Located on the Place Vendôme, this Al-Fayed property sat beside the seat of the French Minister of Justice, both familiar sights to me. The Ritz was where Pamela Harriman had her stroke. At the elegant hotel, we had yet another conference. Frank Klein, the General Manager of the Ritz Hotel, was introduced to us as Mohamed Al-Fayed's man in Paris, who would be charge of the French side of this case. MacNamara was still at the table, and it was clear he was really in charge. It was also apparent, Klein was as nervous as the proverbial cat.

From the outset we had been told while in Paris we would be staying at the Ritz Hotel. Klein nervously told us we would be staying at an apartment in Paris, instead of the Ritz. The same apartment on Rue Arsène Houssaye, near the top of the Champs-Élysées, where Dodi and Diana had been heading to when they were killed. When we got there, we found the baggage we had left at the Park Lane flat. The concierge showed us around this truly grand apartment, occupying the top two floors of the building. There were phones throughout for us to use. With this very controlling crew, we strongly suspected the phones, and likely the entire apartment, were bugged. Our suspicions would be confirmed.

TURNING OVER EVERY STONE

Each of the next four mornings, we would find, just as back at the Park Lane Apartment, the concierge had come in with fresh croissants and started the coffee for us. As nice as that was, this lack of privacy was another reminder we were dealing with a strange and controlling bunch. Each day we got out and about in Paris. We ultimately got to see everyone as we intended. Most people we approached straight up, telling them what we were trying to find out and who had engaged us. Occasionally, I would use a pretext of another investigation I was pursuing to get in the door and eventually bring up the purpose of our mission for Al-Fayed. Turning over every stone, as promised.

These meetings included a variety of police contacts. We had a lunch with a close colleague who was now the Chief of Staff to Martine Monteil, the Paris police chief, whose name was on the lengthy French investigative report. Our colleague had done much of the writing and read the entire document. He assured us of the report's veracity. He, like almost every person we spoke with, acknowledged Henri Paul—because of his position—was likely a source for one or more agencies. But in their entire investigation, we were assured, the French police found no concrete evidence Henri Paul was in collusion with anyone on the night of the accident.

We had an engaging dinner with the individual who had been the CIA's Chief of Station (COS) in Paris at the time of the accident. He and his wife had chosen to remain in Paris for the first few years of their retirement. A former colleague of mine, this individual also knew John Hotis from their time together at CIA Headquarters. He asserted there was no indication of involvement by any intelligence service in Princess Diana's death. Again, more than likely, Henri Paul was somebody's source or asset.

As the former Paris Legat, I secured admission into the US Embassy, just off the Place de la Concorde. But it was John Hotis, based on name recognition alone, who then got us into the inner sanctum of the CIA station. There the new COS welcomed us. He was not surprised by our mission. The CIA's press spokesman back in DC had been issuing denials to Mohamed Al-Fayed's widely reported claims of CIA involvement. As for the possibility Henri Paul had a relationship with an intelligence service, he opined it was highly likely. As a French citizen, Paul would be obliged to cooperate with the DGSE—*Direction Général de la Sécurité Extérieure*—France's equivalent of the CIA, if they wanted to place technical surveillance in the Ritz. Since possible targets, such as Yasser Arafat, often stayed at the Ritz, "Well, you figure it out."

Also, back at the US Embassy, we had similar conversations with my successor as Legat, as well as the US Press Officer, and Military

Intelligence representatives. At the British Embassy we spoke to the Police and Press liaisons. Elsewhere in Paris, we contacted the DGSE, *Direction Général de la Sécurité Extérieure*, who were guarded but pleasant. The DST, *Direction de la Surveillance du Territoire* and the RG, *Renseignements Généraux*, (both then intelligence-gathering divisions of the French National Police) were more forthcoming but still noncommittal.

After five days of "turning over every stone" we went one evening to the Ritz Hotel for a scheduled meeting with GM Frank Klein. The following day we were to return to London. Klein was again a nervous wreck. He told us, "they" were very unhappy with us. "They" said we had been working on other cases and they were displeased with our failure to believe the "truth" of what happened. Clearly, the apartment, and the phones in it, were bugged. We were not surprised. We were told to leave France. We were not to return to London. Klein's hands were shaking as he gave us two one-way business class tickets for the first Air France flight to Dulles Airport the next morning.

THE END OF CONSPIRACY

A few years later, a British police investigation—"Operation Paget"— and a follow-on UK inquest would re-examine the crash. The British police report, released in 2006, ruled Diana's death a "tragic accident." The inquest's jury ruled on April 7, 2008 that Diana and Al-Fayed were the victims of an "unlawful killing" by Henri Paul and the paparazzi. The inquest also declared that Paul was drunk. Sad findings, but no conspiracy.

Significantly, the inquest completely discredited John MacNamara, as he was forced to admit under oath he had no evidence of a conspiracy. On February 14, 2008, he specifically admitted he had no evidence of the involvement of the British nor the French security services, nor the British ambassador to Paris, nor Prince Philip the Duke of Edinburgh, in a plot to kill the couple. All contrary to his earlier pronouncements.

Mohamed Al-Fayed said on April 7, 2008, he would accept the inquest's verdict and abandon his years-long campaign to prove Diana and Dodi were murdered in a conspiracy.

In November 2008, the National Security Agency (NSA) disclosed, in response to a Freedom of Information Act request, that it was holding 1,056 pages of information about Princess Diana. The press reported the NSA intercepts "had gone on right until she died in the Paris car crash with Dodi Fayed." The press reporting also quoted an intelligence official describing the collection of her conversations as "incidental," implying she was not the target of their collection. This disclosure stirred up a storm in the London media but went largely unnoticed in the American press. Such "incidental collection" years later would become an issue in the USA in the aftermath of the ugly Russian collusion narrative.

I am persuaded it is highly likely, as Mohamed Al-Fayed still maintains, that Dodi Al-Fayed and Princess Diana were planning to marry. There is more than the engagement ring. Diana's divorce had become final; she was now free to marry. She was high-maintenance and Dodi was certainly someone who could maintain her in the style to which she was accustomed. Then there is Villa Windsor. What an opportunity to "poke a finger in the eye" of the Royal Family: to take up residence in the former home of the Duke and Duchess of Windsor would be Diana's sweetest revenge on the Royal Family who treated her so shabbily.

But it ended in a traffic accident. Just as I was told in an early morning phone call with the French Police on the last day of August in 1997.

CHAPTER SIXTEEN

DEATH IN A BUNKER

At five o'clock in the morning, on December 3, 1999, Edmond J. Safra, one of the richest men in the world, was awakened with news that two masked men had broken into his Belle Époque building at 17 Avenue d'Ostende in Monaco. His male nurse, who awoke him, was bleeding from three stab wounds. Safra retreated with his female nurse to his steel-reinforced bathroom. The police received a call from the building's concierge, who had seen the male nurse stagger bleeding from the apartment.

When the police arrived, they found the apartment full of smoke. A fire had been started in a wastebasket. Safra and his female nurse, Vivian Torrente, were barricaded in a bathroom bunker. Despite the banging on the bunker door, Safra's paranoia was such that he would not open it. Safra and Torrente died of smoke inhalation.

The Safra family originally came from Lebanon, where they had been traders and then bankers for generations. Starting as a teenager in the family business, Edmond J. Safra left Lebanon and moved first to Europe, then South America, before making it big in New York.

In the 1950s Edmond Safra started the Trade Development Bank, his own private investment bank, with one million dollars. In 1966, he started the Republic National Bank of New York, which operated as a retail bank with 80 branches in New York City and Long Island. It was the third largest branch network in the metropolitan area behind Citigroup and Chase Manhattan.

AMEX'S WHISPERING CAMPAIGN

The Trade Development Bank had grown to $5 billion in deposits by 1983, when Safra sold it to American Express for $550 million. As a term of the sale, Safra signed a non-compete agreement through 1988. However, he grew unhappy over the way American Express was managing the Trade Development Bank. So, he tried to get control back at the same time he activated the rival Republic National Bank Geneva. A legal battle naturally ensued. But American Express management also took it to the street by starting a smear campaign against Safra.

American Express spread countless rumors that linked Safra and his banks to drug trafficking, money laundering, and organized crime. One story circulated on Wall Street that Safra's Republic National Bank would send an armored car to pick up large sums in cash from its more secretive customers. At the time no one knew these rumors had their origin with American Express. It was a global whispering campaign, which planted allegations in a variety of publications. This, in turn, led law enforcement agencies to initiate investigations. At one point US Customs opened an investigation of Safra's banks for money laundering, but no charges were brought.

The Wall Street Journal's financial writers were among the recipients of anonymous faxes, which purported to document Safra's supposedly criminal activity. Understandably, since this material alleged federal crimes, the reporter receiving them shared a fax with the FBI.

The agent in the FBI's NYO, who reviewed the fax, did what may seem simple to some. He noted the line across the very top edge of the fax, the originating number. He determined the sending fax machine was in the fifty-first-floor executive suite of a gleaming skyscraper in lower Manhattan overlooking the Hudson River, the American Express Tower. It all started to unravel.

Bryan Burrough, a *Wall Street Journal* reporter who did not buy the slurs aimed at Safra, now started to report regularly and in detail about the ongoing effort from the top of American Express Company to destroy Safra's reputation. Ultimately, Burrough published a book[16] about the corporate smearing of Safra. Keying off Bryan Burroughs's reporting, Safra proved in court the malign actions of American Express, leading to an apology and a donation of $8 million to Safra's charities.

RUSSIANS ON THE RIVIERA

By the early 1990s, Safra's fortune was an estimated at $2.5 billion. In 1996 he cofounded Hermitage Capital Management with Bill Browder. The fund fast became one of the most important investment companies in Russia. It was a key aspect of the Sergei Magnitsky case, which lead to Magnitsky's arrest and death in Russia, and eventually the Magnitsky Act targeting Vladimir Putin's associates.

Safra also alerted the FBI to a multi-billion-dollar money laundering network during the late 1990s involving the Bank of New York, Russian banks, and the Russian Mafia. The case demonstrated the Bank of New York laundered more than $7 billion for Semion Mogilevich and other Russian Mafia from 1996 to 1999. In 1998 Safra was a cooperating witness in a multi-billion-dollar money laundering operation involving IMF money, Safra's Republic National Bank, and Vladimir Putin.

So, when Safra was killed in his bunker-like apartment, the prime suspect was the Russian Mafia. This was the immediate assumption not just of Monaco's police, but the FBI, the French National Police, the Israelis, and others with an interest. And everybody's investigation proceeded on that premise.

---

[16] Bryan Burrough, *Vendetta: American Express and the Smearing of Edmond Safra* (London: Harper Collins, 1992).

A key witness, as well as a victim of the attack, was Safra's wounded male nurse. A detective—*inspecteur*—in Monaco's police department, Olivier Jude, was assigned to accompany the nurse to the hospital.

TO QUANTICO AND BACK

Olivier Jude is an incredibly talented individual. He is an expert in money laundering and has lectured around the world on the subject. He is fluent in English, French, Italian, and Monégasque. From my very first days as the Legat in Paris, he was my "go-to guy" for whatever was needed in the Principality of Monaco. We secured Olivier an appointment to the FBI National Academy in Quantico, Virginia. In the middle of 1999, Olivier went to that three-month program for police. He was the first, and still the only, member of the Monaco Police to graduate from the FBI National Academy.

Just days before the attack on Safra's apartment, Olivier returned from his sojourn at the FBI Academy in Quantico, Virginia. There—in addition to enriching his English with the American idiom—he took an elective class in homicide investigations, which included a PowerPoint presentation on knife and stab wounds. As a professional police detective, he wanted to learn more about this subject since he had little experience with violent crime in Monaco.

Safra's wounded male nurse was an American, Theodore "Ted" Maher. The Safras liked that Maher had been a medic in the US Army's Green Berets. They thought he could be both a bodyguard and a nurse. Because of his American English language skills, Olivier was chosen to accompany Ted Maher in an ambulance to the hospital. His task was to interview Maher, who was regarded as a key witness, as well as a victim.

When Olivier got a glance at Maher's wounds, he immediately recognized from the PowerPoint presentation at Quantico that they were self-inflicted. So, while literally everyone else in the world was looking at the Russian Mafia, Olivier proceeded with his interview of Maher convinced he was looking at a suspect—not a victim.

After many hours—there is no right against self-incrimination in civil law countries—Olivier got a full confession from Ted Maher. Maher admitted he stabbed himself and started the fire. There were no masked intruders. In an eerie echo of John Hinckley's explanation for shooting Reagan, Ted Maher said his actions were an attempt to win Mr. Safra's respect. He thought he would appear as a hero to Safra. Within two days of Safra's death, Maher was arrested. Several days later, on December 7, 1999, Monaco's chief prosecutor announced Maher would be charged with causing the deaths of Edmond J. Safra and Vivian Torrente, Safra's female nurse.

Safra, fearing his kidnapping or death, had refused to open the bathroom door. The bathroom was under construction and the vents to the outside were closed off. Safra and Torrente died of smoke inhalation from a fire Maher had set as part of his staging.

Maher was imprisoned in Monaco for over two years before his trial began. This delay resulted in more controversy and conspiracy speculations surrounding the case. Once the trial began, Maher testified he acted alone. He admitted to being motivated by fear and panic at losing his high-paying job.

On January 21, 2003, Ted Maher was sentenced to ten years imprisonment. Two months later Maher and his cellmate escaped during the night by sawing through the bars on their cell's tiny window and, using a rope made from garbage bags, climbed down the wall. Maher only made it to Nice, where French police alerted Olivier Jude to his location. Again, Olivier arrested Maher and brought him back to Monaco. Ted, as Olivier now called him, had only been free for seven hours.

Nine additional months were added to Maher's sentence for this escapade. After serving eight years imprisonment in the Principality, he was released in October 2007 and returned to the United States. Since then, Maher has claimed his confession was coerced and he is innocent. I can't imagine anyone believes him.

Edmond J. Safra's obsession with security led him to Monaco and ultimately to his death. With a police force of five hundred officers, Monaco has the highest ratio of police to population in the world and is completely surveilled by security cameras. Safra's penthouse was in a building with a state-of-the-art security system, which also housed three banks. The building sat next to the historic Hotel Hermitage, also heavily secured. His steel-reinforced bathroom was later described to me as "a veritable bunker" by the police commissioner of Monaco.

It was his death trap.

On December 6, 1999, Safra was buried in Geneva. That same day, the Federal Reserve approved the sale of Republic National Bank to HSBC Holdings, netting Safra's estate $2.8 billion. A major philanthropist during his lifetime, he left his wealth to the Edmond J. Safra Philanthropic Foundation, which supports hundreds of projects in fifty countries around the world.

Although the Principality of Monaco has expelled dozens of Russians, it and the entire Riviera continues to be deluged by ostentatious and suspect Russians buying yachts and property for cash.

Olivier Jude remains an active member of the European Chapter of the FBI National Academy Associates (the NAA).

CHAPTER SEVENTEEN

"THAT'S AN ISLAMIST!"

S even Trappist monks from the Abbey of Tibhirine in Algeria's Atlas Mountains were kidnapped on the night of March 26–27, 1996. They were held for fifty-six days and then beheaded in May 1996. Only their heads were found. The GIA *Groupe Islamique Armé*, Armed Islamic Group, claimed responsibility.

France had endured news of violence in Algeria and occasional attacks from the Islamists on their home soil, but nothing so horrified the French as the news of the slaughter of the monks. Every church in France tolled its bells at the same hour in mourning.

The French government did what it could initially to unwind this kidnapping. Jean-Charles Marchiani, who had been an advisor to Interior Minister Charles Pasqua, became deeply involved in efforts to free the monks. Marchiani had a web of contacts and in the past had achieved success in liberating French hostages. He was, however, very opinionated and a bit of a publicity hound. His persistent claims of Iran's involvement with TWA 800 and the Oklahoma City bombing cases caused our Paris Legat office no end of headaches.

A funeral mass for the seven monks was held in Algiers on Sunday June 2, 1996, at the Our Lady of Africa Cathedral—*Notre Dame d'Afrique*—a magnificent structure, which sadly is now only visited by a few brave souls. Pope St. John Paul II sent Cardinal Francis Arinze, an African, as his personal representative to the monks' funeral. The Bishop of Oran, Pierre Claverie, presided. Just two months after the monks' funeral, on August 1, 1996, Bishop Claverie was himself murdered in a terrorist car bombing.

Cardinal Aaron Jean-Marie Lustiger, Archbishop of Paris, was also at the monks' funeral. I would see him eight months later when he presided at Ambassador Harriman's obsequies in Paris on February 7, 1997. Cardinal Lustiger died ten years after the ambassador. My daughter and I—through a fortunate series of happenstance—would be up close and personal at his funeral mass in Paris' Notre Dame Cathedral on August 10, 2007, sitting just rows behind then French President Nicolas Sarkozy. A truly magnificent ceremony with dozens of bishops on the altar.

In December 1991, the Islamists dominated the first rounds of Algeria's legislative elections. The main political arm of the Islamic movement, the FIS *Front Islamique du Salut*, appealed to the angry and unemployed youth of Algeria. Fearing the election of an Islamic government, the authorities intervened on January 11, 1992, cancelling the elections. European and American commentators were initially critical of the Algerian government. An Algerian Gendarme Colonel later pointedly told me, "When the Islamists win an election, it's the last election." Cold logic, but harsh to our democratic ears. The Algerian government banned the FIS, and so began the violent insurgency by the Front's armed wing, the GIA *Groupe Islamique Armé*, who would murder the monks.

Then violence from these Algerian Islamists spilled over into France.

On Christmas Eve 1994, just six months after our arrival in Paris, Air France Flight 8969 was hijacked by the GIA while on the ground at Algiers' Houari Boumediene Airport. The terrorists murdered three passengers and their intention was to blow up the plane over the Eiffel

Tower in Paris. When the aircraft made a refueling stop in Marseille, the GIGN—*Groupe d'Intervention de La Gendarmerie Nationale*—an elite counterterrorist unit of the French Gendarmerie stormed the aircraft, killing the four hijackers.

Hours after the death of the hijackers, the GIA killed four Catholic priests—three Frenchmen and a Belgian—in Tizi Ouzou, Algeria. The unfolding drama riveted our attention along with that of the entire French population over the Christmas holidays of 1994.

ATTACKS IN PARIS

Another wanton attack followed, this time in the heart of Paris, on July 25, 1995. A gas canister bomb exploded in the rail hub beneath the Place Saint-Michel. In this key transportation complex, two suburban commuter train lines *RER* intersected, as did two of Paris' subway system, Métro lines 4 and 10. The blast killed eight and injured 117 others. Eerily like the first World Trade Center attack, just eighteen months earlier, which killed six and injured hundreds on February 26, 1993. A gas device was used in both instances.

The attack at the Place Saint-Michel station happened at 5:30 p.m., the height of the homeward-bound rush hour. The large explosion damaged the four key transportation lines, which immediately shut down the entire subway and commuter rail system throughout the Paris region. Thousands were trapped for hours on trains, most of them in underground tunnels.

Among those trapped somewhere in the vast Parisian transportation web were the staff of our Paris Legat office. I had no idea where they were at that moment and no way to check on them. In those first hours after the initial report of the attack, we did not know how widespread it was or where other attacks might be happening. As I tried to get updates from our harried French police contacts, I was soon being called by FBI Headquarters, where it was only noon, for details of this terrorist incident. I quickly started getting phone calls from the staff's concerned parents in the US, who wanted to be reassured their daughters were safe.

They could not reach them, either. Eventually, FBI Headquarters asked the same question and were not too understanding that I could not yet account for everyone.

We had an understanding among our Legat team when any incident like this happened. We would first contact each other with our own status as soon as possible. For hours this was impossible for those stuck in the Paris métro, hundreds of feet below ground. Although severely stressed out, none of our personnel were injured. It would not be the last time that we would be made aware of the continuing threat of Islamic terrorism.

Only days before the attack at the Place Saint-Michel, FBI headquarters had authorized the purchase locally of cell phones for official use—by the agents. After the attack at Place Saint-Michel, I informed headquarters we had proceeded with the cell phone purchase, but considering our recent brush with terrorism, we purchased phones for the support staff as well as the agents. I got no objection nor any response. Proof of the virtue of not asking permission.

The GIA would continue periodic terrorist attacks in and around Paris throughout 1995 and into 1996. The Parisiens took this constant menace surprisingly well. Bombs exploding in public trash bins along our regular routes to work did introduce unwanted tension into the daily routine of our Legat team and our families.

At the outset, the Islamist terrorists targeted foreign civilians living in Algeria, killing more than one hundred European men and women resident in the country. Women who appeared in stylish European dress on the streets of Algiers or Oran were attacked. Soon, few dared to so dress in public. Throughout 1994 and 1995, more priests and religious sisters were murdered by the Islamists.

In its pursuit of an Islamic state, the GIA sought to destabilize and overthrow the Algerian government to "purge the land of the ungodly." Its slogan inscribed on all communiques was: "no agreement, no truce, no dialogue." The group desired to create "an atmosphere of general insecurity" and targeted not only security forces, but civilians. Between 1992 and 1998, the GIA continued a violent campaign of terror, sometimes wiping out entire villages. Far more than 100,000 people died in this bloody frenzy.

Our Legat Office in Paris had responsibility for liaison in Algeria. Our job of maintaining contacts, getting leads covered, and reporting on the terrorist developments was extraordinarily difficult during those years.

Although incredibly intense and barbaric in Algeria, Islamic terrorism was not limited to that one country. In the 1990s, it quickly became a worldwide phenomenon and eventually coalesced under the banner of Al-Qaeda. US embassies in Africa were bombed on August 7, 1998. More than two hundred people were killed in the nearly simultaneous explosions in in Dar es Salaam, Tanzania, and Nairobi, Kenya.

FBI investigators on the scene in Africa learned one of the attackers involved in the bombing had fled to the Comoros, a French-speaking island nation in the Indian Ocean. During the preceding year, I had established excellent relations with the US Ambassador in Mauritius, who was also responsible for the Comoros. Hence, I was able to obtain immediate Country Clearance to the Comoros for a team of agents to pursue that terrorist. The African embassy attacks were linked to local members of Egyptian Islamic Jihad, which was associated with Osama bin Laden and his terrorist organization Al-Qaeda. On June 7, 1999, bin Laden was added to the FBI's Top Ten Most Wanted List.

In 1999, Algeria held elections. The government had worked to restore political stability to the country. A *Concord Civil* initiative was decreed by President Abdelaziz Bouteflika after his election in April 1999. Many political prisoners were pardoned and large numbers of jihadis were motivated to "repent" under a limited amnesty law in force until January 13, 2000. The AIG disbanded and the level of insurgent violence fell rapidly. But a new group, GSPC—*Groupe Salafiste pour la prédication et le combat*-Group for Call and Combat, a bunch of AIG diehards, continued to wage a terrorist campaign in Algeria.

In October 2003, the GSPC announced its support for Al-Qaeda and took a new name: Al-Qaeda in the Islamic Maghreb. By then the Algerian Government's efforts were given a boost as a result of the

September 11, 2001, attacks. The United States government had previously criticized what were viewed as harsh measures against insurgents. Now there was US sympathy for Algeria's struggle. We were now all in the same boat.

Consequently, US companies were cleared to help and do business in Algeria. In my second career as a consultant, I went back to Algeria to follow-up on the struggle against Islamic terrorism, which as Legat Paris I did only from the sidelines.

BACK TO ALGERIA

One firm I engaged with was Northrop Grumman. They were my client; their customer was the Algerian *Gendarmerie Nationale*, an exceptionally large agency. Larger than any American police force, the Gendarmerie had responsibility for law enforcement over most of the Algerian territory and shared responsibility with the *Police Nationale* in the urban centers. Policing in Algeria was organized very much on the model the French had left them in the 1960s. Little had changed since then. In fact, the urban police were still called *La Sûreté*, a term long in disuse in France.

The project Northrop Grumman had undertaken, and the Algerian government committed to, was a multi-billion-dollar effort to modernize the command-and-control systems of the *Gendarmerie Nationale*. Initially my role was as a consultant working with the gendarmes and the Northrop Grumman team on the scope of operations. I was expected to be a subject matter expert. I also found myself translating in more ways than one. The American engineers were experts in communications and systems management. They had all worked on big projects for the US military. But the gendarmes were at heart a law enforcement agency.

The younger gendarmes, lieutenants and captains were particularly well informed about policing developments in the rest of the world. They knew what they wanted. I was often interpreting their needs, as well as language. An interjection of "*C'est ca*" from an enthusiastic lieutenant letting us know "that's it," would allow us to move on with the dialogue. Although paid by the company, I became in effect an advocate for the gendarmes.

As the years-long project progressed, my own firm worked on some aspects as a sub-contractor. The entire project was in a sense a gigantic effort in change management. As a subcontractor, we assembled a team of coaches and instructors from among former colleagues in the FBI and the NYPD. They were to be a cadre to train the gendarme trainers in "leading change." Here again, I turned to the brilliant network available to me thanks to the NAA and the NEIA.

From 2004 through 2007, I made multiple trips to Algeria. It is a surprisingly beautiful land. Traveling the highways, we saw vistas of orchards and vineyards on gently rolling green hills extending down to the blue Mediterranean. Elsewhere we drove past fields of waving wheat. It is not all the Sahara Desert—the common image of North Africa in the minds of many Americans.

The project brought policing in that vast country from the 1950s to the twenty-first century in one fell swoop, skipping many of the intervening stages of development, which police systems worldwide have endured in the past half century. Many modern states have struggled, for example, with the transition from a 911 system based on landlines to now ubiquitous cell phones. Algeria never had any 911 system, nor an extensive landline system, nor an orientation to logical street numbering, so the new 911 service could be created from the ground up, exploiting the now ubiquitous mobile phones and cell towers being built as part of the project.

The project also granted Algeria its own version of national systems and technologies familiar to the FBI and American law enforcement. Uniform Crime Reports (UCR), National Crime Information Center (NCIC), Major Case Management tools, a National Strategic Operations Center, mobile command posts, and a network of cell towers were among the results of the project.

Tours of the facilities in Algeria often included visits to police stations. In every entry hall or lobby there were dozens of plaques on the wall remembering the gendarmes from that station who died at the hands of the terrorists. The name of the gendarme was above his photo and below it was a very moving remark, such as *père de trois enfants* or *père d'un enfant* (father of three children or father of a child).

On our team bus, as we were traveling to the city of Blida, a young bilingual gendarme was standing in the front of the vehicle providing occasional commentary. As the bus passed slowly though a congested area, our guide pointed to a man with a long black beard, wearing a long white robe, "That's an Islamist!" he hissed. These were the killers of his fellow gendarmes; his tone was close to hate. It struck me, in a country that was 99.9 percent Muslim, there was no hesitation in condemning Islamists. Yet, in the US, condemning Islamists was bizarrely seen as being anti-Muslim. Political correctness shielding us from the reality that Islamists were murdering Muslims.

Just as I had toured Algeria and the facilities of the Gendarmerie Nationale by bus, eventually a delegation from the Algerian Gendarmerie visited the US. In a well-equipped bus, we traveled to the FBI CJIS Division in West Virginia, where they witnessed UCR and NCIC in operation. Then on to Harrisburg, Pennsylvania, to see a model 911 system in operation. Last stop was New York City, where both the NYPD and the FBI's NYO opened the doors to their command posts. In arranging this weeklong odyssey, I again followed the sage advice of Saint Mother Teresa and "just asked." And everyone I asked, federal, state, or local, immediately said yes, and then welcomed us. My client was impressed.

The possibility of Islamist attacks continues anywhere in the world to this day, but it is a very real daily fact of life in Algeria. Nonetheless, the Algerian nation is now far better able to respond to the threat due to a multi-billion-dollar project in which I played a small yet important role.

On December 8, 2018, in a colorful ceremony at the beautiful Shrine of Our Lady of the Holy Cross in Oran, Algeria, the Catholic Church beatified the "Nineteen martyrs of Algeria." Included among the nineteen were the monks of Tibhirine and Bishop Pierre Claverie, who had presided at the monks' funeral twenty-two years earlier.

PART II

THE BAD

INJUSTICE

CHAPTER EIGHTEEN

"ARREST THAT WOMAN!"

W hen working in Alexandria, Virginia in the early 1970s, I investigated a variety of criminal matters. There were then—as now—many government facilities and bases in and around the DC area. Crimes committed on federal property were classified as "Crimes on a Government Reservation." The federal law[17] included any crime "punishable if committed within that state." So, we in the FBI investigated crimes often thought of as local police matters in other communities.

Like most investigators, whether police detectives or FBI agents, we tended to pair off with a partner as we worked our investigations. Jim Siano, who worked on the Mackle kidnapping in Florida, was now the agent with whom I most often paired off with during my tenure in Alexandria.

One day we received a complaint of sexual assault against a civilian from the military police at Henderson Hall, a Marine Corps facility in

---

[17] Title 18, U.S. Code, § 13.

Arlington, Virginia. The victim was a minor female, the daughter of a Marine Corps colonel who had died a hero a year earlier in Vietnam.

The young woman, who had just gotten her driving permit, was shopping after school at the Post Exchange located on the small installation. When she returned to her car, a male who had hidden himself in the vehicle threatened her with a knife. He then demanded she perform a sex act (fellatio) on him.

We got this case the day after the crime happened. Jim Siano and I first went to the provost marshal's office on the Marine base, as they had received the original complaint. The provost marshal at the time was Major Adolf P. Sgambelluri USMC, a very experienced individual and a graduate of the FBI National Academy. Nearly a quarter century later, I would work with Al Sgambelluri again, when he was the chief of police in Guam and I was the Legat in Canberra. That day in Virginia, though, we were all focused on the offense against this schoolgirl. Major Sgambelluri and his staff briefed us on the case. The reality was they had no suspects and no leads to pass along.

Our next stop was the home of the victim and her mother. It was a red brick colonial-style house located in an upper-middle class area of Arlington County. When we arrived in the late afternoon, on the day after the crime, the victim was in her plaid school uniform. The girl's mother was in her late forties, with perfectly coiffed hair, a tailored dress, and wearing heels. Her speech was that of a well-educated woman. She sat very straight in her chair and was all business with us and very protective of her young daughter. She was, in short, the very model of a dignified southern lady. Contrary to what other investigators might have done, neither Jim nor I made any attempt to separately interview mother and daughter. And we also got the vibe that the Colonel's widow was not going to budge from her daughter's side.

The interview took place in their living room. Prominent on the coffee table was a framed formal photo of the deceased father and husband in his Marine Corps uniform. The young victim thought she would be able to recognize her attacker, if she saw him again. Other than that, we came away from the interview with little of lead value.

At this point in time, almost all cooperation between the FBI and local police—and among police agencies themselves—was very informal. The National Criminal Information Center (NCIC) was just coming online and was initially focused on quantifiable information like the license plate numbers of stolen cars. The ViCap program (Violent Criminal Apprehension Program) was still more than a decade in the future. As there were only limited means of comparing cases from diverse jurisdictions, there was little awareness of serial rapists or serial murderers.

A week or two later, we were with detectives at the Fairfax County Police headquarters concerning some other cases. There we overheard a detective expressing frustration at the turn of events in one of his cases. We asked him for details. He related an incident at a shopping center parking lot in Fairfax County, Virginia, which was remarkably like our case of "Crime on a Government Reservation—Sexual Assault."

A woman, thirty years of age and a new arrival from Germany, was accosted in her car. As with our victim, she was confronted by a male who had hidden in her vehicle. He brandished a knife. She told him, "You can put that away; I know what you want." After the assault, the victim had the presence of mind to watch her attacker depart and record his car's license number.

The Fairfax County detectives traced down the subject based on the license plate information. He was an enlisted Marine. The Commonwealth Attorney in Fairfax County declined prosecution as, in his opinion, the victim's comment to her assailant diminished its "prosecutive appeal." It was immediately apparent to us, however, that this enlisted Marine was most likely our subject. That's the very informal way information was exchanged and leads developed back then.

Our experience with an AUSA in the Eastern District of Virginia was quite different than the detective's experience with the county prosecutor. Our attempt at interviewing the subject, however, went nowhere—as had a previous attempt by the Fairfax detective. The subject, in today's parlance, "lawyered up." We got back to Major Sgambelluri at Henderson Hall and he organized a lineup at the Marine facility. It was a textbook perfect lineup. The AUSA, the defense attorney, the victim, the Provost Marshal, Jim Siano, and I were all standing together on one side of a curtain.

When the curtain went up we saw half a dozen nearly identical US Marines: same size, same haircut, and same uniform. It was the uniform that did it. Our victim let out a loud gasp and began sobbing. They were wearing a uniform like her father's. We had not figured on that reaction. Nonetheless, she unhesitatingly identified our subject as her assailant.

Eventually, the case moved to trial. The matter was heard on the second floor in the old federal courthouse in Alexandria. The judge was Oren Ritter Lewis, a long-time fixture in that court. Judge Lewis struck fear into both defense attorneys and the AUSAs who appeared before him, and by extension some FBI agents who had to testify in his courtroom. Judge Lewis was so fierce and his outbursts so notorious that he was known by all as "Roarin' Oren."

The proceedings began. Jim and I were certainly there to assist the AUSA, but much more specifically to support our key witness, the victim. Just a few minutes into the proceedings, there was a rather large huddle in front of Judge Lewis. We could not hear the details. Then the huddle cleared and Judge Lewis made an announcement. The defendant was agreeing to plead guilty. And as just agreed, in lieu of jail time, he would undertake counseling at Bethesda Naval Hospital.

At this point, the victim's mother, that very model of a dignified southern gentlewoman, jumped to her feet and screamed, "This is the biggest crock of shit!" Judge Lewis, true to his "Roarin' Oren" persona, banged down his gavel and roared "Marshals, arrest that woman!" Which they did, as the now enraged mother flailed her arms. Frankly, Jim and I were standing in shocked silence. As we got our wits about us, my first thought was this is a great miscarriage of justice. Not solely because the subject got off much easier than he should have, but because this widow and mother had been arrested.

It took us the better part of an hour, but we managed to get the victim's mother "unarrested." I don't think one can find that term in any law book, and we had been taught it was something that could not be done. But I know it was done on more than this one occasion. Justice perhaps for the mother, but injustice for her daughter.

CHAPTER NINETEEN

A PROMISING YOUNG LIFE CUT SHORT

Donna Sue Oglesby graduated high school in Poteau, Oklahoma, in June of 1969. She moved halfway across the country to Alexandria, Virginia, where she and a classmate, together with a young woman from Texas, became roommates. All three worked at FBI headquarters.

Within months, Donna Sue would be dead.

Because the three roommates worked different shifts, Donna was home alone on February 3, 1970. When her carpool arrived that day, she was not waiting as usual outside the building. A nineteen-year-old man from the group went into the apartment to get her, only to discover her nude body on a rug in the center of the living room. There were stab wounds on her chest and sewing scissors, later found to belong to a roommate, lodged in her sternum. He was so shaken by his discovery that he couldn't recall many details, including whether the door to the apartment had been open when he arrived or was simply unlocked.

Horrible as the crime was—sexual assault and murder—it was not a federal offense. Jack McDermott, the SAC of the then-new Alexandria Field Office, which had about fifty agents, offered the police the FBI's assistance. He was very engaged in the initial investigation, calling an "all agents" meeting soon after the body's discovery.

McDermott opened the meeting by telling us that Director Hoover had written on a note: "Alexandria will solve this!" Someone asked, "What does that mean?" Did he mean the PD or the field office? The unspoken answer was no one questioned J. Edgar Hoover.

A related question at the meeting was whether the police would handle the crime scene processing or whether we would offer the services of the FBI laboratory. The Alexandria field office and WFO, unlike other FBI field offices, would routinely bring physical evidence directly to the laboratory. McDermott replied, "Lieutenant Lee has processed the scene."

Jim Siano and I were among those who immediately began working leads. Early in the investigation, McDermott wanted to get a firsthand look at the apartment, which the police had sealed. Siano and I went with him for the FBI's first direct look at the crime scene.

We got the key to Donna's apartment and found the door covered with crime scene tape. Removing the tape and opening the door, like the young man who discovered Donna's body, we were overwhelmed with the evidence of violence and death. The body had of course been removed and there was black fingerprint powder all over the room. And there was the rug, with its edges underneath pieces of furniture. A massive circle of dried blood and other discoloration on it was staring us right in the face.

"Look at that rug!" McDermott exclaimed. "That's the rug she was on. It's still here!" We rolled it up and took it straight to the laboratory. McDermott was incredulous, repeating, "Lieutenant Lee told me he processed the scene." Lieutenant Lee ran the identification unit at the PD, and when he processed the scene, he just looked for latents, as the fingerprint powder suggested.

Hoover said we would solve it. And in fact, a "full-court press" was undertaken. All of Alexandria's agents worked the case in its initial days, mainly handling "shotgun" leads, looking for that needle in the haystack. The agents accounted for every male who went into or out of the apartment building. It was a big building with a lot of foot traffic. There were telephone company men, furniture movers, and meter readers. Background checks were run on these men and they were interviewed. The FBI used its manpower to cover leads of phenomenal scope. Then the focus widened beyond the building as agents visited neighboring jurisdictions and collected names of possible suspects. These men were located and interviewed, too. The investigation moved still further outward, beyond the Washington DC region.

We know now there was no need to cast such a wide net. This was no needle in the haystack. Agents had interviewed the killers—a pair who acted together—right after the crime.

An FBI employee, Donna Sue Oglesby, was brutally murdered in her Alexandria apartment. The case went unsolved for decades—the coldest of cold cases. But now we do have an idea of who killed her.

Siano and I were assigned, as both interviewer and chaperone, to each of Donna's two roommates. After the laboratory found hairs on the rug, we had to take hair samples from the young women for elimination purposes. We found ourselves standing over them with scissors in our hands. Donna Sue was killed with scissors. That's when it hit me: these young women were being subjected to so much. Their roommate was murdered; their apartment was violated; they had to answer our embarrassing questions; and now two FBI men were chopping their hair with scissors. They were victims themselves. They would soon quit the FBI, as their parents were insisting that they return home.

At the end of June 1970, I left Alexandria under transfer to New York City.

Unbeknownst to me, on August 20, 1970, another young woman, Yvonne Dowdy, was murdered in Alexandria in circumstances identical to Donna Sue Oglesby's killing. Apparently, even those still in Alexandria did not make a connection between the two crimes.

A VERY COLD CASE—REOPENED

These crimes would remain unsolved for decades. But Donna Sue and Yvonne have not been forgotten. In recent years, a compelling explanation has emerged as to who killed them.

Decades after the crime, Jerry Pender was the Deputy Assistant Director at the CJIS Division who brought about Next Generation Identification (NGI). Pender thought this case could be solved by the coming latent functionality in NGI. At his request, WFO reopened the investigation in 2010. The Alexandria Field Office had been consolidated into WFO since the crime; this presented additional challenges, as the FBI material for this case had been lost or misplaced in the office move.

Steve Milefsky, a criminal analyst at WFO, was assigned the case. Milefsky, a retired homicide detective, had a background in cold cases. At both WFO and the Alexandria PD, he dug to recover traces of this crime, particularly the latent prints Lieutenant Lee had collected. He also wanted the autopsy slides, in the hope of finding DNA. Milefsky is a star homicide investigator who cares about the victims. In the Alexandria PD, he found another veteran investigator with the same qualities. Charlie Bailey a retired homicide detective from the MPD ran Alexandria's CSI. Bailey found the autopsy slides, the latents, and the rug.

A problem arose with the slide of the cervical swab from the autopsy. The glue used to secure the slide prevented it from being opened for

DNA testing. In 2012, the Laboratory ground up the slide with the aim of extracting organic material for DNA testing. Disappointingly, this did not yield enough material to search in CODIS, the national DNA data bank. When the rug was processed, DNA from Donna Sue and three others was detected, but the samples were only good enough for exclusion, not searching.

In the spring of 2013, Bailey found another old case in the Alexandria homicide files. It was the Yvonne Dowdy murder. Bailey, an experienced homicide investigator, was struck by the similarities to Donna Sue's case. Yvonne was twenty-one and single. A blonde, like Donna Sue, she had recently moved to the area. She had been living in a one-bedroom apartment where her body was found nude and stabbed several times in the chest with her own kitchen knife.

On April 24, 2014, the latents were run against the CJIS latent file without any hits. There was hope better results would appear with the coming of NGI. On October 28, 2015, the new NGI latent algorithm went operational. All 43,000 unidentified latents in IAFIS would be searched against each other and against the ten-print files. On November 18, 2015, the Oglesby/Dowdy latents were run with no matches returned. A big effort; a big disappointment.

At the end of 2013, Milefsky was transferred out of WFO. Special Agent Erin L. Sheridan of WFO was then assigned the case. She had developed an expertise in murder investigations, particularly cold cases and serial killers. Working together, Bailey and Sheridan came to focus on two suspects who had been overlooked in the original investigation.

Their first suspect was a Bureau employee who had been living in Donna's building at the time of her murder. Six months later, as a married man about twenty-years old, he was living in Yvonne Dowdy's building when she was murdered.

Their second suspect was Michael E. Norris, nineteen and single at the time, who was working as a security guard. He too was living in Donna's building at the time of her murder. Six months later, he too was living in Yvonne Dowdy's building at the time she was murdered.

The fact that this pattern was not noticed at the time is surprising and sad.

Sheridan confirmed that the original canvass of all the males in the building was conducted by the FBI agents. She found a listing of the names (last name only) in the Alexandria PD notes of the case. She mentioned my name—BAKER—was on the list. Both the suspects were contacted "by the agents."

Erin also confirmed the first suspect was interviewed right after the murder along with his girlfriend (soon to be his wife) present. The interviewer's notes indicate the girlfriend answered the door with him (the then Bureau employee) standing behind her. And further she answered most of the questions for the two of them.

Charlie Bailey speculated that the agents may have given Michael Norris "a pass" because he was a security guard and about to become a deputy sheriff. Erin noted that based on criminal profiling developed over the last twenty plus years, being a security guard would today bring more investigative focus rather than less.

Norris did become a sheriff's deputy in Alexandria. After a half dozen years as a deputy, he was elected sheriff. He served as sheriff for eight years. In 1985, he was defeated in his reelection bid. In that election Norris had faced allegations of drug abuse and problems in his personal life. He moved to Florida, where, on May 26, 1990, he died of a self-inflicted gunshot wound. The Fort Lauderdale PD said Norris was a cocaine user.

The other suspect and his wife also moved to Florida. While living there, he was charged with assaulting his wife. The assault charge, like Norris's behavior, adds to his suspect profile. This suspect is now divorced, over seventy years old, and still living free in Florida.

A TAG TEAM OF KILLERS

Now there is a likely explanation for these murders. They appear to be the work of a tag team of killers. The two suspects are incredibly similar. Two law enforcement "wannabes." Both were white males about nineteen and twenty at the time. Both lived in the same buildings at the same times as the murders of Oglesby and Dowdy, two remarkably similar victims. In fact, it might have taken two assailants to overpower these fit young women. The two suspects may have been egging each other on while together, but once they separated, their extreme sexual violence subsided and they found other outlets. Sheridan noted violent criminals have been known to slow down or stop over time.

It is not unknown for killers to work in pairs. Roger Depue, an expert criminal profiler[18] who has studied hundreds of serial offenders, reviewed this case in November 2017. He recalled several cases where two predators worked together on the capture and murder of female victims. They reinforced one another's fantasies as they discussed and planned their crimes.

As for the phenomenon of criminals aging out of their violent behavior, the "Golden State Killer" case provides a high-profile example. On April 24, 2018, Joseph DeAngelo, then seventy-two, was arrested and charged with a series of multiple rapes and murders from some forty years earlier. Like our suspects, he was once in law enforcement. His crimes appear to have stopped after a decade of activity, just as our suspects are thought to have eventually stopped.

Bailey retired from the Alexandria Police Department on April 1, 2014. Sheridan continues to work this case. The Bureau's Deputy Director Paul Abbate, formerly at WFO, has supported Sheridan's investigation for years. He keeps photos of Donna Sue and Yvonne under glass on his desk.

While they are not forgotten, their killer is living free in Florida.

---

[18] Dr. Roger L. Depue, one of the fathers of criminal profiling, is the author of *Between Good and Evil: A Master Profiler's Hunt for Society's Most Violent Predators*. Grand Central Publishing. February 1, 2005.

CHAPTER TWENTY

"DO YOU HAVE YOUR GUN?"

On a crisp bright winter day, two weeks before Christmas 1972, I was walking north on Lexington Avenue in New York City with fellow Special Agents John Connolly and Artie Grubert. We were three-a-breast, John in the middle. He suddenly grasped both our forearms and in a stage whisper asked, "Do you have your gun?" As we answered yes, he was gesturing with his head and shoulders at a tall man in a shiny brown leather topcoat, who had just passed us walking in the opposite direction. "That's Frankie Salemme!" The three of us spread out, and as the subject was crossing the street, one of us shouted out, "Hey Frankie!" The man's head snapped around in acknowledgement.

That's all we needed. We rushed forward; John and I pinning him to a wall, while Artie Grubert had drawn his weapon and was holding it in the air. All four of us were shouting while Salemme insisted we were making a terrible mistake, and the three of us yelled contradictory orders: "Hands up!" "Don't move!" and "Shut-up!" And worse. New Yorkers continued walking by, calmly stepping into the street to get around us. No crowd gathered, but we were excited about who we had just apprehended. Our immediate search of his person yielded a foot-long screwdriver concealed inside that long brown leather coat: a potentially dangerous weapon.

Francis Patrick Salemme, known in the mob as "Cadillac Frank," was a member of the Raymond Patriarca Mafia Family. He was a known killer, or "hitman," suspected at that time in at least eight murders. In 1968, when he was indicted for the car-bombing of attorney John Fitzgerald, he fled and was a fugitive for four years. The FBI issued an Identification Order (IO) for his arrest thus making him an "IO Fugitive" in Bureau lingo. The Identification Order is what is known to the public as a wanted poster or flyer, which in years past hung in post offices across the country.

As we were on foot and ten blocks north of the field office, then at 69th Street, we did what people in Manhattan do: We hailed a cab. As we started to pile in, with Salemme protesting loudly, the cabbie's face revealed he thought he made a mistake in stopping for us. I slid in first, and sat behind the driver, Salemme was in the middle, with Artie Grubert on his right. John Connolly sat in front beside the driver.

With an Italian father and an Irish mother, Francis Patrick Salemme, then in his thirties, had very sharp features; some might call him handsome.

John, sitting beside the driver, pulled out the IO, and held it up for comparison. Across the top of the flyer in bold black letters was *Wanted for Murder, Attempted Murder, and Atrocious Assault.* And just below that, the mug shot with those distinctive sharp features. John was yelling—over Salemme's protests—"This is you!"

When the cab stopped at a light John held the flyer in front of the cabbie, saying, "Look at this, what do *you* think?" the already stressed out cabbie glanced at it and could only see those big black words. His head snapped back instantly, he leaned forward over the steering wheel and he stared straight ahead. One of us in the back exclaimed, "That's a positive ID." As we exited the cab in front of the field office, I was the last one out. As I was sliding across the back, the cabbie reached around and grabbed my arm, "Don't worry," he said. "You boys got the right guy."

None of us had handcuffs. As we entered the FBI lobby, an agent was exiting. We asked him if he had 'cuffs. He did and gave them to us. Now properly handcuffed, we took Salemme up to the sixth floor. Our concern at that point was not so much the possibility that he might escape, but rather being seen by a supervisor with our prisoner un-cuffed. That's a big "no-no" in the FBI. It would have been a shame to be censured for not 'cuffing a prisoner rather than being commended for capturing an "IO Fugitive."

Once up in our sixth-floor office space, we read Salemme his rights and presented him with the printed "warning and wavier" form. Then we fingerprinted him, and the resulting print match ended his shouting. In fact, he pretty much shut up altogether. John, Artie, and I accompanied him—now properly handcuffed—to the Federal House of Detention in lower Manhattan. This trip gave us more time with Salemme, and we were no longer shouting at each other. We had not established any rapport with him, but we were all more relaxed. So, as we were handing him over at the Federal House of Detention, John asked him, "How does your case look?" to which Salemme replied, "I'll beat the one, but they got me pretty good on the other one."

An admission of sorts.

Other agents at the NY field office that evening were coordinating the follow-up investigation. When we stopped Salemme, he had another man's identity and address on his person. From that, agents determined the exact apartment where Salemme was living. It was on the Upper East Side, in a doorman building, very upscale. The team of agents obtained a search warrant and later that night, on December 14, 1972, we joined in the search of the apartment. The investigation at the building established that three men—all fugitives—had been staying there: Salemme, Steven "the Rifleman" Flemmi, and Luigi "Baby Shanks" Manocchio—all multiple killers. We also found passports with their photos and aliases. They had been to France and Italy, among other places, during their nearly four years as fugitives.

Some months later, in 1973, I traveled to Boston to testify in Cambridge, Massachusetts at the John Fitzgerald car-bombing case.

Fitzgerald was the attorney for Joseph Barboza, a mob figure who had turned against the Mafia. Our intelligence was that Raymond Patriarca—then the head of the New England Mafia family—had ordered the Fitzgerald attack. The local authorities charged Francis Salemme and Stephen Flemmi with the bombing.

On the cold morning of January 30, 1968, Fitzgerald was sitting in his car with the driver's door open as he spoke to his wife, who was standing in their home's doorway. When he turned on the car's ignition, there was a massive explosion. As the door was open and his one leg still outside the car, he was thrown from the vehicle and survived. Had he been completely in the car with the door closed, he surely would have been killed, as was the bombers' intention. An immediate second blast of dynamite lifted the car off the ground, throwing debris in all directions, and shattering windows throughout suburban Everett, Massachusetts.

Fitzgerald lost one leg and use of the other.

Salemme was the only one on trial for this outrage, as Flemmi was still a fugitive. The Massachusetts charge was the rather colorful "atrocious assault."

When I arrived at the old Middlesex County courthouse in Cambridge, Massachusetts, I was only briefly introduced to the local prosecutor in the lobby. Minutes later I was called in to testify. The courtroom was somewhat different than others in my experience. Not a lot has changed in Cambridge since colonial times. The witness "stand" was just that: as a witness, I stood on a wooden platform. The prosecutor began and asked me to point out the defendant. I looked at the defense table, where I expected Salemme to be but did not see him. I looked at the other table and then scanned along the front rows. I could not see Salemme. This wasn't good. Then in the far rear of the courtroom, up in what appeared to me as a choir loft, was a man lounging sideways. When we arrested Salemme he had curly black hair. The individual in what I now realized was the "dock" had a bald head. Nevertheless, I pointed up and said, "That's him." As the prosecutor intoned the familiar, "Let the record show," I breathed a sigh of relief.

The prosecutor next asked why we stopped Salemme. "Because we knew he was wanted for murder in Massachusetts," I replied. At that moment, the defense attorney, F. Lee Bailey, jumped to his feet and called for a mistrial.

The subsequent huddle before the judge was mostly within my hearing. It transpired that the murder charge was a separate case; the present matter was an attempted murder, and my response, according to the defense, had poisoned the jury. Although J. Edgar Hoover had died a year earlier, his draconian discipline carried on. If my remark caused local authorities to lose a major case, the consequences for me would be extremely severe. But the judge did not accept Bailey's contention and the case moved on.

Following the prosecutor's lead, I managed to get in the slight admission Salemme had made to us at the Federal House of Detention. I was then cross-examined by F. Lee Bailey, a prominent Boston criminal defense attorney who already had a significant national reputation. Raymond Patriarca was paying Bailey to defend Salemme. Bailey addressed me as "Officer" Baker. I was not sure if he was trying to throw me off, or if he really did not know I was an FBI agent.

Bailey asked me why we did not let the defendant call his attorney. I started to reply that was not so. He cut me off and repeated the question. I again started to respond as he asked the same question several times. At one point he paused, took an audible breath, and proceeded to remind me perjury was a serious crime. I broke eye contact with him and turned my head and shoulders towards the jurors on my left and said "No, he never asked to call an attorney, because if he had, we would have let him."

The witness who clearly made the greatest contribution was the victim, John Fitzgerald. As a result of the bombing attack, he lost the use of his legs. Using his hands along the floor, he painfully pushed himself into the courtroom on a dolly. He had everyone's breathless attention. His physical appearance spoke more than any words about the car bombing.

Salemme was found guilty. He was given a thirty-year sentence for this truly atrocious crime. He was released from prison in 1988 after serving only fifteen years. Over the next decade, Salemme would murder his way to the top of the New England Mafia Family.

John Connolly and I worked together—almost daily—for two years in New York City targeting organized crime. The principal target was La Cosa Nostra, or the LCN in Bureau speak, known to the public as the Mafia. John then served nearly twenty years in the Boston FBI office.

In New York and then in Boston, John had shown a particular talent for developing informants. The information from these informants helped provide the probable cause to enable the government to obtain electronic surveillance against organized crime throughout the nation—not just in New England. In turn, it was the evidence from these electronic intercepts that supported the convictions of major organized crime figures. More than any other "street agent," John Connolly is responsible for the success the federal government had against La Cosa Nostra by the end of the twentieth century.

Former FBI Special Agent Joseph D. Pistone, known to many as "Donnie Brasco," is quoted in the book, *The Ceremony*, which is about one of John's most unique accomplishments: the first-ever taping of a Mafia induction ceremony. Significantly, it was Connolly's documentation of the criminals' efforts to evade court-authorized wiretaps in that case which led the federal courts to deem the "Roving Bug" provision of the Federal Electronic Surveillance Act[19] constitutional. Joe Pistone commented, "If you have a Top Echelon (TE) informant—and Connolly had twenty TEs—you know you are dealing with a killer, but you let them know they will not be protected from prosecution for capital crimes. Anything but murder."

Recruiting killers to penetrate the Mafia was effectively John Connolly's assignment. That's how the FBI's Top Echelon (TE) Criminal Informant Program, as found in the Bureau's Manual of Investigative Operations and Guidelines (MIOG), describes it. Murder

---

[19] Title 18, U.S. Code, § 2518 (11).

is a prerequisite to LCN membership and Connolly's task was to recruit Mafia members. Thus, he recruited killers.

Connolly retired from the FBI in 1990. Five years later, in January 1995, AUSA Fred M. Wyshak Jr., shepherded though the system a major RICO (Racketeer Influenced and Corrupt Organization) case in Boston, which resulted in the indictment of James "Whitey" Bulger, Stephen Flemmi, and Frank Salemme. Wyshak's case collapsed when Flemmi filed an affidavit revealing he was an FBI informant who was authorized by a former Boston United States Attorney and the FBI to engage in gambling and other non-violent criminal activity.

AUSA Wyshak was, somewhat understandably, chagrined at this turn of events, and even more frustrated at the subsequent disappearance of his principal defendant, Whitey Bulger. Wyshak learned that Bulger, like Flemmi, had been a longtime FBI informant handled by John Connolly. Now Connolly would become Wyshak's overarching focus. No longer his targets, the gangsters became tools in Wyshak's twenty-year quest to get Connolly.

The initial allegation against John—still repeated—is that he tipped off Whitey to his indictment. That is a supposition with no factual basis.

In December 1999, Frank Salemme—the very guy we'd sent to prison over a quarter of a century earlier—provided testimony to secure a federal indictment of Connolly. John Morris, a self-admitted corrupt FBI supervisor, also cut a deal for himself in exchange for testimony against Connolly. Morris would never do a day in prison. Salemme told the federal grand jury he and Flemmi had paid Connolly, who in turn tipped them off to grand jury information. All of this supposedly happened after Connolly's 1990 retirement from the FBI.

The RICO statute, a valuable tool in the fight against organized crime, was enacted while John and I were engaged against the mob in New York. Its genius was it addressed the ongoing criminal enterprise, rather than individual criminals. Everyone charged in a RICO must have participated in some fashion in the enterprise. John's alleged role was he protected the gang. He did indeed. Whitey and Flemmi were his—and the government's—informants. Long before Wyshak's arrival in Boston, numerous DOJ attorneys—up to and including Robert S. Mueller III, who was an AUSA, and then the Acting US Attorney during John's tenure in Boston—knew of this relationship. John related more than once, to me and others, conversations he had with Bob Mueller in the 1980s.

After a luncheon at the Locke-Ober restaurant, where Mueller and John had met with a visiting AUSA from San Francisco, they walked back to the US Attorney's Office, then located in the John W. McCormack Federal Office Building. Mueller began talking about John's informants. John was uncomfortable with Mueller speaking with such familiarity about these matters, particularly out on the street. But what really alarmed John was Mueller's indiscreet fascination with Whitey Bulger's informant status—while Whitey's younger brother, William Bulger, was the president of the Massachusetts State Senate. William Bulger enjoyed an outstanding reputation and would later serve as President of the University of Massachusetts.

After that street-side exchange, John went straight to Jeremiah T. O'Sullivan, head of the Organized Crime Unit of the US Attorney's Office to complain about Mueller's promiscuous chatter regarding the Bulger brothers. In that confrontation, O'Sullivan asserted that many prosecutors in the office were aware of Bulger's informant status. He reminded John that he (O'Sullivan) and his then boss, Gerald McDowell, had protected Bulger and Stephen Flemmi "from prosecution" in a Race-Fix case in exchange for the "probable cause" they provided against the Mafia. This was, in fact, documented in the January 29, 1979, RICO prosecution memorandum in the Race-Fix case. O'Sullivan, red-faced, said he couldn't keep something from the boss that so many others in the office knew.

Yet, in December 1999, nine years after his FBI retirement, John Connolly was indicted for RICO. His alleged role in that ongoing criminal conspiracy was protecting Bulger and the other informants. His prosecution was abetted by what we would learn was the perjured testimony of Salemme and Morris.

Wyshak's lead investigator, Massachusetts State Police Colonel Thomas Foley, said he had warned prosecutors before the trial that

Salemme had "lied about murders he committed and shouldn't be trusted as any sort of witness." Colonel Foley said he told them of "Salemme's falsehoods and strongly advised them not to use Salemme as a witness against Connolly."

They used Salemme anyway.

On May 17, 2002, Salemme testified against Connolly in the Boston federal case. Salemme also testified he himself had absolutely nothing to do with the murders of eight individuals. John Connolly sat shocked in court, knowing Salemme had killed them all.

On September 16, 2002, Connolly was found not guilty of nine of the fourteen "predicate acts" of the RICO case. Significantly, he was found not guilty of causing the death of John Callahan, a charge he would again face in Florida. Connolly was sentenced to ten years in federal prison for the five remaining predicate acts. Convicted, we now know, on the perjured testimony of Salemme and Morris. Later, in a deposition in Florida, John Morris would recant pivotal testimony that he had given in Connolly's 2002 federal trial.

Not surprisingly, Wyshak used the DEA as well as the Massachusetts State Police as investigators in his ongoing crusade against Connolly and other FBI agents. On October 29, 2003, DEA agents completed a lengthy interview of Stephen Flemmi, Salemme's old fugitive roommate in Manhattan. Connolly had already been in federal prison for almost a year when Flemmi talked to the DEA. Flemmi said that Connolly was never paid money and Connolly never tipped them off to grand jury information. Flemmi explained that Salemme wasn't even aware he and Connolly knew each other until 1997, when Flemmi "outed" himself as Connolly's informant. As for the eight murders Salemme denied committing on the stand, Flemmi said Salemme was in fact the perpetrator of all of them, and that he (Flemmi) was personally involved in three of the murders, including the Peter Poulos murder, which happened during their sojourn in NYC.

This DEA information would have exonerated Connolly.

But Wyshak did not provide these DEA-6 debriefing reports to Connolly's lawyers until years later, after John had been indicted in Miami—for a crime he was acquitted of in the 2002 Boston federal trial.

A year later in a separate matter, Philadelphia FBI agents were conducting a prison interview of Roger Vella, a Mafia member and government witness. Vella volunteered that his fellow inmate, Frank Salemme, had told him he'd framed Connolly with perjured testimony. The agents' FD-302 dated October 7, 2004, memorialized that as well as Vella's retelling of Salemme's admission to nineteen murders. Salemme also told Vella he never paid Connolly any money. Wyshak did furnish that ten-page FD-302 to Connolly's defense. He could not easily withhold it, as it was obtained by an independent team working on other matters in Philadelphia. Too many FBI agents and AUSAs were aware of Vella's exculpatory information. However, Vella was a "third party," who had never participated in a crime with Salemme. Hence, his information was not as potent as that contained in the Flemmi DEA-6 reports.

But the team that obtained Flemmi's DEA-6 information was working for Wyshak, and in what can only be seen as a flagrant Brady[20] violation, he buried those DEA-6s for three years. The FD-302 information from Vella would have corroborated the DEA-6 reports had they only provided in a timely manner.

After seventeen years as a fugitive, Whitey Bulger was arrested early in the evening of June 22, 2011, by the FBI in Santa Monica, California. Later that evening, as he was being processed at the Metropolitan Detention Center in Los Angeles, he told two FBI agents Connolly was "framed," he never paid Connolly money, and John Morris lied at Connolly's federal trial. Two days later, on June 24, 2011, as Bulger was sitting in a US marshal's aircraft, awaiting his transport back to Boston, he was advised of his rights and signed the Waiver of Rights form. He then told two other FBI agents and a deputy US marshal that Connolly was "framed," supplying additional details. Copies of the FD-302s of

---

[20] *Brady v. Maryland*, 373 US 83 (1963), holding that in a criminal trial the prosecution must reveal to the defense any potentially exculpatory evidence in its possession.

those interviews were immediately hand carried to Robert Mueller, whose prurient interest in the Bulger brothers had accompanied him from the US Attorney's Office in Boston to the FBI Director's office in Washington DC. In what was a flagrant Brady violation, these FD-302s were not then furnished to Connolly's defense team.

Seven years later in May 2018, at the Annual G-Man Golf Tournament in Palm Springs, a charity event, several former agents known collectively as "Friends of John" attended. An active agent from the LA field office casually commented to one of the former agents, marveling that the exculpatory comments from Bulger had never helped John.

"What comments?"

From there it started to unfold. Connolly's defense team was made aware of the FD-302s. Eight years old and heavily redacted, the FD-302s were finally furnished after demands from the defense team.

John V. Martorano was, like Frank Salemme, a mob hitman. He too had spent years living as a fugitive. Eventually captured in Florida, he was in jail when he learned two of his underworld partners—Bulger and Flemmi—had been informants for decades. Now out to save his own skin, Martorano became a government witness. He fingered Bulger and Flemmi in twenty-some murders. Martorano was the trigger man in most of those crimes. The 1982 murder of John Callahan in Florida was one of them.

Martorano never mentioned Connolly when he first began to cooperate. Ram Nyberg, a Miami-Dade detective, recorded in December 1999, "Martorano had no idea of anyone else besides (himself and) Bulger and Flemmi who were involved in the conspiracy to kill Callahan." Later, in a March 2006 deposition, the detective stated, "Neither of Mr. Martorano's proffers included any information on John Connolly." AUSA Wyshak sat beside the Assistant State's Attorney at the prosecutor's table during the Florida trial.

Wyshak ran that prosecution.

In 2005, Connolly was indicted in the Florida case. The Miami murder charge against him alleged that he somehow caused the death of

Callahan—a charge Connolly was acquitted of in his 2002 federal prosecution. With Wyshak down in Florida on the case, Martorano's tale evolved to claim that Connolly had issued the warning about Callahan being a potential liability.

A centerpiece of Wyshak's pursuit of Connolly was the continuing allegation that, four years after he retired from the FBI, Connolly tipped off Bulger to the 1995 federal indictment causing Bulger to flee.

Teresa Stanley testified at the Miami trial there was no warning from Connolly about Bulger's 1995 indictment. Stanley, who was Bulger's girlfriend at the time, testified she and Whitey were on the outskirts of Boston on January 5, 1995, when they heard about his indictment on their car radio. That's when he dropped her at her home and fled.

The reality and the speciousness of John's Florida trial is there for all to see. The entire process was a special broadcast on NBC's Dateline. Admitted murderers, including the actual killer, were recounting secondhand information from the missing man, Whitey Bulger, implicating John and saving their own skin. It is plain to see.

On January 15, 2009, John was invited to address the court in Miami prior to sentencing. He stood facing the judge, but instead whirled on a shocked Wyshak, accusing him of withholding the evidence provided by Flemmi back in 2003, which would have exonerated him in his 2002 Boston federal conviction. Caught on film by NBC's *Dateline* and documented in the court transcript, the off-balance Wyshak unwittingly conceded Connolly was right, that exonerating evidence was withheld. Wyshak effectively admitted in court transcripts he knew Connolly was convicted in his 2002 Boston trial on perjured testimony.

Appeals of John's Florida conviction continue. Two lower Florida courts found John "legally correct" in maintaining his innocence and ruled the conviction for a crime he played no role in must be tossed out. Florida's highest court overruled them. The lower courts have held it is "undisputed" John wasn't even in the State of Florida, when Martorano, who admits he never met John, killed the victim in Fort Lauderdale.

The reality is John was convicted in Florida for something with which he had no involvement. Even the trial Judge has now acknowledged as much. John was not even in the state when the crime occurred. How did we get to such a point?

People—jurors—are willing to believe the worst when someone is portrayed as corrupt. John's conviction for Second Degree Murder While Armed can be seen in that light. The assumption, that he is corrupt, bolsters the credibility of witnesses who would otherwise not be worthy of belief. Two professional killers testified "Whitey told them this, that John said that." To get out of jail free, better men have lied to more. There is no direct evidence; nothing even remotely approaching the electronic intercepts John helped to secure as evidence against La Cosa Nostra.

Mistakes were made. Because John was so productive in the criminal informant arena he was kept in that single line of work, when in retrospect it might have been prudent to rotate him to other duties. He may have made mistakes in judgment and gotten too close to these criminal sources, true. It is also very understandable—almost to be expected—that if a government agent is allowed (much less encouraged and ordered) to associate with the same criminals for twenty plus years, mistakes *will* happen.

It is ironic in all the news reporting and other "noise" surrounding this matter, the allegation has been made—and is believed by some—that our arrest of Salemme on December 14, 1972, was "set up" by the Boston mob to make John look good. The fact is it was me who urged John to leave the office that day, and I chose our destination. Artie Grubert and I dragged John along with us. We were going to the newly opened Bloomingdales on 86th Street, to buy our wives Christmas gifts. For John Connolly and the Boston mob to have engineered that encounter would have been impossible. But this is where we are when someone is portrayed as corrupt and conniving.

Martorano, the admitted killer of Callahan, was released from prison in 2007 with a gift of $20,000 to help him start a new life.

John spent nearly twenty years of his life in prison.

CHAPTER TWENTY-ONE

BLACK MASS: THE MOVIE VS. THE REAL DEAL

The film *Black Mass*, starring Johnny Depp as James "Whitey" Bulger, claims to be a true story. It is often cited, along with Martin Scorsese's *The Departed* as an accurate cinematic rendering of John Connolly's misadventures with the Boston mob. Even though *The Departed* never claimed to be about the Connolly/Bulger imbroglio, its setting in South Boston and theme of informants and undercover agents led many to that conclusion.

The Departed is in fact an adaptation of the Hong Kong movie *Internal Affairs*, which was based on a story of police corruption in that Asian city. *The Departed*, released in 2006, was the earlier of the two and by far the better movie. It won four Oscars and grossed twice the revenue of *Black Mass*.

But since *Black Mass* claims to be a true story, it is far more damaging to John's cause and the FBI's reputation. The 2015 release distorts enough key facts to render it wholly inaccurate. As *Black Mass* was based on an eponymous 2001 book, which had some fundamental errors, I was reluctant to patronize this film. In the book's text, there is the implication that some old-time Boston agents somehow steered us towards the arrest of Salemme in 1972, while in the book's notes there is the contradictory canard that Flemmi tipped the FBI to Salemme's location in New York.

Aside from those two outrageous lies, the book *Black Mass* repeated, and hence helped to perpetuate, some widespread myths. First was the tale that John's transfer to Boston from New York was a reward for the capture of Salemme. It was not. But the repetition of that myth adds credence to the fable that either the mob or old-time agents engineered the Salemme arrest to get John to Boston. In fact, John's was a hardship transfer, which came the following year. I am certain of this since I helped draft the letter pleading that John be transferred to Boston to assist his infirmed parent. The other myth repeated in *Black Mass* is that John and Bulger were childhood friends. In fact, Bulger is eleven years older than John. Whitey Bulger went to federal prison in 1956, when John was a young teenager, and did not get out till 1965, after John had graduated Boston College.

When I went to see the movie in a multiplex—I paid for a ticket to *Mission Impossible*—and sat down to watch *Black Mass*. I did not want to give a dime to it. As for the so-called factual story, it was worth what was paid for it.

As to the "art" end of the movie, I will leave that to others. But I can say the following: The movie was violent. I don't like gratuitous violence at all, but frankly, I have seen much worse. The language was bad as well, with nonstop use of the "F" word. I don't care for that either, but it is how gangsters speak. A lot of the scenes and settings do capture the favor of the place and time.

They compressed time terribly. I know some of this must be done, but this was excessive. John was in Boston for eighteen years and they made the period look like a few "linked" episodes from '81 and '85. (Dates displayed on screen as sub-titles.)

And they compressed characters terribly. I know some of this must be done as well, but again, this was excessive: All the FBI executives—SACs,

ASACs, and HQ personnel—were represented in the one character played by Kevin Bacon.

The inclusion—and exclusion—of certain personalities was puzzling. For instance, there was no mention whatsoever of Frankie Salemme, a key protagonist.

On the other hand, Marianne, John's first wife, is a major character. Actually, they divorced in 1982 after having been separated since 1978. John Connolly was single during the early 1980s. He married his second (current) wife, Liz, in 1988. I know because I was at their wedding. By the time of his retirement, in 1990, they already had three young sons (one set of twins). The dinners in the movie shown "chez Connolly" *all happened at the home of Connolly's supervisor*, John Morris. We now know Morris was personally much closer to Bulger than Connolly ever was because Bulger said so at the time of his 2011 arrest.

Fred Wyshak, the "bulldog" AUSA, played by Corey Stoll, did not get to Boston until 1989, and John retired in 1990. There was not much overlap between them. Yet, in the movie Wyshak is there while this is all happening and is seen as raising the first questions about it. Connolly is shown attempting to make friends and to perhaps divert Wyshak's attention from Whitey, but Wyshak bluntly refuses and demands the FBI arrest Connolly—something that did not happen till 1999, nine years after John's retirement. It was reported in the *Wall Street Journal* that Wyshak was a source for the movie and was on the set during filming.

It shows.

Some scenes are total fabrications. Again, I know some of this may be necessary for dramatic effect or for character development, but scenes showing Whitey with a young son or Whitey touching Marianne never happened. And then Whitey in church! Most damaging of all is the placement of John in Florida, when Martorano murders Callahan. It has been established and agreed to by all sides in judicial proceedings that he was not in Florida. The killer, Martorano, played in *Black Mass* by W. Earl Brown, fled in 1979 and remained a fugitive for sixteen years. He was not apprehended until 1995. Martorano's other key victim, Roger Wheeler, is played in *Black Mass* by David DeBeck. Martorano saved his own skin in that case by falsely implicating another retired FBI agent, H. Paul Rico.

As for the acting, it is hard for me to be objective, but I must say Johnny Depp did not appear to "act" at all. Rather he was dressed in a costume and make-up and posed as a look-alike Whitey Bulger. Others did act well, portraying the various personalities involved.

Former NYPD Detective Sonny Grosso of "French Connection" fame and a friend of John's told us that now disgraced Hollywood producer Harvey Weinstein originally optioned *Black Mass* for Ben Affleck and Matt Damon through Miramax. Sonny provided frank advice to Weinstein in their meeting about the then potential film project. Sonny was never hesitant in letting it be known he was one of many former cops and FBI agents who believed Connolly will one day be proven innocent. Weinstein listened to Grosso and then dramatically jettisoned the *Black Mass* manuscript right into a nearby trash bin.

Sonny Grosso also relayed information about another Hollywood producer to us. According to Sonny, "Scorsese and *The Departed* film people deliberately avoided portraying Connolly or the FBI in any un-flattering manner." They took that approach, Sonny told us, because prominent Boston-bred actors—Affleck, Damon, and Denis Leary—are all very aware, from their own sources in Boston, that "people are polarized, with many believing Connolly took the fall for higher-ups."

CHAPTER TWENTY-TWO

"IT TAKES TWO, BABY, IT TAKES TWO"

William Dredge was facing the stark reality of going to prison. He had been indicted for distributing quaaludes. Like many others in that position, he wanted to make a deal to keep himself out of prison. Unlike many others, he had something good to trade. Dredge knew a Washington, DC attorney who could fix cases in a federal courtroom—Judge Alcee Hastings' courtroom in Miami.

Dredge started talking to the FBI in July 1981. Among other information, he alleged Santo Trafficante, the La Cosa Nostra boss in Florida, had agreed to pay $600,000 to Hastings through the DC attorney to fix a case. What he was describing was the classic relationship of a "bagman" and a corrupt public official—a criminal conspiracy, which at a minimum takes two individuals. Typically, the bagman collects the bribes and shields the corrupt official.

William A. Borders Jr. was the corrupt attorney. Borders had raised huge sums of money for Jimmy Carter's presidential campaigns. Carter appointed him to the District of Columbia Judicial Nomination

Commission, a selection panel for Superior Court judges in the Capital City. Later, in 1979, the Carter administration created a national search committee for federal district judgeships. Borders, as part of that search committee, urged Alcee Hastings' nomination. Hastings was quickly nominated by Carter and confirmed unanimously by the Senate as a US District Judge for the Southern District of Florida.

Dredge had a degree of credibility, as FBI agents had already observed Borders meeting with Trafficante, though their conversations were never monitored. Dredge said Borders had recently asked him to approach Frank and Thomas Romano. They were brothers who had been convicted of defrauding a Teamsters' pension fund. Borders wanted a bribe in exchange for low sentences and the return to the brothers of property, which Judge Hastings had ordered forfeited.

The Romanos themselves declined to get involved in bribing a federal judge. They would rather take their chances with the charges of misusing Teamsters' pension funds and filing false tax returns.

At this point, The FBI's Miami and Washington Field Offices were both on the case. We jointly decided on an undercover (UC) operation exploiting the opportunity that the Romanos demurring presented us. The bribery case against the corrupt federal judge, Alcee L. Hastings, started.

FBI Headquarters was aware of this developing case, as it was targeting a federal judge. It was what is now called a "sensitive investigative matter." FBI Director William H. Webster, a former federal judge himself, reminded us at the outset and throughout the investigation that we must be on very firm ground when "interfering" with the judiciary. As the ASAC in the Washington Field Office, with responsibility for criminal investigations, this case was now my baby.

To play the role of Frank Romano, we would need as the UCA (undercover agent) an "Italian-American type." The problem was the Romano brothers were well into their sixties and looked older than any onboard agent, since the mandatory retirement age for Bureau agents was then fifty-five.

A solution was found in retired FBI agent Harold Paul Rico. He was so well thought of he was brought out of retirement for this role as the principal UCA in the case. Dredge made the introduction, and the sting was on. Borders took the bait. Rico, now posing as Romano, met multiple times with Borders. Agents recorded their conversations and later those Borders had with Hastings.

Borders was cagey and careful, but Rico eventually got the details of the deal recorded in a series of meetings between the two of them in Washington, DC and Florida. Rico, in his Romano role, would pay Borders $25,000 if the lawyer got Hastings to release the forfeited property within ten days. "Romano" would then pay an additional $125,000 once he was confident Hastings would reduce the sentences.

The undercover agent told Borders he wanted to be sure he (Borders) could deliver the judge. The test would be to see if Borders could get Hastings to meet at a particular spot in the Fontainebleau Hotel in Miami Beach at a set time. Of course, this would also be further proof of the judge's involvement in the plot. When the appointed time came, Hastings showed up and Rico, satisfied, paid Borders the first $25,000.

At a follow-on meeting, Borders was to be paid the rest of the money. Borders was specific; the Romanos should drop their current appeal and simply file a motion for an amended sentence. Borders assured Romano that Judge Hastings would respond with an order for probation. It was a clear indication the judge was part of the conspiracy.

Hastings didn't immediately issue the order to release the Romanos' assets. So, Rico protested to Borders. An hour later, Borders called Hastings, and this time the Bureau was on the call.

They talked in code, but it sounded like they were discussing the order to release the Romanos' assets. The monitoring agents commented it sounded like these two had done this all before. And, in fact, the day after the recorded conversation, Hastings ordered the release of most of the Romanos' assets. The money was paid, and the property released seventeen days after the payoff. Rico, as Frank Romano, then arranged to come to Washington to pay the remaining $125,000 to Borders.

Hastings also traveled to DC to meet with Borders. We managed to place a female UCA from the Washington Field office on the flight with Hastings on a seat right beside him. She learned nothing material to our ongoing bribery case, but later she related the judge's overt sexual propositions made during their flight.

A foretelling of the kind of behavior that would later land him in hot water as a US congressman.

We had, over the preceding months in the Washington Field Office, worked to establish a surveillance squad devoted to criminal investigations. That squad was now up and running under Supervisor Tom Renaghan. On October 9, 1981, Romano and Borders were to meet at the Twin Bridges Marriott in Arlington, Virginia. We learned Borders had made Hastings' hotel reservation across the Potomac River at the L'Enfant Plaza Hotel. Tom Renaghan's team had Borders and Hastings under observation, as they spent the morning together at L'Enfant Plaza.

Then Borders went to meet "Romano" at the Twin Bridges. At the Marriott we had Romano's room completely wired with video and recording devices. The surveillance teams were watching both men and both locations. I was anxiously waiting and listening in the field office. Borders, however, had a mind of his own. Rather than going to the hotel room he ordered "Romano" into his car. In case of just such an eventuality Rico was wearing a wire. The hope was we could surveille Borders back to the judge and maybe, just maybe, see the money change hands, which would be an airtight violation of the federal bribery statue.[21]

But that was not to be.

There was now a fear for Rico's safety. And, since it appeared Borders was not going immediately back to the judge, we didn't want to lose sight of the $125,000, either. Even without the transfer of the cash to the judge, it still looked like a good circumstantial case. Borders was arrested shortly after taking the money. I was not the only one closely watching this case unfold. Director Webster and others in his office were

---

[21] Title 18, U.S. Code, § 201(b).

closely following the events that afternoon and I had to respond to more than one unwelcome phone call asking for an update.

On March 29, 1982, William Borders was convicted of obstruction of justice and conspiracy to solicit a bribe. He was sentenced to five years imprisonment and ordered to pay a $35,000 fine. The Washington, DC bar would never allow him to practice law again. He died in 2018. Borders' friend, Alcee Hastings, had been indicted with him. It does take a minimum of two for a conspiracy. As a reminder, when Borders alone was convicted of conspiracy, some agents started singing in the office "It Takes Two," the 1965 hit by Marvin Gaye and Kim Weston, which was again popular in a Tina Turner redo.

Some even danced to it.

On his last day in office, January 20, 2001, President Bill Clinton granted Borders a pardon. The unconditional pardon was one of a flood of controversial pardons Clinton issued that day. The pardon listed Borders's crime as a "Conspiracy to corruptly solicit and accept money in return for influencing the official acts of a federal district court judge [Alcee L. Hastings], and…traveling interstate with intent to commit bribery."

Like we kept saying: It takes two for a conspiracy.

Hastings, however, managed to get his case separated from Borders' case and moved to Florida. In 1983, after a two-week trial in federal court in Miami, the jury deliberated for over seventeen hours but disappointingly concluded that the government had not established guilt beyond a reasonable doubt.

Hastings had won and was back on the federal bench.

But William Terrell Hodges and Anthony Alaimo, two of Hastings' fellow judges on the 11th Judicial Circuit, must have wondered, if Borders was guilty, how could Hastings be innocent? So, these two good judges took the extraordinary step of requesting an investigation into whether Hastings had lied and falsified evidence at the trial. The 11th Judicial Circuit Chief Judge, John Godbold, then filed a complaint against Hastings with the US Courts Judicial Council.

The judges' complaint resulted in an independent, four-year-long investigation by John Doar, a former departmental attorney. An 11th Circuit panel accepted Doar's findings: Hastings had committed perjury, tampered with evidence, and conspired to accept bribes.

In essence, the same evidence and charges as in our criminal case.

The US Judicial Conference, on March 17, 1987, informed the House of Representatives that Hastings should be impeached. The House, acting out their constitutional role, passed seventeen articles of impeachment on August 19, 1988. Then on October 20, 1989, following his trial, the Senate found Hastings guilty. The first article, which charged the conspiracy, passed sixty-nine to twenty-six.

Alcee Hastings became only the sixth federal judge in our nation's history impeached by the US Congress and removed from the bench.

Paul Rico worked on this case for eight years. He testified in US District Court, in the House of Representatives, and at the trial in the US Senate. His work was performed under a personal services contract, which paid him one dollar. In January 2004, Paul Rico died at seventy-eight years of age, while chained to a gurney in a hospital in Tulsa, Oklahoma. He had been falsely accused of helping to arrange the 1981 murder of Roger Wheeler, an Oklahoma businessman, who owned World Jai Alai.

Paul Rico, an outstanding agent, did not live long enough to defend himself against the charge he helped gangsters.

Alcee Hastings, the impeached former judge, was elected to the US House of Representatives in 1992, where he served fifteen terms until his April 6, 2021, death.

CHAPTER TWENTY-THREE

HE DIED IN CHAINS

T he bombing of attorney John E. Fitzgerald's car went to court in the summer of 1973.

I traveled to Boston to testify against Francis Salemme in that case. Harold Paul Rico came from Florida for the court session as well; this was the first time I met him. Dennis M. Condon, Rico's old partner, picked us up. Both men were decades older than me and could not have been more gracious. They were both extremely pleased Salemme would finally be "going away" for his crimes and justice would be served. Dennis Condon spent a day driving H. Paul Rico and me around Boston—Bunker Hill, Old Iron Sides, all the historical sites—while at the same time the two of them talked about the web of crimes and criminals involved in this case. Two fine gentlemen, willing to share their insights and experiences with a junior colleague.

During the 1950s and early 1960s, Paul Rico had worked general criminal matters in Boston, often bank robberies, then the Bureau's "meat and potatoes." In the mid-1950s he arrested the then little-known, James "Whitey" Bulger for a series of bank robberies. Bulger served nine years, from 1956 to 1965, for those federal crimes. He was released early.

When in the early 1960s the Bureau's focus shifted to organized crime, Paul Rico was assigned to the Criminal Intelligence Program (CIP). Rico developed outstanding informants. One of them was John J. "Red" Kelley, who had been used by the La Cosa Nostra (the LCN) as an armorer. Kelley's information and later testimony led to a conspiracy to commit murder conviction against New England LCN boss Raymond Patriarca. Kelley also provided information, which led to an indictment of Carlo Gambino, head of New York's Gambino Crime Family.

What led to our present discussion and tour of Boston had its origins in Rico's conversion of Joseph "the Animal" Barboza from a defendant to a cooperating witness. Joe Barboza eventually testified against several LCN members and helped to convict Patriarca in a federal conspiracy to commit murder. Rico's two sources, Barboza and Kelley, were the first two individuals to enter what is popularly called "witness protection." The current program, known as the Witness Security Program[22] (WITSEC), was established in large part because of Paul Rico's efforts.

When Rico gained Joe Barboza's cooperation, he was not technically an informant; he was a witness already facing criminal charges. Hence, he was represented by an attorney, John E. Fitzgerald, who occasionally participated in the debriefings of Barboza conducted by Rico and Condon. In 1968 the LCN mounted the car-bombing attack against Fitzgerald, which was carried out by Francis "Cadillac Frank" Salemme and Stephen "The Rifleman" Flemmi.

Rico had recruited Stephen Flemmi as an informant in 1965. When he became aware of Flemmi's involvement in the attempted murder of Fitzgerald, Rico discontinued his informant status. Rico was largely responsible for the charge against Flemmi. Once they were indicted for the car bombing, both Flemmi and Salemme fled. Four years later, we discovered shortly after our arrest of the fugitive Salemme in New York City that Flemmi had been staying with him in the same apartment.

---

[22] Title V of the Organized Crime Control Act of 1970; codified as Title 18, U.S. Code, § 3521.

Salemme was the only one being tried that day in 1973, as Flemmi was still a fugitive.

In the end, Salemme was the only one ever convicted for the bombing.

Rico was transferred to Miami, Florida in the spring of 1970. His efforts had so infuriated some elements of the LCN that discussions of a "hit" on Rico were picked up by the Bureau. This was an extremely dangerous and unusual step to discuss. One move taken by the Bureau in response to the threat was Rico's transfer out of Boston. For five more years in Miami, Paul Rico would continue his outstanding work against organized crime.

A few months after our meeting at the Fitzgerald car bombing trial, I again got to spend some quality time hearing about the tangled web of New England criminals from H. Paul Rico. By the fall of 1973, I was assigned to the FBI Academy at Quantico teaching Police Management. Rico was there for a weeklong Organized Crime In-Service class. Among his classmates were agents from New York, with whom I had worked during the past three years. I was invited to sit in on some of their sessions.

It turns out friends of Rico from his Boston days were then my neighbors in Burke, Virginia. So, one evening I drove Paul from Quantico to their home and then back again the next morning. The whole time I was listening to and questioning this successful senior investigator. Again, as Yogi Berra might have said "You can learn a lot by listening." I would not see Paul Rico again until 1981 when, as a retired agent, he showed up in his undercover role as "Frank Romano" in Washington DC.

After five years in Miami and a total of twenty-four years in the FBI, Paul Rico retired on May 1, 1975. He became the vice president and eventually the general manager of World Jai Alai, which was based in Florida. During the following twenty-two years he was at World Jai Alai, Paul Rico kept the operation clean, having as many as a half dozen former agents on the staff. Each of them had their own circle of contacts and sources of information.

The owners of World Jai Alai hired John Callahan, an accountant from Boston, to serve as president of the company. Only a year after

Rico started at World Jai Alai, he learned from his or others' sources that Callahan was associating with mob hitman John V. Martorano in Boston. Paul Rico promptly brought this information to the board of directors of World Jai Alai, which led to Callahan's dismissal.

Roger Milton Wheeler, Sr., the principal investor/owner of World Jai Alai, lived and worked in Tulsa, Oklahoma, where he was both the chairman and CEO of Telex Corporation. On May 27, 1981, as he got behind the wheel of his Cadillac after finishing his regular Wednesday round of golf, Wheeler was shot dead. Roger Wheeler, Jr. became the head of World Jai Alai operations upon his father's death. He kept Rico on board in Florida. Roger Wheeler, Jr. and Paul Rico became close friends and Roger Jr., never believed Paul had anything to do with his father's murder.

Paul Rico retired from his second career in 1997, at age seventy-two, after twenty-two years at World Jai Alai.

The investigation of Roger Wheeler's death dragged on for years. It was handled mainly by an Oklahoma detective who was hardworking but naive and credulous. He entertained the wildest unsubstantiated stories and rumors. His probe eventually led him to Boston. There his credulity was wickedly exploited by Fred Wyshak, the driven Boston federal prosecutor, who simply believed the FBI was corrupt. Wyshak was zealous and very skillful. In 2000, he handed the Oklahomans Stephen Flemmi as a witness against Rico. The fact that Wyshak knew Flemmi was a repeat perjurer did not cause him to hesitate.

On March 14, 2001, Whitey Bulger, Stephen Flemmi, John Martorano, and John Callahan were indicted in Oklahoma for Roger Wheeler's murder. The Oklahoma detective wanted Rico included in that murder conspiracy indictment, but the Tulsa DA said he needed something more. The detective—with Wyshak hovering figuratively behind him—was then cleverly exploited by two very savvy mob killers. Bulger was a fugitive and Callahan was dead. Flemmi and Martorano, however, spent months in jail, where they created a prosecution theory implicating the FBI, which they knew the detective and Wyshak wanted to hear.

And they wanted a deal.

John Martorano, the admitted triggerman, said Callahan asked Bulger and Flemmi to have Wheeler murdered. Callahan was murdered by John Martorano in 1982. Martorano also said Callahan told him the details about Wheeler came from Rico. A big hole in that tale is that Paul Rico had never been to Tulsa.

Stephen Flemmi's story was that Callahan told him that he and Rico wanted Wheeler killed. It defies logic that Callahan would make common cause with Rico, the man who got him fired years earlier.

It was a very weak case, most of it secondhand information from a dead man, Callahan. But neither the detective nor the DA showed any skepticism nor made any effort to test the statements from these witnesses eager to say what they wanted to hear. And so, they made a deal.

Paul Rico was never indicted. His case never went to a grand jury, where some obvious questions would surely be asked. Instead, a complaint was very irregularly sworn to before a Family Court Judge and an arrest warrant issued.

In a pre-dawn raid at his Florida home on October 10, 2003, Paul Rico was arrested by the Tulsa detective along with Florida law enforcement. The seventy-eight-year-old retiree, who suffered from congestive heart failure and other ailments, was denied bail. In the Dade County Florida jail he was put in general population, where he suffered terribly. He was beaten so severely by other inmates he was twice hospitalized. He lost fifty pounds during his incarceration.

In January 2004, the seriously ill Rico was transferred from Florida to Tulsa. In an Oklahoma hearing bail was again denied as was a request from his attorney that his shackles be removed. He was desperately sick and suffering, yet he was kept in four-point restraints on a gurney. Just hours after that hearing on January 16, 2004, which denied both requests, H. Paul Rico died. He was also denied a chance to defend himself against the false accusation he helped kill Wheeler.

In the plea deal, Martorano confessed to twenty some murders, including those of Wheeler and Callahan. Released in 2007, Martorano is a free man today.

CHAPTER TWENTY-FOUR

A TALE OF TWO ATTORNEYS

Francis Lee Bailey Jr., known to the world as F. Lee Bailey, had cross-examined me in the Fitzgerald car bombing case. We knew Mafia boss Raymond L.S. Patriarca, who ordered the bombing, was paying Bailey to lead the defense. Bailey's efforts over the years, however, went beyond a simple attorney-client relationship with these mobsters. Far from it. He took on the role of undoing the accomplishments of federal law enforcement and the courts in the war on organized crime.

John J. "Red" Kelley, an armorer for the LCN, was one of Bailey's early clients. Kelley was acquitted in the notorious Plymouth mail robbery, but then convicted in a Brinks' armored car robbery. In both cases, he was defended by Bailey. Shortly after his conviction, Kelley became an FBI informant largely through the efforts of Special Agent H. Paul Rico. Kelly's testimony resulted in the August 1969 conviction for murder of New England LCN boss Raymond Patriarca and a few of his cohorts. Kelley was one of the first to enter the federal witness protection program. Like others, he eventually found it too confining and left the program in 1980.

Bailey later testified he talked to Kelley, "many times after the trial was over," a strange and inexplicable activity. But then in 1983, Bailey handled Kelley's "recantation" of his 1969 testimony against Patriarca and his mob associates. At that point, seventeen years had lapsed since Kelley's original testimony, and he was clearly suffering from early onset Alzheimer's. He may have also wanted to avoid the wrath of the mob now that he was back out on the street. Kelley did escape death from the mob, but not from Alzheimer's, which he finally succumbed to on February 10, 2000.

Joseph "the Animal" Barboza was a cooperating witness who also testified against LCN members and helped to convict Patriarca in another conspiracy to commit murder. On August 25, 1970, Bailey filed a petition claiming Barboza wanted to "recant" his testimony against the mob killers. Barboza's brother called the FBI saying he needed to talk to agents. Wisely, since Bailey was allegedly Barboza's attorney, the agents did not respond. Instead, they told the US Attorney's office about the call. AUSA Edward F. "Ted" Harrington and another prosecutor went to see Barboza. They reported in writing to the DOJ that Barboza said Bailey "made me" sign the petition and he had no desire to recant his testimony. Further, Barboza reported he was given money to recant, and Bailey was speaking for Patriarca in negotiations for the desired recantation. AUSA Edward F. Harrington, later Federal Judge Harrington, testified Bailey came to Barboza as Patriarca's representative offering a cash bribe for the recantation.

Barboza, the government witness who testified against mob bosses, was gunned down in February 1976, on the street in San Francisco by three shotgun blasts. Bailey's comment regarding his one-time client's death: it was "no great loss to society."

Yet again in 2006, in a civil matter involving one of the murders about which Barboza had testified, Bailey offered up the hearsay of an alleged "recantation" by Barboza, which he could not do while the witness was alive.

The US House of Representatives Committee on Government Reform in 2001 held a series of hearings targeting what it called "injustices" in the FBI's use of informants in the war on organized crime. Bailey testified as to his take on the Barboza and Kelley matters. This led to some questions about H. Paul Rico, who had recruited both of those sources and got them into the witness protection program. This gave Bailey an opportunity to curry favor with the congressmen, while getting some petty revenge on Rico. Gratuitously he testified, "… knowledge I have of Mr. Rico's activity was one of which I am highly suspicious, and that was in his attempt to convict your colleague, Alcee Hastings. [Rico] was up to his ears in that." Pretty rich indeed, given former US Judge Hastings already had been impeached by the House of Representatives.

In 1995, F. Lee Bailey came to France twice. I was then serving as the Legal Attaché at the US Embassy in Paris. An AUSA assigned on temporary duty (TDY) to our office had liaison responsibility for F. Lee Bailey, whose visits were connected to a major federal drug trafficking case.

Claude Louis Duboc plead guilty in May 1994 in Federal District Court in Gainesville, Florida. Duboc was a drug smuggler who dealt in marijuana—lots of it. Bailey represented Duboc in the drug smuggling case and he worked out a deal with prosecutors whereby his client would plead guilty and forfeit all of his assets to the federal government. Duboc ended up being sentenced to prison for life. Some deal.

When he was in Paris, Bailey stayed at the Plaza Athénée, an extraordinarily expensive hotel. We now know it was all paid for out of the forfeited funds from his client. At a social event we chatted about his cross examination of me in the Salemme case. He referred to Salemme as "the boss in Boston" in a tone that caused other listeners to comment that he sounded like a gangster himself.

The original case that brought him to France was a US Customs matter. What was astounding to me, and the Customs Attaché, was Bailey pled his defendant and was then appointed by DOJ to oversee the liquidation of the defendant's forfeited assets in France. At the time the only French assets I knew about involved two expensive pieces of real estate; houses with a combined value of more than $40 million.

Bailey told us, in his braggadocios manner, that he'd gotten a percentage of the sale price as his fee. Having a defense attorney dispose of assets in this manner was extremely unusual; if not irregular. I believe the customs guys made a complaint about it to their headquarters, which may or may not have found its way back to the DOJ or to the Northern District of Florida. They noted the possible miscarriage of justice—Bailey plead Duboc guilty and then shared in his assets with the government. Was the defendant being properly represented?

We now know there was even more property involved than the two mansions in France Bailey bragged about to us. Federal prosecutors in the Northern District of Florida (Tallahassee) had considered all property belonging to Duboc to be profits from his drug smuggling, and hence subject to forfeiture. Much of the property, which included a $2.8 million yacht, a $500,000 yacht slip in Cannes, a $500,000 Jaguar XJ220, and the two houses, were in France, thus costly to maintain while waiting to be sold. To help maintain the property Duboc transferred about 600,000 shares of stock in Biochem Pharma to Bailey. The stock would continue to appreciate, while Bailey used some of it to pay expenses on the other forfeited properties until they could be sold. Bailey was expected to return the stock and its profits to the government, less maintenance expenses.

Bailey later claimed he should be allowed to keep the appreciation on the Biochem stock, which amounted to millions of dollars, as part of his fee. He refused to return those assets to the court. Eventually, in April 1996, Bailey was sent to jail at the Federal Detention Center in Tallahassee on a civil contempt order. There Duboc, who had, not surprisingly already dismissed him as an attorney, was also a resident. Bailey's brother helped get him out of jail when he finally gave up the funds.

Nonetheless, in 1999, complaints were brought by the Florida Bar, which found numerous rule violations by Bailey in his handling of this whole affair. The Bar recommended his disbarment. Later, citing his mishandling of the stock forfeited by his client, the Florida Supreme Court agreed ruling Bailey should not be permitted to practice law, finding he put his financial interests above those of his client. In an unsigned unanimous opinion, the court concluded Bailey was guilty of "the most serious and basic trust account violations."

In November 2001, Bailey was disbarred in Florida and subsequently in Massachusetts. Justice had finally caught up with Francis Lee Bailey, Jr.

AUSA Fred M. Wyshak Jr. began his career as a prosecutor in the Brooklyn District Attorney's office. He then became a federal prosecutor in the District of New Jersey, before transferring to the District of Massachusetts in 1989. Contrary to the cinematic rendering in *Black Mass*, Wyshak had little or no personal dealings with Special Agent John Connolly, who retired from the FBI in 1990. Wyshak displayed a strong dislike for the FBI from his arrival in Boston. Some in the law enforcement community speculated Wyshak may have had a negative experience with the Bureau in New York or New Jersey. While that might help to explain his hatred of the FBI, there is no excuse for his arrogant and obnoxious behavior.[23]

Early in Wyshak's tenure in Boston, the FBI field supervisor in charge of the Organized Crime Squad, James A. Ring, received numerous complaints from agents about Wyshak's insulting behavior. Ring requested that the Organized Crime Strike Force no longer assign FBI cases to Wyshak. This was an unusual move by a field supervisor. Having served in that role myself, I can't imagine doing anything like Jim Ring did. But then, I was always blessed to work with great US Attorneys and AUSAs.

In January 1995, Fred Wyshak was largely responsible for a major case in Boston, which resulted in arrest warrants being issued for James "Whitey" Bulger, Stephen "The Rifleman" Flemmi, and Francis "Cadillac Frank" Salemme. Whitey Bulger and Frank Salemme fled. Flemmi did not. Salemme, by now the boss of the New England crime family, was arrested in August 1995 in Florida. Bulger would remain a fugitive until June 26, 2011.

---

[23] Commentary from law enforcement sources. Also, Wolfinger, *RICO* (Telemachus Press, 2012) 163–172.

The initial allegation against John Connolly still repeated in interviews by Wyshak, is that he tipped Bulger off about to his indictment. Repeating it does not make it so.

Bulger's girlfriend during that time, Teresa Stanley, was interviewed by the FBI. She said she and Bulger were driving back from a mini vacation in New Orleans on January 5, 1995, when they heard about the indictments on their car radio. There was no warning from Connolly. The agents who interviewed her believed she was telling the truth. But Wyshak did not accept her explanation.

AUSA Wyshak also learned both Bulger and Flemmi had been longtime FBI informants, last handled by Special Agent John Connolly. Fred Wyshak's zeal would now be fully directed at FBI agents. Formerly the targets, the gangsters would become the tools in Wyshak's decades' long quest to nail FBI agents.

Wyshak was hostile towards everyone in the FBI. There were numerous witnesses to his openly questioning the honesty of even newly assigned SACs. After an FBI spokesperson finished speaking at a law enforcement conference, Wyshak was heard to say, "Here's the FBI lying again." His charges ranged across the board, at one point accusing an agent of corruption for closing an informant file. That brought an internal investigation down on the agent's head, which was eventually closed.

The investigation of Roger Wheeler's 1981 murder in Tulsa was handled by an Oklahoma detective whose probe led him to partner with AUSA Wyshak. Both Wyshak and the detective had set their sights on former FBI agent H. Paul Rico as a conspirator in the murder. In 2000, Wyshak handed the detective Stephen Flemmi as a witness against Rico. Wyshak knew by then that Flemmi was a repeat perjurer, but he did not hesitate. A witness such as Flemmi at that point was thoroughly impeachable: he lacked all credibility. Using someone like this seems close to a Giglio violation.[24]

---

[24] *Giglio v. US*, 405 U.S. 150 (1972), holding that the finder of fact (jury or judge) in a criminal trial must be informed if a witness has been promised immunity from prosecution.

Roger Wheeler Jr. remained close friends with Paul Rico and did not believe the former agent had anything to do with his father's death. Wyshak wanted to shock Wheeler Jr. into becoming a believer in his crusade. At a June 2003 interview Wyshak asked Wheeler Jr. to view his father's autopsy photographs. There is no possible reason for a son to have to look at those awful photos twenty-two years after his father's death. Another example of the cruelty of Fred Wyshak.

On May 17, 2002, Frank Salemme testified against Connolly in the Boston federal case. Salemme told the jurors he and Flemmi had paid and were tipped off by Connolly to grand jury information. Twelve years after his FBI retirement, John Connolly was convicted on what we would later learn was the perjured testimony of Salemme.

As discussed earlier, the prosecutors had already been cautioned by their lead investigator, Massachusetts State Police Colonel Thomas Foley, that Salemme had "lied about murders he committed and shouldn't be trusted as any sort of witness." In what was likely yet another "Giglio" violation, they used Salemme anyway.

We of course now know from those DEA-6s—which Wyshak in a flagrant Brady violation, hid for three years—that Salemme did lie in his May 17, 2002, testimony against Connolly. Salemme's partner in crime, Flemmi, revealed in those DEA-6s that he never paid Connolly money in 1993, that Connolly never tipped Salemme off to Federal Grand Jury information in 1994, and that Connolly never tipped off Salemme to the 1995 indictment, all contrary to Salemme's testimony.

During the time I served as Legal Attaché in Paris, there were ongoing Bureau investigations of Connolly. Then Bulger became a "Top Ten" fugitive, and a full court press was on. At Legat Paris—along with all other Field Offices and Legats—we were receiving and disseminating information about Bulger. At various times leads were circulating through Bureau channels that Bulger might be somewhere in Europe. I learned Wyshak received a lead that Bulger was in Paris. He forbade his team to share this lead with us, and further threatened them with prosecution for obstruction of justice if they advised the Bureau.

The Legal Attaché's office enjoyed excellent contacts with the French authorities. That's why we were there, that was our job. But Wyshak secretly undertook plans to send Massachusetts state police officers to France to find and apprehend Bulger. They had no contacts or awareness of the situation on the ground, and they certainly had no authority to make an arrest in France.

Wyshak's actions made me wonder if he'd learned at some point that I was close to Connolly and, hence, wanted the Legat kept out of the picture. Or it could just have been his general hatred for and distrust of the FBI. Possibly both.

On October 29, 2003, DEA agents completed their lengthy interviews of Stephen Flemmi. Connolly had already been in federal prison for nearly a year. Flemmi told the DEA that Connolly was never paid money and never tipped them off to grand jury information. This DEA information was exculpatory as regards Connolly. But Wyshak did not provide these DEA-6 debriefing reports to Connolly's lawyers until years later, after Connolly was indicted in Miami. Most AUSAs and Special Agents would consider the DEA reports Brady Material, which is exculpatory material that must be made available to the defense.

On January 15, 2009, in his Florida trial, Connolly was allowed to stand and make a statement to the court. He took advantage of that opening, whirled around to face Wyshak and accused him of withholding the exculpatory material provided in 2003. It was quite a scene, and the entire process was broadcast on NBC's Dateline. Caught on film and documented in the court transcript, a shaken Wyshak conceded Connolly was right. Wyshak effectively admitted in court transcripts he'd committed a "Brady" violation.

In the Florida proceedings, AUSA Wyshak sat beside the Florida assistant state's attorney at the prosecutor's table. Wyshak ran that prosecution. And he permitted myths to be repeated. The words came out of the Florida prosecutor's mouth, but they were Wyshak's as he sat silently listening. The story was that Connolly was schooled in corruption by H. Paul Rico. This was a variation of the myth, told in *Black Mass* and elsewhere, that old-time agents engineered the Salemme arrest to get Connolly to Boston. The repetition of the myth leads to its acceptance. In fact, it's not true. Paul Rico and John Connolly never worked together. They were of two different generations. Fred Wyshak certainly knew that, yet he let the words flow from of the mouth of his co-counsel.

When the FBI finally apprehended Bulger in 2011, he told two agents that Connolly was "framed," he never paid Connolly money, and there was perjury at Connolly's federal trial. Two days later, sitting in a US Marshal's aircraft, Bulger was advised of his rights and signed the Waiver of Rights form. He then told two other FBI agents and a Deputy US Marshal that Connolly was "framed," supplying additional details. The FD-302s reflecting those two interviews were not furnished to Connolly's defense until 2019, eight years after the fact. Brady violation, anyone?

The attacks—not mere innuendos—against a broad range of FBI agents by Wyshak continued long after the killers had made their deals and the former agents were imprisoned. In interviews in 2017 and 2018, Wyshak spoke of "many agents" being corrupt and "other agents" being corrupt. Fred Wyshak, unlike Bailey, is not motivated by lucre. But he is blinded by his hatred and suspicion of the Bureau.

Justice caught up with F. Lee Bailey. But Fred Wyshak has not yet been called to account for his atrociously malign decisions favoring stone-cold killers in order to "get" FBI agents. Nor has he been called to justice for his repeated Brady and Giglio violations.

Both attorneys had a role to play; one as a criminal defense lawyer, the other as a prosecutor. One was motivated by greed; the other was a zealot driven by a dark obsession. Both led to injustice.

CHAPTER TWENTY-FIVE

"YOU JUST KEEP DIGGING, GARY"

Stopping his car to pick up the newspaper at the bottom of his driveway, as he did every morning, Sidney J. Reso could not have known that within seconds he would be kidnapped and shot.

On that April morning in 1992, Reso was the chief executive officer of Exxon International, then based in Florham Park, New Jersey. A man and a woman tried to force Reso into a van as he was bent over to pick up the newspaper, but he resisted. In the ensuing struggle, he was shot. The bullet entered his wrist and ripped through the entire length of his forearm before exiting. The kidnappers tied him up, gagged him, and forced him into a coffin-like wooden box, which they locked away in a rental storage unit.

Claiming to be environmental activists and styling themselves "The Rainbow Warriors," the criminals contacted both Exxon and Reso's wife, Pat, to demand a ransom of $18.5 million dollars. The kidnappers' pseudonym mimicked the name of the Greenpeace flagship, *Rainbow Warrior*, which had been sunk about seven years earlier. And it had been only three years since the catastrophic Exxon Valdez oil spill. So, in the spring of 1992, eco-terrorism was an explanation the Bureau initially took seriously.

The actual kidnappers were a suburban couple, Art and Irene "Jackie" Seale. They had been married for twenty-five years and had two teenage children. He had been a police officer and then a security advisor for Exxon. She was an attractive athletic blonde who enjoyed jogging and keeping up her tan. They had tried their hand at several business ventures and enjoyed the good life, driving matching white Mercedes convertibles. But business failures lead them into bankruptcy and they turned to crime.

The couple they targeted, Sid and Pat Reso, had been married for thirty-six years. Pat had accompanied her husband on numerous moves around the US and across the globe, as he diligently climbed the corporate ladder at Exxon. The youngest of their five children was now away at school and it was, Pat said, "our time."

The two opposing central couples in this case were in a sense mirror images of each other. Both were in long-term marriages to their high school sweethearts. Both had grown or nearly grown children. Each wife in her own way was devoted to and dependent on her husband. Yet, one couple succeeded in life and lived somewhat below their means, while the other overspent, got into debt, and ended up in prison.

Reso's taking was a classic case of kidnapping for ransom and it was to become a classic FBI kidnapping investigation. A tape recording of Reso's voice and a series of ransom notes were received. The first pay-off attempt was readied; the kidnappers frustratingly failed to show. Hundreds of FBI agents were dispatched to New Jersey to aid in the hunt. Eventually, the case would surpass the 1960 kidnapping of Adolph Coors III to become the Bureau's third-largest kidnapping case after the Patty Hearst and Lindbergh baby cases.

The FBI SAC in New Jersey was Gary L. Penrith. He is a lifelong friend and a great FBI leader. Gary established a close bond with Pat Reso very early in the investigation. Even now, nearly thirty years later, he sensitively recounts his conversations with her at the Reso home, where the FBI had established a command post. Gary's emotional commitment to this case was real. Years earlier his father was killed by criminals, at the foot of their family driveway, while resisting a home invasion.

Pat Reso underwent a terrible ordeal. She alternated from being pleased that the FBI had set up camp in her home—they were doing something and they were good company—to resentment her home had been invaded. Prayer was her refuge. She was always a devout Catholic, as was her husband. On the morning of the kidnapping, after their coffee together and kissing Sid goodbye, she began her morning meditation. Pat was already in prayer as Sid was being abducted 200 feet away at the bottom of their driveway. During the stressful days of waiting, she resorted to writing out her prayers and messages to Sid.

Gary Penrith had as much experience as anyone in the FBI with kidnapping. He was deeply involved as a field agent in the Patty Hearst kidnapping investigation. As a supervisor in the Criminal Division at FBI headquarters, he oversaw kidnapping investigations nationwide. My parents, who were then living in New Jersey, were fond of Gary and followed his every press conference. My Dad was even moved to write a letter of support to the *Asbury Park Press* commending Gary and the FBI "for their unrelenting efforts" in this case.

Yet weeks went by without word from the kidnappers. The investigation continued. For the first time, surveillance teams used technology that enabled the tracking of mobile phones. The FBI's Behavioral Science Unit, as if looking into a crystal ball, summoned up an eerily accurate vision of the kidnapping couple.

But no one was happy. Penrith was under enormous pressure. Some of it surely self-imposed, but FBI headquarters wanted results. Attorney General William Barr, then in his first turn at that post, was in close contact with FBI executives. And the Resos, having spent much of their life in Houston, had become friendly with fellow oilman George H.W. Bush, who in 1992 was resident in the White House. Even the President had questions about the case's progress.

Gary Penrith, who managed the investigation of Exxon CEO Sid Reso's kidnapping, and me with FBI Director Mueller at a NEIA conference in Sun Valley, Idaho. One of several venues where Mueller told us of his humiliating post 9/11 confrontation with President George W. Bush.

As the case grew more intense, the FBI received several calls. It was time for the drop. Throughout the night of June 18, a wild chase unfolded. The kidnappers used numerous notes and pay phones to send agents and police from one location to another. At one point a rental car used by one of the kidnappers was spotted long enough for a license plate to be recorded. It all finally started to fall apart for the kidnappers. If the fast-moving events of that evening took place in a novel, they would strain belief. The New Jersey US Attorney, Michael Chertoff, hailed Penrith's work as a "textbook perfect investigation."

But even the best investigators in the world can't rescue someone who is already dead. Reso had been left, gagged, inside that box in the metal storage locker, still dressed in his suit and tie for work. The bullet that shattered his arm had driven fabric into his flesh and fragments of bone out the exit wound. For each of the first few days he was given a mere cup of water. The temperature soared to one hundred degrees inside the metal storage unit. In just three or four days, he died in his own waste. After his death, Jackie and Art hid Sidney Reso's body in a shallow grave in the Pine Barrens of New Jersey.

The investigators had to find the victim's body. They focused on Jackie as their best hope of finding out what had happened. In her interview with the agents, she provided a detail that lets us see into her soul; her complaint was "jail was ruining her tan." Neither the US Attorney, Chertoff, nor the FBI SAC, Penrith, were happy with cutting any break for Jackie. But they wanted to find Sid's body for Pat Reso's sake. So, they made a deal.

Jackie's directions to the burial site in the New Jersey Pine Barrens were not all that precise. The digging and digging led to media criticism fueled by the "Pineys;" rural backwoods families, habitués of the vast Pine Barrens, known by that demonym, who resented the government intrusion in their backyard.

Gary Penrith, likely more than a little bit down, was sitting behind his SAC's desk in Newark when my mother's phone call got through to him, "Don't you listen to those Pineys, Gary, you just keep digging." He said it made his day.

The similarities to the kidnapping of Barbara Jane Mackle decades earlier, which Gary had studied, are eerie. A man and a woman mercilessly forcing a victim into a coffin-like box; the FBI desperately digging for the victim in the soft soil of a very rural area. But the outcomes were so different.

There are at least three intertwined tales in this kidnapping case. It is still a virtual manual on how to run a major investigation. It was a love story between Sid and Pat—and even Art and Jackie—and it is also a true tale of horror, with Sid's ghastly ordeal and death inside that box.

The investigators, prosecutor, and judge all became emotionally involved in the case and its outcome. And why not? They were good human beings. Much of the public became emotional, too, when the case moved into the courtroom. From there the details of Sid Reso's death were revealed to all though the media.

In imposing a ninety-five-year sentence with no possibility of parole, US District Judge Garrett Brown said to Art Seale the "mercy you will be given is the same you gave your innocent victim—none."

But for her cooperation, Jackie Seale was rewarded with twenty years in federal prison and a concurrent state sentence. She was released after only seventeen years confinement, during which time she had taught Pilates to keep her shape. She soon remarried.

The sentencing judge was prescient when he told Jackie, "You got away with murder."

CHAPTER TWENTY-SIX

LIFE AND DEATH IN IRAN

A teenaged boy answered the doorbell in his parents' home in suburban Bethesda, Maryland, on July 22, 1980. A man in a postman's uniform said he had a special delivery package requiring the signature of the boy's father. When the father came to the door, the "postman" pulled a 9 mm Browning semiautomatic pistol from the bottom of the package and fired three times. The impact caused dust to fly off the father's clothes as he fell backwards.

Ali Akbar Tabatabai, the Shah of Iran's last diplomat in America, was pronounced dead forty-five minutes after being shot. His assassin, David Theodore Belfield, an American convert to Islam, was an agent of the new Iranian regime.

I had started my assignment as the ASAC at WFO in charge of criminal investigations just a few months earlier. Ali Akbar Tabatabai's office was in the District and his assassin and accomplices all were residents of Northwest DC. Although the murder happened just over the DC line in Maryland, this case would become my responsibility. The federal offense involving murder or assault of a diplomat[25] was unusual. They occur rarely and usually only in Washington, DC or New York, cities with a large diplomatic presence.

The Iranian hostage crisis was underway and it was a constant shadow over our investigation. As with any criminal case, we wanted to pursue the investigation to its logical conclusion. But we did not want to upset the delicate negotiations underway for the lives of the American hostages held in Iran. At WFO, we were regularly reminded of this by FBI headquarters and the US Attorney's Office. They themselves were regularly reminded of this by the White House. Happening in the nation's capital, crimes like this received far more high-level attention than if they happened elsewhere in the nation.

The assassin, David Theodore Belfield, was born on November 10, 1950, and grew up in a Baptist family on New York's Long Island. After graduating from high school, he attended Howard University in Washington, DC. Ironically, it is the same university where his victim, Tabatabai, obtained his college degree.

Belfield frequented an Islamic student center at Howard and converted to Islam at the age of eighteen. During the early 1970s, he spent time visiting prisons around Washington, DC as a missionary of Islam to the Black inmates. In the process he met and befriended some of those who would become his accomplices in the murder of Tabatabai.

The response to the assassination was immediate. The Montgomery County Police, the Washington Metropolitan Police, as well as our FBI team at WFO all swung into action. There was great law enforcement cooperation. The Federal Bureau of Prisons, an agency I had not worked with previously, was also involved as the investigation moved forward. They possessed valuable intelligence on the web of Islamic extremists formed in the prisons.

As rapid as the law enforcement response was, it was not fast enough. Belfield made his escape. With the help of accomplices, he rapidly made his way to Canada, and from there to Europe. After stops in

---

[25] Title 18, U.S. Code, § 1116.

France and Switzerland, the thirty-year-old Belfield reached Iran on July 31, 1980. He has been there ever since.

Our investigation quickly identified Belfield as the assassin. He had been working as a security guard at the Iranian Interest Section (IIS) in Washington. For several months, since the establishment of the Islamic government in Iran, their diplomatic interests were handled by the Algerian Embassy in DC. But the Algerians were wise enough not to let these revolutionaries into their own embassy building. The IIS was in rented office space in a commercial building on Wisconsin Avenue NW. Early in this investigation, I found myself on several occasions joining groups of agents posted across the street from that building.

From the first news of the assault on Tabatabai, we assumed the new Islamic government of Iran was behind it. Investigation soon confirmed our initial assumption. We were careful with the press and with public statements considering the ongoing hostage crisis. As Belfield had made his escape, our investigation now focused on Horace Anthony Butler, the individual who provided Belfield the postal vehicle and the murder weapon. Over the following months, the scope of the murder plot and the wider network of Islamic state sympathizers became clear.

Belfield was indicted on murder charges in Maryland. Our investigation of the plot to murder a diplomat resulted in a federal indictment of four individuals, including Belfield and Butler, in the District of Columbia. We were able to arrest three of them on federal warrants. Others, who had come to our attention as part the network of prison-bred Islamic state sympathizers, were over time arrested on a variety of other charges. But Belfield was already secure in a country that did not have an extradition treaty with the United States. There he took the name Dawud Salahuddin and began his life as a celebrity.

Today, Dawud Salahuddin has an Iranian wife and lives in a comfortable garden apartment in a suburb of Tehran. He is courted by international media and over the years has given interviews to outlets ranging from 20/20 to the *Financial Times* and *The New Yorker*. He himself worked for years at PressTV, Iran's state-run English-language media network.

Robert Alan Levinson's time in the FBI spanned many of the same years as mine. Our trails crossed on a few occasions. Bob started his career in federal law enforcement with what is now the DEA, which was then the Bureau of Narcotics and Dangerous Drugs. In 1972, we worked in the same few blocks of East Harlem in New York City. He was chasing drug dealers while I was watching the bookmakers, often the same individuals.

After his retirement from the FBI, like many of us, Bob undertook a variety of consulting assignments. In 2007, he traveled to Kish Island, a free trade zone in the Persian Gulf. It's the only Iranian territory US citizens may enter without a visa. Initially, it was reported Bob was there on behalf of the British American Tobacco company, investigating cigarette smuggling in the Persian Gulf region. Many of us suspected he was there as a CIA contractor. The one role did not preclude the other. Then Bob Levinson vanished on Kish Island.

We soon learned Bob was there to meet with David Belfield, now known as Dawud Salahuddin. Bob and his CIA contact had high hopes Salahuddin could be developed as a source, or at least provide some insight into Iran. While admitting he met Bob on Kish Island, Salahuddin always contended he has no information about what happened to Levinson after their encounter.

Salahuddin's employer at the time, PressTV, Iran's state-run English-language media network, published a report several weeks after Levinson's disappearance, saying Bob was being detained but would likely be "freed in a matter of days." Other Iranian authorities denied having Levinson in their custody or that they had any knowledge of his whereabouts.

At one point the United Nations passed on to the Levinson family a report that Bob Levinson was alive and facing trial in Iran. "According to the statement of Tehran's Justice Department," the report said, "Mr. Robert Alan Levinson has an ongoing case in the Public Prosecution and Revolutionary Court of Tehran."

A proof-of-life video was sent to the family in late 2010, followed by photos early in 2011 in which Bob looked gaunt and was wearing an orange jumpsuit. The efforts of the US government agencies to recover Bob, or find out what happened to him, have varied greatly over the years, but he was not included in the side agreements of the Iran Nuclear Deal. Some hostages were returned in connection with that pact, but not Bob. His wife, Chris, learned that from TV news reports. No one from the Obama administration thought to give her a phone call.

The most egregious transgressions were the CIA denials of its relationship with Bob and their lack of assistance in trying to find him or find out what happened. The public revelation—Levinson was a CIA contractor on an assignment from the CIA—did not come until 2013. Even then, the agency claimed his was a rogue operation, one not sanctioned by the CIA hierarchy. An absurd explanation. When one is dealing with a CIA contact, one does not ask at each exchange, "Has this been cleared by the hierarchy?"

The CIA tasked him, the CIA paid him, and the CIA accepted his reports. Bob's CIA contact was Anne Jablonski, formally their lead Russian Organized Crime analyst, whom I had met in Paris. Bob also first met her when they were working Russian Organized Crime. Agency apologists have demeaned her—and hence Bob's mission—because she came from the analytical side of the CIA. A meaningless distinction to most, but something we heard from them before.

Salahuddin and Levinson had several phone conversations in 2007 before meeting at the Maryam Hotel on Kish Island, where Levinson stayed. In a number of press interviews he has since given since, Salahuddin said they talked for hours. The presence of two Americans in that tiny alcove likely drew the attention of the Iranian authorities. According to Salahuddin, Bob was detained by Interior Ministry officials. Salahuddin is the last person known to have seen Bob alive.

Robert Alan Levinson, husband, father of seven, retired FBI agent, seventy-two years old in March 2020, died in Iranian captivity.

David Belfield, aka Dawud Salahuddin, the admitted murderer of Ali Akbar Tabatabai, continues to live the life of a celebrity in Tehran, Iran.

PART III

THE UGLY

THE FALL OF THE FBI

CHAPTER TWENTY-SEVEN

MUELLER CHANGED THE CULTURE

Robert S. Mueller III was at Camp David the Saturday morning after the September 11, 2001, attacks. Just days into his tenure as FBI director, he was humiliated when President George W. Bush dismissed his reporting and said he wanted him to prevent another attack. After his experience at Camp David, Mueller resolved and resolutely set about to change the FBI "culture." That's the word he used. He was going to make it into an intelligence agency, or in his repeated terminology, an "intelligence-driven" organization.

Although Mueller as a federal prosecutor had worked with dozens of Special Agents—case agents—in both Boston and San Francisco he did not know FBI culture nor how the Bureau functioned. He also displayed a hostility to SACs, the Special Agents in Charge of each of the Bureau's fifty-plus field offices.

Mueller did not understand the Bureau's Office of Origin—"OO"—system, which had been in use for nearly three quarters of a century wherein one field office runs the case as the office of origin,

sending out leads to other field offices—the Auxiliary Offices (AOs) —
who report back.

In the case of the 9/11 attacks on the Pentagon, the World Trade
Towers, and in Pennsylvania, the logical OO would be New York or perhaps the Washington Field Office. Both had experienced international
squads. The NYO had two, squads I-45 and I-49, which had famously
chased Al-Qaeda suspects around the world for years.

But Mueller wanted centralization. Everything back at FBI
Headquarters, all information and decision making. Headquarters'
compartmentalization is a hallmark of intelligence agencies. Mueller's
predecessor, Louis Freeh, who had been a field agent, strongly believed
in empowering the field offices. Not Mueller. He accelerated the centralization; he also believed SACs—the few he had encountered—presided over their territory like "dukes." His word.

In the week after Mueller's Camp David meeting, Barry Mawn,
who succeeded James K. Kallstrom as the Assistant Director in Charge
(ADIC) of the NYO, tried to explain to Mueller that FBI Headquarters
was never meant to be an operational entity. Further, he argued, the
NYO had the investigative capacity; it was near the Ground Zero crime
scene; and it had been the OO for the entire Al-Qaeda case up to now.
Mueller just cut him off.

PENTTBOM, the bureau's codename for the 9/11 investigation,
would thus become the first case in the history of the FBI run from
headquarters. It set a bad precedent, which would yield poisonous fruit
in the Hillary Clinton email investigation and then in the Russian collusion fiasco.

After the attacks of September 11, President Bush ordered the Office
of Personnel Management to allow retired federal law enforcement and
intelligence officers to return to active duty—security clearances and
all. Mueller was the only head of a federal law enforcement or intelligence agency who refused to enact the order. The CIA, we learned, went
in whole hog, reinstating those who had language—or country-spe-
cific—skills and experiences. There were former agents with those skills.
Robert "Bob" Quigley was both a bomb expert and an Arabic speaker.

He volunteered; the FBI did not respond. Mueller was changing course and he didn't want anyone around who was less likely to buy into his centralized, "intelligence-driven," paradigm.

To run the 9/11 investigations, Mueller strangely passed over FBI executives who had extensive counterterrorism experience. Scotbom's Dick Marquise, by then SAC of the Oklahoma City office, would have been a logical choice. He had shepherded the wide-ranging international investigation from shortly after the bombing on December 21, 1988, over Lockerbie, Scotland, and finished with a terrorist conviction on January 30, 2001. More than ten years of effort, with the aircraft's debris scattered across the width of Scotland, it presented evidence-collection challenges very much like those faced by the PENTTBOM investigators.

Mueller made numerous other moves to change the culture of the FBI, many of which had negative consequences. Replacing agent executives, he brought in "professionals" to take over key headquarters positions; perhaps enhancing short-term technical proficiency in those positions but losing long-term commitment and an invaluable knowledge of the institution and its culture.

Hence, in the Mueller/Comey years we saw non-agents running public affairs, congressional affairs, and serving as general counsel. All positions where the ugliness of Crossfire Hurricane and its aftermath were manifest. So, as John Durham's September 15, 2021 indictment of Hillary Clinton lawyer Michael Sussmann showed us, we had FBI General Counsel James Baker, a non-agent, accepting misdirection from Sussmann. An agent would have known how to interview Sussmann. Baker, sitting alone with Sussmann in his Hoover Building office, didn't even think to bring an agent into the room.

And in the summer of 2021, the IG reported on the misconduct of Jill C. Tyson, another non-agent who was brought in to run congressional affairs. She carried on a sexual liaison with a subordinate, which disrupted the workplace and demonstrated cultural rot at FBIHQ.

A HAPPY EXCEPTION

Perhaps the exception that proved the rule was Mueller's appointment, in September 2005, of John Miller as Assistant Director of Public Affairs. Miller, the veteran CBS reporter who'd famously interviewed Osama bin Laden and bounced around New York City nightspots with John O'Neill, understood the Bureau's culture. He lectured at FBI programs and for over a decade was a regular participant at the annual retreat of the FBI National Executive Institute Associates (NEIA) in Sun Valley, Idaho. That was where I first met him. Miller's deputy in Public Affairs was Mike Kortan, an agent I had worked with in both Public Affairs and International Relations earlier in our careers.

At the end of the summer in 2008, the FBI was commemorating its 100th anniversary. Miller and Kortan asked me to come back to help mark that event. I'd managed the Gala at the Washington Hilton for the Bureau's 75th anniversary and they wanted to draw on that experience. I'd get to work with the Public Affairs staff, some of whom had been there with me for the 75th anniversary, but there were some challenges. The tenor of the times had changed over twenty-five years and appropriated funds would not now be used. Although this event would have to be privately funded, the Bureau did not want to be in a position of soliciting funds. That role now fell to me.

Here again the wise words of Saint Mother Teresa were instructive. The venue for the black-tie evening would be the Newseum, a short walk from both the FBI and DOJ Buildings. Catering at the Newseum was handled by Wolfgang Puck and his eponymous restaurant. We planned on a crowd of twelve hundred and, following Mother Teresa's advice, we just asked. Yes, the Newseum and Puck would do for $40,000 what usually costs $100,000. To raise the $40,000, again, we merely asked. Northrop-Grumman, with whom I was working with as a consultant at the FBI's CJIS Division, gifted $25,000, and the Justice Federal Credit Union did the same for the remaining $15,000. The event was a success, though Director Mueller and Attorney General Michael B. Mukasey ran late and didn't have time to change into black tie. Nonetheless, we had a lot to celebrate and be proud about—the deleterious effects of Mueller's change in culture were not yet manifest.

Miller left the Bureau in October 2009 for a job with the director of national intelligence, and Kortan moved up to become the assistant director of public affairs, a post he held till February 2018. He was the last agent in that post. Director Christopher Wray has since had a series of outside PR executives trying to fill John Miller's big shoes.

TIME TO DO DAMAGE

Mueller had sufficient time to do his damage. His ten-year term was to end in September 2011. The US Congress passed in July 2011, and President Barack Obama signed into law a special exemption granting Mueller an additional two year term. He served a total of twelve years, a term exceeded only by J. Edgar Hoover.

With FBI Director Robert Mueller and Attorney General Michael Mukasey at the celebration of the FBI's 100th Anniversary. An event that proved again the benefit of Mother Teresa's wisdom, "if you want something, just ask for it."

Mueller recruited James Comey to be his successor as FBI Director. In 2013, Mueller regaled the executive conference—a meeting of the Bureau's most senior executives—with his account of a conversation with Comey. Then the Deputy Attorney General—the DAG—Comey expressed hesitancy in accepting a "demotion" to become FBI Director. Mueller demonstrated how he drew an organization chart on a napkin, showing the Director reporting directly to the AG, bypassing the DAG. According to those in his audience, Mueller seemed to find that funny. What is not funny is the amount of damage Comey proceeded to inflict on the FBI until he was dismissed by President Trump on May 9, 2017.

Mueller's change in culture—from a law enforcement to an intelligence mindset—was greatly exacerbated by Comey's poor leadership, leading the FBI into the ugly morass of the Russian Collusion narrative.

CHAPTER TWENTY-EIGHT

A TALE OF TWO CONSPIRACIES

There is no question that Moscow conspired to interfere in the 2016 US Presidential election and that Putin and Russia conspired to diminish and discredit Hillary Clinton, who they believed would be the next US President. It is also now evident that former CIA Director John Brennan and others conspired from the outset to undermine Donald Trump, in order to promote Hillary Clinton, who was their candidate. The conflating of these two conspiracies lead to the Russian collusion narrative. This collusion chimera led, in turn, to abuses of US citizens' rights.

RUSSIA'S CONSPIRACY

Russian hacking and disinformation were aimed at weakening American democracy in general and diminishing the presidential heir apparent, Hillary Clinton. That was the original view of the NSA and FBI. Initially, only Brennan's CIA asserted that the Russian efforts were directed to help the Trump campaign. In December 2016, when reports surfaced that the CIA believed Russian interference was designed to aid

Trump, former FBI Deputy Assistant Director Peter Strzok's texts provided insight: "Our sisters have begun leaking like mad," he messaged Lisa Page on December 15, "scorned and worried and political, they're kicking into overdrive."

The Russian effort deployed only modest resources, in financial and personnel terms because Russian disinformation could amplify messages that were already circulating domestically in America's political media. Their effort relied on entities and persons outside of Moscow's regular intelligence apparatus. The Russians believed, as did most American political pundits, that Hillary Clinton would win.

Special Counsel John H. Durham's November 3, 2021, indictment of Igor Y. Danchenko, sets forth a November 7, 2016 (the day before the 2016 Presidential election) email from a Russian conspirator to a Hillary acolyte declaring, "tomorrow your country is having a great day" with a big Hillary victory.

Two years after the beginning of the FBI counterintelligence case, in July 2018, Special Counsel Robert Mueller indicted twelve Russians for hacking the Democratic National Committee and the Clinton campaign. That indictment detailed Russia's efforts to foment chaos. Then in October 2018, charges against Elena Alekseevna Khusyaynova, a Russian national, were unsealed in the Eastern District of Virginia. Those charges documented a Russian conspiracy, beginning in January 2016, to sow discord and undermine faith in our democratic institutions. Significantly, neither set of criminal charges alleged that any American knowingly took part in the conspiracy.

THE SECOND CONSPIRACY

The second conspiracy was designed to facilitate Clinton's victory. It involved Obama Administration officials from the intelligence community, the State Department, and the Department of Justice. Their activities were briefed to President Obama. According to his recently released notes, in July 2016, John Brennan told President Obama that Hillary Clinton gave "approval" to a plan to "vilify Donald Trump" by "claiming interference by the Russian security service." Then Peter Strzok, the former FBI official, texted after attending one interagency meeting about the investigation of Trump's campaign, "the White House is running this."

Along with those in government agencies, a cozy, interconnected, clique of Washington, DC old hands collaborated in the second conspiracy. They stepped close to and often over legal boundaries. John Durham's twenty-seven-page indictment of Michael A. Sussmann documents much of this behavior. Sussmann was an attorney at the Perkins Coie firm. He also had been a long-time DOJ employee. Perkins Coie was the law firm for the Hillary Clinton's presidential campaign and also represented the DNC in connection with the hacking of its email servers by the Russian government. As part of its efforts to ensure the expected Clinton victory, Perkins Coie, retained Fusion GPS, described in Sussmann's September 16, 2021, indictment as a "U.S. Investigative Firm."

John Durham also provided us with a thirty-nine-page indictment of Igor Danchenko, which documents the deep involvement of Clinton associate Charles Dolan in fabricating the Steele Dossier. Danchenko and Dolan were looking for "any thought, rumor, allegation" for their "project against Trump." Durham filed a further information on Friday, February 11, 2022, detailing how Sussmann engaged tech experts on behalf of Perkins Coie and the Clinton campaign to exploit access to Trump's internet data. According to the tech expert, the goal was to create an "inference" and a "narrative" about Trump that would please Perkins Coie and the Clinton campaign. In an April 4, 2022, follow-up filing, Durham tells us these parties acted as a "joint-venture" and formed a conspiracy.

A central figure in the second conspiracy is John Brennan, a determined partisan. Before his nomination as CIA Director, he was a close adviser to President Obama. Since leaving his CIA post in 2017, he has bragged about prodding the FBI to initiate an investigation of the Trump campaign and has been unsparing in his vitriol towards the former president. On July 21, 2017, at the Aspen Institute's annual

Security Forum, the former CIA director engaged in a disrespectful dia-tribe about the then sitting US president, which was shocking to the ears and souls of the security professionals who were present.

The activity leading up to the FBI's case opening was carried out in Britain under John Brennan's direction. Gina Haspel, Brennan's succes-sor as CIA director, was then the agency's chief of station in London. She was "kept in the dark" about this operation by Brennan. The source for that remark also told us, "Brennan ran the whole Op over there."

THE SPECIAL RELATIONSHIP

To defeat Trump, Brennan turned to British intelligence. The close rela-tionship between British and US intelligence is part of what is known as the Five Eyes, abbreviated in government communications as FVEY. The roots of this group go back to World War II, when the US and Britain began their "special relationship." In the post-war era it was expanded to include Australia, New Zealand, and Canada. The relation-ship was formalized by a series of agreements over the decades, many of them secret. As with other aspects of intelligence, these arrangements intensified in the aftermath of 9/11.

At its most basic, there are two aspects to the Five Eyes arrangement. First, there is an ironclad agreement not to spy on each other. Second is an agreement to share all intelligence, including tasking of one another. Information collected on one another's citizens—deliberately or inadver-tently—can be shared with each other. Concern has been raised about this most often in the arena of electronic surveillance—carried out by the National Security Agency (NSA) in the US and by the Government Communications Headquarters (GCHQ) in the UK. In both the US and UK there are regulations against monitoring their own citizens. In the Five Eyes protocols, however, Britain provides information it has collected on US persons to the American government. The US performs a similar service for the UK government. In this way the "special rela-tionship" evades the intelligence oversight regulations of both countries.

The Guardian, a UK newspaper, reported that British intelligence was suspicious about contacts between associates of Trump's campaign and possible Russian agents. This prompted Robert Hannigan, then the head of Britain's GCHQ, to pass information to John Brennan in 2016. Likely, Brennan tasked Hannigan and GCHQ for any possible intercepts. British intelligence services have long been considered "the hand on the arm of the CIA." Brennan used this British intelligence to push the FBI into an investigation of a major party's presidential campaign.

On January 23, 2017, about the time of Trump's inaugural, Hannigan unexpectedly resigned, giving just a few hours' notice. Only fifty-one years old, the career civil servant was expected to fulfill his four-year term of office. Many in the community of former intelligence officers speculate that Hannigan's resignation was related to his role in birthing the FBI's collusion investigation.

CONFLATION INTO RUSSIAN COLLUSION

The FBI counterintelligence investigation of the Trump campaign "Crossfire Hurricane" officially began on Sunday, July 31, 2016, when Peter Strzok both drafted and signed-out the Electronic Communication[26] (EC) opening the case. Strzok and another agent were in London on August 2, 2016, just two days after the case was opened, to interview Alexander Downer about his conversation with George Papadopoulos. Everything about this case ties back to Britain. After his return from London, even Strzok expressed skepticism about this case texting, "I cannot believe we are seriously looking at these allegations."

When this FBI counterintelligence case was later folded into Special Counsel Robert Mueller's collusion probe, the Trump-hating Strzok again surprises us with his candor in a text: "There is no there, there" explaining his reluctance to join Mueller's team.

---

[26] An Electronic Communication, or "EC," was a formatted document, introduced during Louis Freeh's tenure as FBI Director, which replaced almost all the previous forms of paper communications, such as memos and teletypes.

In the summer of 2016, Brennan, whose animus is evident, briefed then Senate Minority Leader Harry Reid—separate from other members of the congressional "Gang of Eight," who are usually briefed on intelligence operations—telling him the Agency had referred the case to the Bureau. This was clearly part of his personal effort to get the FBI to move on the collusion investigation. Senator Reid, joining Brennan's cabal pushing the collusion narrative, wrote a letter to Comey demanding action. It immediately found its way to the media.

Brennan is clearly a biased actor who prodded the Bureau into pursuing a counterintelligence investigation to aid his candidate, Clinton, by discrediting the ultimate winner. Durham's filings on February 11, 2022, further document how Sussmann fed Trump's internet data details to the CIA to create an "inference" or a "narrative" of Russian involvement. Meanwhile, Putin's Russian hackers in the first conspiracy were trying to undermine the credibility of whom they believed would be the next President, adding more fuel to the collusion fire.

Others in this second conspiracy followed the same track of hoodwinking the Bureau into pursuing an investigative trail and then telling the media about the fact of the investigation. Michael Sussmann did this when he sent the Bureau off on a wild goose chase after an email linkage to a Russian bank. Then he and his firm quickly leaked the existence of the investigation to the media. That's why he was indicted albeit with the mundane sounding charge of "Making a false statement." Although a DC jury failed to convict on that charge, the trial was a window into the machinations of the second conspiracy.

Mueller's efforts as Special Counsel resulted in the indictment of Russian actors who sowed general discord though social media during the run-up to the election. After their assessment of Clinton as winner proved wrong, the Russians' attention turned to Trump's team. In December 2016, Russian Ambassador Sergei Kislyak, used unsecure lines—which he knew were monitored—to report his conversations with General Michael Flynn. In the past, Kislyak had utilized encrypted communication lines.

THE RABBIT HOLE

The CIA led the FBI down a rabbit hole into its counterintelligence investigation of Donald Trump's 2016 presidential campaign. According to the *New York Times*, Special Counsel John Durham has been asking in interviews "whether CIA officials might have somehow tricked the F.B.I. into opening the Russian investigation."

Although the FBI's investigation officially began on July 31, 2016, there were reports of contacts by an alleged informant and others with individuals connected with the Trump campaign before that date. That activity was carried out in Britain by, or under the direction of, John Brennan's CIA. This is highly problematic because of long-standing agreements that the United States will not conduct intelligence operations in Britain, but it may explain the FBI's early stonewalling of congress as it relates to the origin of the inquiry.

The initiation of an FBI investigation requires certain "predicate information." Many veterans of the Bureau have expressed doubts about the sufficiency of the information in this case. What we now know about the case's origin certainly does not meet the threshold required by the Attorney General Guidelines. These have been revised several times since September 11th. But the standard for opening this type of inquiry has always and still does require sufficient predicate information, which is defined as articulable facts.

All of what passes for predicate information in this matter originated in Britain. Stefan Halper, identified in the counterintelligence investigation as a "confidential human source," is an American who runs the Centre of International Studies at Cambridge. He is described as a close friend of Richard Dearlove, a former director of British Overseas Intelligence (MI6). Halper and Dearlove, in fact, are partners in the Cambridge Security Initiative. Significantly, Brennan is also identified as a close friend of Dearlove. Halper, whose father-in-law was Ray Cline, a well-known long time CIA officer, has been identified as a CIA source in the past.

Halper met Carter Page at a Cambridge conference in early July 2016. Halper also contacted Trump campaign aide George Papadopoulos. It would be highly unusual for the FBI to maintain an informant in Cambridge, England. It is far more likely that during the springtime lead-up to the opening of the FBI's case, Halper was instead a source who was providing intelligence to the CIA or directly to Brennan, who had begun creating the collusion chimera.

It was Joseph Mifsud, another UK-based academic with ties to Western intelligence, who met with Trump campaign aide George Papadopoulos on April 26, 2016 in London. In that encounter, Mifsud fed the line about "dirt" on Hillary Clinton to Papadopoulos. Then, on May 10, 2016, Papadopoulos met in London with Australia's High Commissioner to Britain, Alexander Downer, to whom he related the rumor about "dirt" on Clinton.

In his memoir, former FBI Director James Comey mentions only the conversation in London between Papadopoulos and Downer as predicate information for the opening of the counterintelligence investigation of the Trump campaign. That conversation happened a full two months before the July 31, 2016 initiation of the inquiry by the FBI. As Strzok later wrote in an April 2017 text, "I'm beginning to think the agency [CIA] got info a lot earlier than we thought and hasn't shared it completely with us."

Prior to the July 31, 2016, case initiation, the FBI apparently lacked any predicate whatsoever to open a counterintelligence investigation into the Trump campaign. The ensuing case has never been shown to derive from any FBI or other US-sourced information.

However, a referral from the CIA, particularly in the post-9/11 world, would cause some in the FBI to believe they had to act—particularly if the agency's information originated with our major foreign intelligence partner. The FBI was led down a "rabbit hole," losing sight of the time-tested Attorney General Guidelines requiring sufficient predicate. This sourcing—a CIA referral—would explain why the investigation began on July 31, 2016 with no real articulable facts as predicate.

As the FBI's counterintelligence investigation progressed, it utilized a FISA warrant against Carter Page, a member of Trump's campaign, who had been in contact with Stefan Halper at Cambridge. This may be one reason why the early reporting on the FISA aspect came from the British media. The FBI used the dossier provided by Christopher Steele, formerly of MI6, to obtain the FISA warrant.

Although Brennan has exposed himself as a partisan, the CIA has escaped criticism for their role in using only thinly-sourced information from British intelligence to snooker the Bureau. Potentially most embarrassing of all, it appears possible that the CIA may have itself undertaken intelligence activities in Britain—rather than asking MI5 or MI6—in violation of longstanding agreements with this important ally.

And that may be what was really being withheld from congress.

CHAPTER TWENTY-NINE

TRANSPARENCY AND INSTITUTIONAL FAILURE

Greater transparency from the FBI in the Russian collusion investigation was something many wanted. Be careful what you wish for.

We got a glimpse when five months of text messages between Peter Strzok and his paramour former FBI attorney Lisa Page were released. These texts from December 16, 2016 through May 23, 2017—which initially the FBI said it could not recover—were unearthed by the DOJ Inspector General. If you have the time, and the stomach, you can read them. They are not an easy read.

All the redactions, the use of jargon, and abbreviations make it a challenge. But what makes it a particularly difficult read for someone like me, part of the FBI family, is the realization that some so-called leaders of the Bureau were totally lacking in character.

After reading these texts, Jack Nicholson's quote from *A Few Good Men* comes to mind: "You can't handle the truth!"

We knew Strzok and Page were biased against President Trump. That was at least part of the reason Mueller removed them from the special counsel's investigation. But it was revolting to find that the two of them behaved in ways that, to many current and former Bureau staff, appeared juvenile, self-absorbed, narcissistic, sycophantic, and foul-mouthed.

A current assistant director of the Bureau told me recently—by way of explaining former FBI Deputy Director Andrew McCabe—that there were simply "bad" people around "Andy." Partly true, perhaps. But these months of texts clearly point to at least three people in this relationship.

In the texts, Strzok and Page appear constantly concerned with what "Andy" thinks and thinks of them. They worshiped him—"I am so proud of Andy," one text reads—and, along with him, "we are a great team." Their texts about others are replete with expletives not fit to print. They disdain members of congress who ask questions about the "unmasking" of Americans; they demean hardworking field agents of the FBI, who don't think strategically "like we do."

Reading these texts, what we suspected becomes clear: A small group, near the top of the pyramid at FBI headquarters, was doing it all. They texted about "going to London," and about meeting with someone "from British [three characters redacted]." One has only to wonder if they are referencing MI5 or MI6. Shortly after James Comey was fired as FBI director, they texted about opening a case they had previously discussed, "while Andy is acting." They chose investigations, made decisions on the direction of investigations, and often did the investigating. Who was reviewing their work product? This was sheer folly. It was bound to end badly.

The hundreds of personal texts in this release lead to another issue. In the federal government, there have been long-standing rules against the use of any government property for personal purposes. In the DOJ and FBI, these rules were strictly enforced, to the degree that the personal use of a cell phone or copying machine could place an employee in jeopardy.

Janet Reno, the U.S. Attorney General from 1993 to 2001, issued humane guidance stipulating occasional use of government property should not expose an employee to discipline. What she—and the Bureau officials who would enforce this rule—understood was this was to apply to emergency circumstances, as when one had to work late and could not pick up a child. Her directive came to be known as the "Reno Rule."

One cannot imagine she had in mind these forty-nine pages of conspiracy, sex, and expletives between Strzok and Page. No one I knew in the FBI would ever have corresponded so coarsely with a colleague, nor with such contempt for elected officials. I wonder if this is a byproduct of the cultural change at the FBI or whether it was perhaps a manifestation of the coarsening of American society overall. Of course, both explanations can be true at the same time.

Transparency is good, necessary, and healthy. It can also be painful. The Strzok/Page texts provide a window into "what went wrong at the FBI." I and others in the FBI family are deeply embarrassed by their tone and content—these people were among those calling the shots at the Bureau during a critical time in our nation's history.

As disturbing as it is, the truth and its lessons must be faced. A thorough housecleaning was in order. Then new FBI Director Christopher Wray and Attorney General Jeff Sessions made a good start with the firing of McCabe and the appointment of well-regarded leaders as deputy director and associate deputy director. And please, let's re-emphasize "the Reno Rule"—so that, in future inquiries, we can be spared some of these stomach-turning texts.

The debacle at the FBI was the failure of an institution's leadership.

FAILURE OF OUR INSTITUTIONS

In his recent book, *A Time to Build*, Yuval Levin examines the ongoing failures of our institutions, which is shaping up to be a major threat to America's welfare and security. As the editor of *National Affairs* and the director of social, cultural, and constitutional studies at the American Enterprise Institute, Levin is well-suited to address the concern. *A Time to Build* continues the work of Levin's earlier book, *The Fractured Republic*, which looked at the broader divisions in American life since the mid-twentieth century.

Levin's analysis is deeply rooted in the Judeo-Christian view of man's fallen nature, straight out of the book of Genesis. He has a very Old-Testament view of man: "It begins from the premise that human beings are born as crooked creatures prone to waywardness and sin, we therefore always require moral and social formation, and formation is what our institutions are for."

Institutions thus perform an important task. They form the people within them by structure and habits. Individuals who've absorbed the ethic and ideals of the institution, Levin posits, are those inside the institution who've been properly formed. The institution shapes behavior and character, building integrity. In his positive take on the word, *insiders* are those hardworking individuals who have been formed in character by their institutional experience.

The problem, at least according to Levin, is not merely that people have lost trust in institutions, but that institutions have shifted from being primarily formative—molding the character of those who live and operate within them—to serving as a platform for individuals to gain attention and promote themselves.

In *A Time to Build*, Levin examines the failings of a broad range of institutions. The three branches of our federal government, universities, and organized religions are all assessed under his very critical microscope. But for the most part, his analysis is broad, leaving it to the reader to apply Levin's analysis to one's own organization.

FAILURE OF LEADERSHIP

In defining an institution, Levine suggests it must perform an important task. Certainly, the FBI does; enforcing the law.

He repeatedly stresses how the institution forms the people within it. It shapes behavior and character, building integrity. The FBI did this under past directors. William Webster insisted "We must do the work the American people expect of us, in the way the Constitution demands of us." Louis Freeh emphasized, "The bright line" could not be crossed into bad behavior. J. Edgar Hoover warned, "don't embarrass the Bureau" with your personal conduct.

Levin tells us that institutions were historically trusted because people had absorbed their ethos. We trusted the FBI in the past because the people in the Bureau were formed with integrity as a core value. Now, thanks to the behavior of FBI leadership throughout the Trump collusion investigation, we've lost faith in the FBI. We no longer believe key people within the Bureau are trustworthy.

Peter Strzok opened the case, then traveled the next day to London to investigate George Papadopoulos' conversation with Alexander Downer. His activity violated numerous Bureau norms and traditions. Lack of oversight, judgment, and reflection hardly begin to describe his behavior.

Andy McCabe repeatedly engaged in deceitful and dastardly behavior. Aside from ordering an obstruction of justice investigation of Trump, seemingly as retaliation for Trump firing Comey, he also ordered the FBI to investigate the President to determine if he'd been working with the Russians against American interests. Other than Comey's firing, McCabe offered no predicate for either of these investigative initiations, which was FBI procedure in the past and is required by the Attorney General Guidelines.

The ultimate offender is Comey. The demonstrated abuse of power by Comey, McCabe, Strzok, and others has undermined public trust in the FBI. And a law enforcement agency depends on public trust to be effective in a democracy.

Comey is also a prime example of Levin's narrative on institutions: He's a celebrity who has used the institution as a stage to elevate himself. As FBI director, Comey continually substituted his own moral interpretation over established norms and precedents. His virtual declination of prosecution in the Clinton email matter, usurping a prosecutor's role, is a case in point. His management style was remote and detached. Those who worked with him at the Bureau describe him as "floating above it all."

The distinct previous guardrails at the Bureau—especially the expectation of caution before starting political investigations and briefing congress on sensitive investigations—were ignored by Comey. He never even briefed the Gang of Eight, during their quarterly meetings, about the Crossfire Hurricane investigation. When asked, during testimony on March 20, 2017, why congress had never been briefed, he replied it was too "sensitive," again substituting his own moral judgment for the rules and regulations.

And Comey continues to promote his "holier than thou" celebrity.

Institutional dereliction, a theme of Levin's, has occurred under recent FBI directors (Mueller and Comey), who didn't focus on "forming" trustworthy people. In the past, each new agent was provided a pocket copy of the US Constitution. They were encouraged to keep it with them, next to their heart, so they wouldn't veer from its principles. Under Mueller and Comey, new agents were no longer provided a copy of the Constitution. A small, but highly symbolic example of this dereliction.

Levin provides examples of institutions which try to mask the failings of their people. FBI Director Christopher Wray did this when he hid behind the inspector general's finding that opening the case against the Trump campaign met the "very low" legal bar, even though it was not the "right" thing to do. Wray's continuing response, that those involved in the abuses of Crossfire Hurricane are "no longer with us," seems to dodge the need for broader institutional reform.

INTELLECT IS NO SUBSTITUTE FOR CHARACTER

An entire chapter of Levin's book is devoted to an examination of elites, who are often, but not always, synonymous with the "outsiders" who today use institutions as platforms for their own celebrity. Levin explores the old WASP elite, who were centered in the Northeast. That near-aristocracy was at the apex of American political, cultural, and economic life until the mid-twentieth century. Although some of them abused their positions, they did have a code of *noblesse oblige*, which was at least partly rooted in their realization that they were lucky to be born into this aristocracy.

At the NEIA reception during the IACP meeting in Philadelphia, I first met Christopher Wray, shortly after he became Director. He continues to stress that the "rotten potatoes" are no longer with us, seemingly ignoring the underlying cultural problem.

Today's elites are the meritocracy who have passed all the tests. They are—in Levin's crisp telling—far more dangerous because they believe they have won their positions through merit, rather than luck. Levin observes the "new aristocracy is in some important respects less reticent about its own legitimacy" in that they believe they possess power by right, rather than the privilege of the old WASP aristocracy. Because of this view, they tend to impose few restraints on their use of power and lack the code of conduct the past aristocracy tried to uphold. This lack of restraint can be seen in the promiscuous "unmaskings" that came to light in the Flynn matter.

Today's meritocracy implicitly substitutes intellect for character. Often, they are the graduates of the elite schools who go on to use our institutions as—you guessed it—platforms for their own celebrity. Comey and Mueller certainly fit that description. Levin, in his analysis, contrasts those elitists with others who work their way up inside the institution, absorbing its values.

In the hopefully prescient conclusion to *A Time to Build*, Levin writes "Abuses of power . . .are beginning to compel some real moments of reckoning." This is what we hope for from leaders in the executive and legislative branches as they begin to reform our FBI.

The Strzok/Page texts, along with the McCabe and Comey books, portray a clique furthering the cultural rot in the Bureau and the country, so well described in *A Time to Build* and from which we must recover.

CHAPTER THIRTY

THERE WAS NO OBSTRUCTION OF JUSTICE

T he Mueller Report established there was no collusion between the Trump campaign and the Russian government. Concomitant with that is a total lack of any real predicate for the initial FBI investigation into collusion. Yet, the cloud of obstruction of justice remains even though there was never a good reason for initiating an obstruction of justice inquiry.

Let's look at how that cloud was formed: Obstruction of justice was quickly added to the investigation by Andrew McCabe after the firing of FBI Director James Comey on May 9, 2017. This was during the truly short window in time when McCabe was the Acting FBI Director. Within days, on May 11, 2017, McCabe testified to the Senate Intelligence Committee there had been "no effort to impede our investigation to date." In his book, *The Threat: How the FBI Protects America in the Age of Terror and Trump*, McCabe cites the firing of Comey as the sole reason for his initiation of the obstruction of justice inquiry.

But shortly before his firing, Comey testified before the Senate Judiciary Committee (May 3, 2017) to state repeatedly that Trump administration interference in the counterintelligence investigation "had not happened." When fired, Comey messaged all FBI employees, reminding them the President had the right to fire him "for any reason, or for no reason at all."

Andrew McCabe's book *The Threat*—and his February 2019 *60 Minutes* TV interview promoting it—has sadly further embarrassed the Bureau and those of us who love the institution.

Granted, McCabe makes a very good—even impressive—appearance on TV. He garnered some sympathy from the public. His need to defend himself and get "his side" of the story out there is understandable, but in his book he takes cheap shots at former Attorney General Jeff Sessions. This is not at all becoming for a former acting director of the FBI. Jeff Sessions was a gentleman who had already suffered too much indignity at the hands of President Trump. Again, some may say it was understandable for McCabe to strike back at the former attorney general who signed off on his firing. All that said, I think McCabe's already tattered reputation suffered further.

In addition to ordering an investigation for obstruction of justice, McCabe also ordered the FBI to investigate the president to determine if he had been working with the Russians against American interests. Other than the firing, McCabe offers no predicate for either of these investigative initiations, which is required by the Attorney General Guidelines. In his *60 Minutes* interview, McCabe explained he did this to ensure there would be an ongoing investigation even if he was forced out. But what does that tell us about those in the chain of command behind McCabe? Were others not seeing things the same way as he?

Special Agent William J. Barnett, one of the Crossfire Hurricane case agents, told US Attorney Jeffery B. Jensen in a September 17, 2020, interview that it was only a "get Trump" attitude that allowed Comey's firing to be interpreted as obstruction. He explained it could just as easily have been that Trump did not like Comey and wanted him replaced.

After all, like all other FBI directors before him, Comey served at the pleasure of the president.

The initial counterintelligence case itself should not have been launched on July 31, 2016, as there was never any real predicate. The idea that the president could be involved in obstruction of justice for firing a subordinate was fully debunked in the June 8, 2018, memorandum Bill Barr prepared for Deputy Attorney General Rob Rosenstein. According to Barr's analysis, the president was exercising decision-making authority "invested in him by the Constitution."

So much of what McCabe has since said just does not make sense. It is truly embarrassing. He alleges conversations involving Deputy Attorney General Rob Rosenstein concerning Trump's possible obstruction of justice. But it was Rosenstein who wrote the detailed memo setting forth the reasons for Comey's firing. McCabe's concern about being fired right behind Comey is also a bit misplaced, as he was one of only four Bureau executives interviewed by Trump for the director's job.

NO REASON AT ALL

Yet, obstruction of justice, which was introduced by McCabe "for no reason at all," we might say, was folded into Special Counsel Robert Mueller's inquiry, which started a few days later, on May 17, 2017. Mueller's appointment removed McCabe from the investigation's chain of command. The findings of the DOJ's Inspector General led to McCabe's further sidelining. Ultimately, on March 16, 2018, McCabe was fired. The man who put obstruction of justice into play was out the door; yet the obstruction inquiry rolled on.

Once the investigation was in the hands of the Special Counsel, the obstruction aspect focused on the earlier conversation between the President and Comey about General Michael Flynn, as well as Comey's actual firing. When it became known obstruction was being looked at, William Barr—months before he would be nominated for Attorney General—prepared his nineteen-page memorandum. In a tightly reasoned legal argument, Barr explained why Trump couldn't be prosecuted for obstruction of justice over the 2017 firing of James Comey as director of the Federal Bureau of Investigation. He furnished this memo to Deputy Attorney General Rob Rosenstein.

And Bill Barr knows something about firing an FBI Director. He is one of the few people who have been involved in so doing.

The only FBI director ever fired before Comey was William Sessions. While Barr was the attorney general during the final year of George H. W. Bush's presidency, Sessions' ethical lapses were becoming widely known among FBI management, with whom Barr had a great working relationship

Because of their confidence in Bill Barr, in 1992 senior Bureau management told him of their concerns over Sessions. The issues were widely known among agents and were sapping morale.

In January 1993, AG Barr finished his report, finding lapses in judgment and ethics on the part of the then director. The hope was Sessions would resign, but he did not. Barr's successor, Janet Reno, confirmed his findings, Sessions still did not resign. President Clinton finally fired him on July 19, 1993.

Yes, the Sessions and Comey firings are different. Sessions' dismissal involved personal failings. Comey's was based on work-related judgments. But Bill Barr is in a better position than most anyone to express an opinion regarding the firing of James Comey.

Barr's June 8, 2018, memorandum to Deputy Attorney General Rod Rosenstein argued that attaching obstruction-of-justice charges to Comey's firing was "fatally misconceived." The President's comment—as reported later by Comey—that the case against General Michael Flynn might be "let go" could be seen as an expression of hope. Barr's memo concludes the special counsel may be expanding the obstruction laws to reach actions taken by the President in exercising the decision-making authority "invested in him by the Constitution."

Federal law[27] defines "obstruction of justice" as an act that "corruptly or by threats or force, or by any threatening letter or communication, influences, obstructs, or impedes, or endeavors to influence, obstruct, or

---

[27] Title 18, U.S. Code, § 1503.

impede, the due administration of justice." To be guilty of obstructing justice, a person must have the specific intent to obstruct the administration of justice.

In the end, Mueller could not find proof of obstruction, but somehow could not bring himself to say there was none. It must have been a fascinating discussion, when Mueller sat down with Barr and Rosenstein, who had no doubt thoroughly chewed over Barr's lucid memo, to present that part of his report. Later when Mueller publicly expressed exception to Barr's characterization of his findings, Barr famously said, "Bob, just pick up the phone."

ALL TALK, NO ACTION

Roiling through the pages of the second volume of the Mueller Report is the President's frustration with the unfairness of it all. He was—as we now know—an innocent man frustrated and angry with being investigated for a crime he did not commit. So he strongly expresses himself, shifting in the report's pages from anger with those investigating him to disappointment with those whom he felt should be protecting him. But it was all talk, no action. President Trump never did anything to interfere. Not with the original FBI counterintelligence investigation, nor later with the Special Counsel's inquiry.

Soon, Bob Mueller, in response to a congressional subpoena, would testify before a House Committee about his report. He promised to limit his comments to what was in the report. Committee members from both sides would try to get him to say something more but he resisted. One simple question should have been asked about his investigation "What could you not do that you wanted to do?" The answer to that would have likely been "nothing." That would have set aside any question of obstruction of justice.

HOW TO HANDLE IT

Comey, who arrogantly attended a one-on-one dinner with the new president, could have learned a lot from his predecessors.

Louis Freeh, who succeeded Sessions, made it a point never to be alone with President William Clinton, who was under FBI scrutiny during their combined tenure. Freeh turned down numerous invitations to the White House. Even State Dinners were declined. Meanwhile, Clinton seemed determined to meet up with Freeh. Early each morning, accompanied by a few FBI Agents, the director jogged on the Mall. Their route ran from 9th Street towards the Lincoln Memorial. Upon learning this, Clinton took up jogging. The president, accompanied by a phalanx of secret service agents, would be spotted in the pre-dawn darkness, jogging on the Mall towards the oncoming FBI contingent. At which point Freeh, or one of the Bureau agents, would shout "about-face!" and they would head back to their locker room in the FBI Building.

Again, I recall the good example Janet Reno gave us of handling an awkward expression of optimism, which is certainly not the same as obstruction. While Reno was visiting France, when Pamela Harriman was the US Ambassador, a minor federal criminal case was underway against the French celebrity—Régine Zylberberg. Harriman asked Reno: "Can you make Régine's case in Boston go away?" The AG said absolutely nothing in reply. So, I spoke up, "Madame Ambassador, the attorney general can't comment on that." The idea of obstruction never arose then, nor should it have with Comey and Trump.

Rob Rosenstein, the man who appointed the Special Counsel, has clearly said that the Mueller Report does not show obstruction of justice. But justice does take some funny turns. Andy McCabe, the man who introduced obstruction without any real basis into the collusion narrative, was fired for lying. Although he has since had his pension restored, the record will always reflect he lied.

CHAPTER THIRTY-ONE

THE WORST FBI DIRECTOR

After a December 2019 Senate Judiciary Committee hearing, Senator Lindsey Graham declared that "James Comey has done more damage to the FBI than anyone since J. Edgar Hoover." That's an unfair comparison: Hoover had a full half-century to accumulate questionable actions that tarnished his legacy. Comey managed to do his damage in just a few short years as FBI director.

James Comey, in published defenses of his record as FBI director, demonstrated what a veteran instructor at the FBI Academy warned us about over the years: "First you're good. Then you think you're good. Then you're no good." In other words, don't get too enamored with your own virtue; it can lead you astray. Clearly it has with Comey.

He was first good, cast in a virtuous role during his time as deputy attorney general. When he subsequently served as FBI director, he was initially well liked for his humanitarian concern for Bureau employees. His management style was very hands off. A Bureau executive, waving his hand over his head, described Comey to me as "floating above it all." Quite the opposite of Bob Mueller and Louis Freeh, who were both very much hands-on. Comey, in his published commentaries and on-air appearances, continued to act as if he alone was heroically protecting "our vital institutions" from unwarranted criticism.

On May 28, 2019, in an op-ed in the *Washington Post*, Comey offered a self-serving response to the harsh critique served up in the DOJ Inspector General's report. As he did in his book, he again described the sole origin of the FBI's counterintelligence investigation of the Trump campaign as based on a report "from an allied ambassador" of an encounter in London between a Trump adviser and "a Russian agent." That was his characterization of George Papadopoulos' meeting with Joseph Mifsud, a pan-European academic. Mifsud told the then Trump aide the Russians had "dirt" on Hillary Clinton. Comey piously huffed that it would have been "dereliction" not to proceed with a counterintelligence investigation based on that report. But to proceed with such an intrusive investigation on so little was the real abuse.

A secondhand rumor should never be enough to justify opening a counterintelligence investigation of any American, much less a presidential candidate. That's the concern held by many of us who served in and loved the FBI. This off-handed conversation initiated a counterintelligence case that dogged a presidency. Like directors before him, Comey should have said, "We need more."

Comey tried to bolster his case by branding Mifsud a Russian agent. That remains to be seen, as it is more plausible that Mifsud was a British or CIA asset. In that first encounter, there was no mention of emails. Only after the WikiLeaks disclosures was an assumption made by both Australian High Commissioner Alexander Downer, Comey's "allied ambassador," and Papadopoulos, that the "dirt" was in the emails.

Comey focused on the critics who call the FBI corrupt and the few who call the offending agents traitors. The FBI is *not* corrupt, and it is certainly not treasonous. But when Comey served as director, he allowed it to pursue investigations into one or more US citizens without sufficient predicate. Comey's indignant complaints about treason and corruption allegations are an effort to distract from a legitimate inquiry into some dangerous and faulty decisions made on his watch. He is not that good, and his initiation of the counterintelligence investigation was no good at all.

Without naming Attorney General William Barr, Comey seemed to attack Barr's characterization of campaign "spying." Comey's semantic discussion of "spying" versus "surveillance" is rather silly. When American intelligence officials are assigned overseas to an embassy, as I was, we expect to be surveilled, both electronically and physically. We have always called it spying. When our FBI follows or listens in on foreign diplomats assigned in the US, we call it surveillance.

Comey justified the spying—electronic surveillance—of Carter Page, a US citizen, by writing that a federal judge granted "permission." We now know the FISA Court was seriously misled.

In defending his decision to reopen the Clinton email investigation, Comey failed to mention his initial usurpation of the prosecutor's role in declining prosecution in that case. The usurpation could be described as his "then you're no good" moment, and was spelled out in Deputy Attorney General Rob Rosenstein's memo justifying Comey's firing.

Comey also tries to deflect from his responsibility by claiming it all happened "seven levels below" him. That is simply not true. The Deputy Assistant Director for Counterintelligence, Peter Strzok, drafted and signed out the communication initiating the probe. Strzok's texts demonstrate he answered to Andrew McCabe, who was deputy director and Comey's direct report. It was McCabe who set up the interview with General Michael Flynn and it was Strzok who conducted the interview. These people were not seven levels down from Comey. They were his inner circle, mere steps away from him on the seventh floor of the J. Edgar Hoover building.

It was Comey himself who wrote a memo of his conversation with Trump and then leaked it. He, and only he, did that. What was he thinking?

Here was the FBI director trying to incriminate the president.

Throwing everyone else under the bus, Comey claimed FBI procedures failed him. But it was Comey who signed three of the four applications for FISA coverage on Carter Page. And it was Comey who set the tone, by declining to brief the Congressional Gang of Eight. He tried to distract from his failings by attacking those who called the Bureau treasonous or corrupt. In reality, the FBI is not either of the two. But under Comey, it was poorly led. That is something he, so sure of his own goodness, appeared to find hard to face. He was just not that good.

Naming Attorney General William Barr, Comey attacked those who legitimately questioned the FISA justification, as well as the initial opening of the case. Comey seemed particularly aggrieved that the attorney general continued an investigation into the origins of both. He expressed surprise that Barr would criticize the Department of Justice or the FBI at all, even though both institutions are under the attorney general's purview. Perhaps if Comey's management style had been a bit more hands-on and critical, the FBI wouldn't have found itself in this mess in the first place.

When Comey served as FBI director, he led the investigation of one or more American citizens without sufficient predicate. With the semantics of "spying," "treason," and "corruption," Comey has sought to distract with fake issues. The lack of justification for initiating the investigation is what truly matters.

History will ultimately judge Comey's performance as FBI director, but his initiation of a counterintelligence investigation against a presidential campaign was the most damaging decision to the FBI's reputation to date and has jeopardized our liberties in this nation.

CHAPTER THIRTY-TWO

THE FBI WAS LUCKY TO HAVE BILL BARR

The February 2019 confirmation of William P. Barr for the second time as attorney general of the United States was good news for the FBI—and our country. Bill Barr knows and understands the Bureau from his earlier service as attorney general under President George H.W. Bush. He understands the Attorney General Guidelines, because he oversaw an FBI that was guided by them during his first tenure as attorney general. If the Attorney General Guidelines had been considered at all, Andy McCabe would never have ordered the investigation of a president for "working against American interests."

Bill Barr saw how the FBI operated in the pre-September 11 world—as a law enforcement agency that stayed within legal guidelines. Having served during Bill Barr's first stint as attorney general, I was glad he came back. He knew what the FBI had been and could be again. After all the damage and embarrassment the Comey/McCabe clique had caused, there was hope again for those of us who loved and valued the Bureau and for all Americans who wanted this vital institution restored. Barr had the character and experience to get it back on track.

HE'D SEEN THIS ALL BEFORE

The deployment of federal agents on the street during civil unrest, the employment of tear gas, federal civil rights charges against local police, and an attorney general in the FBI command post—William Barr has seen it all before. During his previous tenure as attorney general he was in the thick of it.

On Aug. 21, 1991, 121 prisoners rioted at the Federal Correctional Institution in Talladega, Alabama, taking eight male and three female hostages. The situation dragged on for ten days. FBI management invited Bill Barr, who had been acting attorney general for only three days, into their command post. There he made the tough call authorizing the Hostage Rescue Team (HRT) to retake the prison—which it did, with no loss of life. With the clouds of smoke still hanging in the air over Talladega, President Bush called to congratulate Barr and the FBI. The die was cast: Barr would become the permanent attorney general, although the official nomination was more than a month away. Bill Barr had showed no fear. That became his reputation among agents.

On April 29, 1992, the Rodney King riots erupted in Los Angeles. The spark that set off these disturbances was the acquittal in local court of white police officers who had been video-taped beating King, who was Black.

On the evening of May 1, 1992, the third day of continued rioting, Barr ordered a force of 2,000 federal agents into Los Angeles to help control the situation. In addition to the FBI, the force included ATF agents, US Marshals, and others. A cadre of FBI SACs, under the overall command of Oliver "Buck" Revell, was sent in to run the Feds' field command post in LA. At the same time, Barr's Justice Department initiated a federal civil rights case against the just-acquitted LA police officers.

Although limited to just one city, the 1992 riots were in a sense even worse than 2020's multi-city unrest. The number killed in Los Angeles was sixty-five, and the injured over 2,380. The presence of federal agents on the ground helped stop the looting after two days, although shooting at first responders continued for almost a week. The FBI faced a challenge it had before and would again: While working beside the police to restore public order, they were also investigating members of the LAPD for civil rights violations. But the FBI proved then, and would again, they can "walk and chew gum."

The civil rights charges against the officers, violations of Title 18, § 242, US Code, Deprivation of rights under color of law, concern a person under the authority of state or local law acting to deprive someone of their constitutional rights. It's the statute that usually covers incidents of police brutality. The charges were made and the case went to court. In April 1993, three months after Barr left office, two of the LAPD offices were found guilty in federal court of depriving Rodney King of his civil rights.

By the time of the LA riots, Barr already had a great working relationship with FBI agents and management. Barr's reputation for fearlessness, along with his appreciation of the Bureau's capabilities, both rose out of the smoke of the Talladega prison siege.

A SECOND TURN AS ATTORNEY GENERAL

As attorney general in the Trump administration, he continued to live up to his reputation. A case in point is the explosive issue of police killings of Black men. After the July 2014 death of Eric Garner while being arrested by the NYPD, the decision whether to bring civil rights charges against New York officer Daniel Pantaleo banged around the halls of justice for five years. As in any encounter in which a white officer's actions led to a Black man's death, there was a sustained cry for action against the officer. It would have been politically expedient to bring charges but, unlike in the Rodney King incident, the facts of the case didn't merit it. Barr finally made the tough call and took the heat. There would be no federal civil rights case concerning Eric Garner's death.

Nonetheless, Attorney General William Barr came under harsh attack from Democrats, the media, and former officials such as John Brennan, who ran the Central Intelligence Agency under President Barack Obama.

This opposition to Barr centered on his effort to learn the predicate—if there was one—for the unprecedented investigation into Trump's presidential campaign. Comey and Brennan repeatedly and publicly questioned Mr. Barr's motives. They and their media allies warned that declassifying documents from the inquiry would set a dangerous precedent. Barr did not back down. Before completing his second tour as AG, he made John Durham a special counsel, ensuring the facts would eventually come out.

Those who worked under Barr during the Trump presidency speak of him the same way we did during his first tour: "He knows no fear." His willingness to confront what went wrong in the collusion investigation will, one hopes, lead to changes in how the FBI handles politically sensitive investigations in the future. The process of applying for Foreign Intelligence Surveillance Court (FISA) warrants will be reformed.

Some ripples will be—and *should* be—felt by the entire intelligence community.

Barr also looked at the culture of political correctness at the DOJ, which has caused the FBI and other agencies to slink away from a frank discussion of the Islamist threat. For example, Eric Holder, Barrack Obama's Attorney General, had mandated that the appropriately descriptive term "radical Islamist terrorism" be replaced with the vague term "violent extremism." But at the Bureau, this had gone far beyond the knee-jerk PC of "watch your words." During the Mueller and Comey years, the FBI allowed advocacy groups, like the Council on American-Islamic Relations (CAIR), to get their noses under the FBI tent.

GEORGE FLOYD'S DEATH

As in the Rodney King case, Barr's Justice Department opened a criminal civil rights inquiry into George Floyd's death at the hands of police within hours on May 25, 2020, using the same "color of law" statutes.

Barr also issued a directive that the agents of the WFO deploy on the streets of the District of Columbia in a "show of force." In leading the federal response to the threat to law and order over the summer of 2020, he leaned on lessons learned. Among other DOJ components joining the WFO agents "on the street" were the Bureau of Prison's Special Operations Response Teams, a much-improved riot response unit, thanks in part to Barr's initiatives after Talladega. Barr continued to demonstrate his fearlessness by walking around the streets of DC to observe the federal response. Current Bureau officials told me he was a regular in the WFO Command Post.

But, in a sense, he'd been there before.

He formed as close a bond with Bureau management during his second tour as he had in his first. He was doing the work that still needs to be done to restore the Bureau's reputation. The FBI was lucky to have Barr as attorney general for a second time, as was our country.

The actions for which he was praised in the past—judicious use of non-lethal tear gas, putting federal investigators "on the street," and being present in their command post—now evoke criticism from some quarters. A sign of the times, perhaps. Yet, true to past form, Bill Barr proceeded fearlessly. He was the right man, well prepared, for that moment.

CHAPTER THIRTY-THREE

THE ABUSE OF GENERAL FLYNN

The revelations detailing the abuse of General Michael T. Flynn's civil rights by a cabal of FBI executives is shocking. Truly ugly. Even more concerning is a further indication of a cultural shift at the Bureau, which threatens far more than one man's liberty.

Jeffrey B. Jensen, then the US Attorney for the Eastern District of Missouri, was called on by Attorney General William Barr to reexamine the case against General Flynn. Jeff Jensen spent ten years as an FBI agent. Those who knew and worked with him in the Bureau all use the word "character" when describing him. Later he worked as an assistant US Attorney for ten years.

It was the efforts of Jensen's team that brought to light documents in the General Flynn matter. As is appropriate, they were redacted and turned over to Flynn's defense team. Many aspects of the investigation and ultimate interview of General Michael Flynn are shocking and demonstrate an undeniable drive to simply "get him."

SA William J. Barnett was the case agent for "Crossfire Razor," the FBI code name for the Flynn investigation. On September 24, 2020, he was interviewed by Jensen and his team. The FD-302, which memorialized the interview, has been partially declassified and made available. The case agent traditionally has a key role in the FBI. Barnett, assigned to WFO, would be expected to decide the direction of the investigation. Not so in today's FBI. Barnett's FD-302 makes clear, that he thought the predication for the investigation was "not great" and he did not find any illegal activity on the part of Razor (General Flynn). Hence, he was not consulted about nor asked to participate in the January 24, 2017, interview of Flynn, and was only told about it the following day. The Flynn interview was conducted by a deputy assistant director—Peter Strzok—and a special agent supervisor. Barnett was, in his own words, "cut out" of the interview.

A case agent not handling the interview of his subject is out of the norm. Many other aspects of the interview of General Michael Flynn by Strzok are bizarre. Not just those highlighted in media reports.

ALTERATION OF AN FD-302

One item that has escaped much mention is the alteration of one agent's account of the Flynn interview. For more than half a century, FBI agents have been required to preserve any information which might become testimony using a form called the FD-302. Most commonly, this information is the result of interviews. It was always considered the interviewing agent's FD-302. That is, supervisory personnel and others never modified it. It should reflect what the agent observed and heard from the witness or suspect. As a supervisor at several different levels in the FBI, I reviewed hundreds, likely a thousand or more, FD-302s. Other than an occasional grammatical correction, I never changed a word. After all, I did not hear nor see the witness or suspect.

Shortly after the attempted assassination of President Reagan, while I was serving as the ASAC of WFO, a secret service supervisor asked me to change some agents' FD-302s. I simply replied, "No, we just don't do that." And he was a friend. So, it was shocking for me to read, in Jensen's report, that Peter Strzok "completely" rewrote another agent's

FD-302 of the Flynn interview. Even more shocking, Lisa Page, a non-agent attorney, who was not even at the interview, provided edits.

What makes this even more difficult to fully comprehend is the FD-302 that was eventually provided to the court was not actually that of the agents' interview of Flynn. It was instead a FD-302 of an interview, done months later, of Peter Strzok about his recollections of the original interview. Truly bizarre.

MISUSE OF § 1001

Some have commented on the use—or abuse—of Title 18, § 1001, US Code. Lying to the FBI, commonly referred to as "a thousand and one" violation, involves making a false statement to a federal agent in "any matter within the jurisdiction of the federal government." Most interviews are conducted without informing people about the consequences of lying to the FBI. There is no standard warning about "1001." Agents would from time to time invoke "1001" to encourage witnesses to be forthcoming. I did.

This lying violation was seldom prosecuted. In this instance the case agent, Barnett, believed Flynn simply wanted to save his job. That should have set aside any notion of invoking "1001." Over the decades, there have been many frustrated agents pounding their fists on the desk of an AUSA as they were told this would not be prosecuted because "everybody lies." In more recent years, it's been an "add-on" offense, when prosecutors have already nailed down the substantive offense. This is often seen in celebrity cases, á la Martha Stewart, Bernie Madoff, and Scooter Libby.

In the Flynn matter it was a perversion. Rather than using a warning about this violation to get at the truth, a trap was set for a lie, to manufacture a "1001" violation. That is ugly and was unimaginable in my FBI.

Some editorial commentary has also emphasized the lack of a Miranda warning to Flynn. In this set of circumstances, I do not see the missing Miranda as an issue of concern. Flynn was not then a suspect, and it was not then a criminal matter. It was supposedly a counterintelligence investigation. Although, confusingly, in his testimony to congress later that spring, Comey referred to the "criminal case" concerning Flynn, he could have simply been mistaken; this remark being another instance of his "floating above" the day-to-day management of the FBI.

The Flynn aspect of Crossfire Hurricane is another example of the "Headquarters Special," which has the same people making the decisions about investigative direction also doing the actual investigation. This bypasses traditional FBI field case management with its levels of review and independent judgment. Barnett, the case agent, told Jensen he believed Deputy Director McCabe was running the Razor investigation. Barnett found he did not have the authority to close his own case; Strzok was able to close the Razor investigation.

Even in the Reagan Assault investigation, we had field agents—not bosses—interview the President.

Many are calling for indictments against past Bureau officials and others who engaged in the abusive behavior against General Flynn. That may be warranted and may yet happen. But more fundamental is the need for cultural reform in the FBI. The constitutional guiderails that were respected in the past need to be restored. The integrity of an Agent's FD-302 and the appropriate use of "1001" are just two examples.

UNMASKING, WHAT'S IT ALL ABOUT

Attorney General William Barr was forthright about his concern over the "unmaskings" that took place during the 2016/2017 presidential transition. Pushing back, Barr's media critics were quick to cite "Intelligence Community sources" in stressing unmasking is both legal and routine. Not quite so.

The CIA and the National Security Agency (NSA) are not allowed to spy on Americans—or to target a US citizen or even operate in this country. If they accidently pick up information concerning an American, known as "incidental collection," they are charged with protecting that individual's identity through a process called "masking," in which the tag [US PERSON] or similar is substituted for the American's name in the information that is disseminated to other agencies or allies. If the information recovered by these agencies indicates the American is engaged in a crime or activities against national security, the information is furnished to the FBI, with no masking of the individual's identity so that an appropriate investigation can be pursued.

The rubric "US Person" encompasses legal aliens and US corporations, as well as US citizens, who all share in the fourth amendment's "right to be secure" against "unreasonable searches."

The FBI, in turn, has the sole responsibility for conducting counterintelligence investigations in the US. Using the Foreign Intelligence Surveillance Act (FISA), the Bureau maintains electronic surveillance on foreign agents living in the United States. During the Bureau's ongoing coverage of these individuals and establishments, most of the phone calls involve US Persons. These conservations are often boringly routine, e.g., ordering pizza, making airline or dinner reservations. At the field office level, the Americans' names are masked and are almost never unmasked.

Americans are to be unmasked only for a genuine operational need. In the case of the Bureau's FISAs, the "operational unmasking" is often done at the field office level. For example, a foreign commercial attaché at an embassy in DC calls someone in Colorado asking about the price or availability of a strategic commodity. The identity of the American in Colorado is unmasked so an FBI agent can intelligently interview the citizen about this contact.

What genuine operational need could Joe Biden (then vice president), CIA Director John Brennan, or the 21 other Obama administration officials named by the Office of the Director of National Intelligence (DNI), have had in revealing the identity of General Michael Flynn? Likely none.

These people did have the authority to request the unmasking—albeit if asked, they would have been hard pressed to provide a genuine operational "need to know." They may have acted out of curiosity. More likely, they were motivated by domestic politics. In any case, they were abusing their authority and the US Person's fourth amendment rights.

Former UN Ambassador Samantha Power is one of the Obama officials identified as an unmasker. According to the DNI's information, she is responsible for 260 unmasking requests, including seven of Flynn. She has since testified under oath that she has "no recollection" of these Flynn requests. Something is wrong. Another issue that needs to be resolved.

NSA collects and processes vast amounts of communications from all over the world. They often provide verbatim conversations to other agencies, always masking Americans. As a legal attaché, I provided hundreds of their text passages, known as "cuts," to our allies. I was never asked who's who.

Those who pushed back against Barr, claiming that unmasking is routine, cite a statistic from the DNI that between September 2015 and August 2016, there were 9,217 unmasking requests. When one considers the immense volume of material provided by just the NSA to other government agencies and allies, that is an exceedingly small number indeed. It undermines rather than underscores their claim.

The *Washington Post*, among other Barr critics, have claimed the Flynn call was intercepted by the Bureau, not NSA, and therefore, the unmasking issue is somehow irrelevant. Yes, it is *possible* that Flynn was never masked when picked up on the Bureau's ongoing FISAs of the Russian Ambassador. But we do not know *for sure*. If, as has been reported, Flynn was outside the US (in the Dominican Republic) during one of his conversations with the ambassador, likely that call was also picked up by NSA, who would have masked him in reporting to other agencies. So, both NAS and the Bureau may have picked up the same call. That happens.

There were promiscuous unmaskings of Flynn and other Americans without any valid operational reason during the 2016 election cycle. A clear abuse of authority. A crime was also committed. Flynn's intercepted phone call with the ambassador would have been highly classified. Someone in the Obama administration leaked that call to the *Washington Post*. That's a felony.

From what can be discerned between the redactions in the documents Jensen provided, it appears Flynn asked about the unmasking of his conversations. The person responsible for that breach has yet to be identified. It also looks like Flynn remarked to the interviewing agents, something like, "You know what was in the call."

Pride, ego, arrogance, or something similar was likely involved on Flynn's part, of course. How else to explain his not registering under FARA[28] or lying to the FBI if he did? Maybe having been a general officer and an agency head for so long, he simply thought someone else had handled this rather mundane task. His behavior on some occasions does boggle the mind, yet it is still not deserving of the treatment he received.

Three principal abuses came to light in the Flynn matter. Two of these are matters directly pointing to a cultural problem at the FBI: the alteration of an agent's FD-302 and the abuse of section 1001. FBI management, with strong backing from the DOJ, must restore the guiderails against abuse. The unmasking issue is government-wide and is a matter for congress and the executive branch to address with clearer guidelines and penalties for abuse.

Thank God we had Attorney General William Barr at least for a while. He ordered the inquiry by Jensen, a former agent who operated under those guiderails. Jensen's findings led to the dismissal of the changes against Flynn by the AG. Barr wrote in his recently published book, "I concluded the handling of the Flynn matter by the FBI had been an abuse of power that no responsible AG could let stand." Barr also ordered the related investigation into the origin of the counterintelligence case against the Trump campaign by Special Counsel John Durham.

There is hope for all Americans who want to get to the bottom of the Russian collusion hoax.

---

[28] Foreign Agents Registration Act (FARA), Title 22, U.S. Code, § 611 et seq.

CHAPTER THIRTY-FOUR

NEED FOR INTELLIGENCE REFORM

Brennan's Russian collusion chimera led to a counterintelligence investigation that enabled abuses against US persons—specifically the rights abuse of Carter Page, General Flynn, and likely Papadopoulos. The need now is for a long-term fix to prevent a recurrence of these abuses.

Intelligence operations always attract criticism in democracies. Suspicion of abuse has been a perennial feature of American political discourse since the 1960s—at least. Although intelligence agency misconduct has happened before, the recent misconduct—involving interference in a presidential election—is unprecedented.

Interference in elections by our own intelligence community is far more dangerous than any foreign intervention. It has inflicted damage on our governmental institutions and on American democracy itself.

When Attorney General William P. Barr divulged to congress his intention to examine the origins and predicate for the original FBI counterintelligence investigation of the Trump campaign, he got people's attention. His follow-on comment, "I am not talking about the FBI necessarily, but intelligence agencies more broadly" may not have been as widely reported, but it surely set off alarm bells in certain precincts.

Barr assigned the job to John Durham, now a special counsel. According to the *New York Times*, the Durham investigation is looking into "intelligence that flowed from the CIA to the F.B.I in the summer of 2016."

John Brennan and other critics of the Durham investigation claim it will harm the intelligence community's morale. This argument has not held sway in the past. The Church and Pike Committee hearings in the 1970s spotlighted intelligence abuses, which led to institutional reforms. Members of the affected agencies have told me they welcome this new cleaning of the Augean stables.

The argument that the investigation could disclose classified information and jeopardize relationships with friendly foreign intelligence services does not hold water, either. Under our legal and political traditions, compliance with the law and protection of civil liberties is of far greater importance and justifies limiting the tools of government.

It is essential to understand what made past reforms possible. Serious congressional inquiries, like the Church and Pike investigations, are necessary. Perhaps establishing a presidential commission, like those that investigated the Iran-Contra Affair and the 9/11 attacks, is needed.

The misdeeds that occurred during the 2016 presidential election cycle cut across the range of intelligence activities. They involved more than one agency. The FBI has taken much of the blame, but Brennan's CIA was the original culprit. The interagency process within the government has been compromised. Misuse of the Five Eyes arrangements, particularly with Britain, has been exposed.

We have seen this all before. In 1978, after the Church Committee revealed abuses by the intelligence community, including the FBI's COINTELPRO, significant reforms of America's intelligence community were undertaken. These gave us the Foreign Intelligence Surveillance Act (FISA) and its creation, the Foreign Intelligence Surveillance Court (FISC).

And as important as they were, the Church Committee reforms were not the first. In the immediate post World War II years, a new intelligence structure was established. The CIA was created, with a specific—overseas—mission. The "special relationship" with Britain, which was forged in the stress of WWII, was codified. Boundaries were established. The National Security Agency (NSA) and the Central Intelligence Agency (CIA) were to focus overseas, while the FBI was to be the sole entity responsible for domestic efforts against espionage.

After revelations that these boundaries were overstepped—the Church Committee gave us even more explicit guidelines. FISA was imposed by congress and the DOJ and FBI themselves developed the "Attorney General Guidelines" for domestic and international intelligence investigations. Former federal Judge William H. Webster, who became the FBI director in 1978, the same year that FISA was enacted, set the gold standard for its use and implementation. Later, as CIA director, Judge Webster endeavored throughout his tenure to codify the borders of the CIA though a "charter."

The trauma of the 9/11 attack was a shock to the system for our intelligence agencies. Then a ricochet was sent vibrating though the intelligence community with the findings and recommendations of the September 11 commission. The FBI and CIA both received blame and criticism for withholding information and missing clues. Failure to "connect the dots" became a mantra.

While the response to the scathing September 11 Commission Report and the ensuing "war on terrorism" gave us an FBI and CIA operating in much closer concert, there were unintended consequences. The FBI is now more likely to accept and act on any referral from the CIA—with consequences that are the subject of this book.

Bill Barr tried to "lay down the law" and ensure that in the future the opening of a counterintelligence case against a US person is based on sufficient predicate, not a mere referral from the CIA. Bill Barr's initiative, appointing a special counsel, was a step in the right direction. But we can't expect John Durham to do it all. The problems go well beyond the purview of the Justice Department.

THE FIVE EYES THREAT TO OUR LIBERTIES

Yes, our FBI has gotten a lot of blame, much of it justified. But the murky origins of the counterintelligence investigation of the Trump campaign go well beyond the Bureau. In the third paragraph of the Mueller Report introduction, the case's origin is explained as a "foreign government contact[ed] the FBI about the May [2016] encounter of George Papadopoulos." If the origin of the case was in Britain, the use and likely manipulation of the long-standing agreements between American and British intelligence need to be re-examined.

"Five Eyes" is an intelligence alliance between the US, UK, Australia, New Zealand, and Canada which stipulates they would all share intelligence and would never spy on each other. Accordingly, either American intelligence was misled by the British in the opening of the case or John Brennan was conducting an operation in the UK in violation of the "Five Eyes" agreement. The abuse of this unique agreement should have been part of any review of "intelligence agencies more broadly."

On Monday, September 17, 2018, President Trump ordered that certain documents from the Russian probe be declassified. These were to include the FISA Court order, the application for the monitoring of Carter Page, and the still unredacted texts of some of the key players. By Friday, September 21, only four days after issuing his order, the President canceled it. He cited the calls of "key allies" as a reason for his reversal. The U.K.'s *Daily Telegraph* reported on November 21, 2018, that these appeals came from MI6.

The releases would have pointed to the origin of the original counterintelligence investigation. Pointed only, as the originating EC (electronic communication) dated July 31, 2016, which congress wanted to see, was not part of Trump's order. Still, the text messages would have showed Strzok and others' contacts with British intelligence. In any event, these disclosures would be embarrassing to the FBI, likely showing that they were snookered by Brennan into a counterintelligence investigation of US persons without the necessary predicate.

In turn, the reversal by President Trump—unusual in such a strong-willed, opinionated individual—demonstrates the influence of the "special relationship" with Britain, particularly the influence MI5 and MI6 have on their US counterparts. This reversal also demonstrates the influence of the entrenched bureaucracy at the CIA, which Trump might call the deep state.

A sharing of all intelligence, including tasking of one another, is fundamental to the Five Eyes agreement. Information collected on one another's citizens—deliberately or inadvertently—is shared. Hence, the "special relationship" provides a back door for the sharing intelligence that would not be otherwise allowed. This came to light in 2008 when the National Security Agency (NSA), in declining a Freedom of Information Act request, acknowledged that it held over a thousand pages of information about Princess Diana. More recently, we learned that the conversations of TV personality Tucker Carlson were leaked by the NSA. Whether the NSA or British intelligence originally collected Carlson's conversations is still an open question.

Relationships with foreign intelligence services should be reexamined to ensure that activities performed on behalf of the U.S. are not used to sidestep rules against spying on Americans. As a part of our agencies' reporting, there should be a certification that outsourcing is not being undertaken for political purposes. Five Eyes, and particularly the British, should not be a backdoor to do what is not otherwise permitted.

LIMIT FISA TO SURVEILLANCE OF FOREIGNERS

The application, operation, and renewals of the FISA warrant against Carter Page was an abuse. Department of Justice Inspector General Michael Horowitz, in his first report on the FISA warrant targeting Page, made that clear. Nonetheless, he found the process legal. Perhaps that is all we can expect from a narrowly proscribed Inspector General (IG). Still, if something is wrong, being legal does not make it right.

The Inspector General did, however, identify questionable judgment and mistakes made during the FISA process. The principal failing highlighted in Horowitz's first report is the alteration of an email by an attorney then employed by the FBI, which was used in one of the FISA renewal applications. Other instances of poor judgment and lack of attention to detail include failings in disclosures and corroboration in the application itself. Shortcomings found in the review process for approval before submission to the Foreign Intelligence Surveillance Court (the FISC) are a departure from past practice.

In his second FISA report, Horowitz documented a number of inaccuracies in the FBI's warrant applications. As shocking as such sloppiness is, it is not the major problem with these warrants, nor the biggest threat to Americans' civil liberties.

As the FBI's counterintelligence investigation progressed, it would utilize, in October 2016, a FISA warrant against Carter Page, a US citizen. Page, a member of Trump's campaign, had been in contact with Stefan Halper at Cambridge. This may be one reason why the early reporting on the FISA aspect came from the British media. The FBI used a dossier provided by former MI6 operative Christopher Steele to obtain the FISA warrant. We now know, from the November 3, 2021, indictment of Igor Danchenko, that the dossier was a deliberate fraud. Yet, without the "Steele dossier" there would be no FISA application.

As he had in his first report about the Carter Page FISA warrants, the IG March 2020 report identifies numerous inaccuracies and instances of missing documentation during the FISA process. The principal failing highlighted in the second report is the serious errors in the FBI's factual accuracy review ("Woods" procedures). The IG's staff took a sample from a dataset of more than 700 applications relating to US Persons from eight FBI field offices over a recent five-year period. In each of the files that were then reviewed, they found errors, inconsistences, and lack of documentation. Shortcomings of this magnitude are shocking and prompted the IG to issue a preliminary report before completing his audit.

Just three days after the IG's second report, Chief Judge of the Foreign Intelligence Surveillance Court James E. Boasberg issued a rare public order. Judge Boasberg referenced the court's comments on the Page matter, which "calls into question reliability of other FBI applications," stating the second IG report "provides further reason for systemic concern." The judge went on to order the government to undertake several steps to ensure the accuracy of FISA applications. But accuracy is not the only issue.

This use of FISA against a US citizen presents a fundamental threat to Americans' civil liberties. It essentially suspends the Constitution. In 1978, reforms in response to the Church Committee's revelations gave us the FISA and FISC. For more than two decades they were used solely, as their names imply, to gather intelligence on foreign agents living in this country.

In addition to the arduously detailed preparation of the FISA application by the case agents, Director Webster had a team of law clerks painstakingly review each application before it was presented to him for signature. The original act had mandated that each application be signed by the FBI director and then by the attorney general. That has since changed and the final sign-off authority has been extended to an ever-increasing number of officials.

The original thinking was if an American is suspected of being an agent of a foreign power, the proper way to pursue that individual was by the espionage act, a criminal statute. That would preclude the use of a FISA warrant against the US person. The criminal code (Title III) would then be the basis for any necessary electronic surveillance (*Elsur*). This requires a higher probable cause standard than FISA, as the information gathered would be evidence for use in court.

The number of FISA warrants has greatly expanded over the years. The FISC reports only 200 warrants in 1979, its first full year of operation, but by 2000, the number had risen to 1,000. In reaction to the September 11 attacks there was a tremendous increase in the number FISA warrants—to over 2000 a year—with a looser approach to their approval.

The coverage of a FISA warrant has expanded as well. At first, what is commonly understood as "wiretapping" was authorized. In recent years, the coverage includes all sorts of electronic communications beyond voice: texts, emails, and instant messaging are now included in *Elsur*. Additionally, FISA can authorize physical entry and searches. The nature of today's data communications also means that FISA surveillance can look "backwards" at older data remaining on servers and other storage facilities.

Over the years, and particularly since September 11, FISA has been amended numerous times and now allows for the surveillance of Americans. But there were safeguards. One safeguard is a requirement the government must show the FISC that a less intrusive technique cannot produce the desired information. As Page had cooperated earlier with both the FBI and the CIA, clearly this safeguard was fudged. It was also Bureau practice, before 2016, to use FISA coverage only on Americans who had a security clearance, possessed national security information, and had shown a willingness to share information with a foreign power. Page did not even hold a security clearance. The IG said that this was legal; but it was not right.

The second, March 2020, IG report's review of 700 FISAs against US Persons, by just eight FBI offices in the recent five-year period, indicates a now routine use of this intrusive tool against Americans. Its increasing use has led to FISA being handled in a perfunctory fashion. Further, the FISA process—unlike Title III criminal warrants—is done in secrecy. The now quotidian FISA has led to promiscuous spying on Americans, as evidenced by the findings of both IG reports.

These IG reports have focused on what was included in the FISA applications. Separate from the IG reports, we now know from declassified documents of Stephan Halper's reporting to the FBI what was not in the FISA applications. Halper, at the direction of the FBI, had recorded conversations with Carter Page in which Page denied collusion with Russia. These tapes, material clearly exculpatory to Carter Page, were withheld from the FISC.

On September 30, 2021, a major new IG report—his third—on the FBI's use of FISA was released. It was extensive and found numerous errors and omissions. The IG concluded the FBI had not taken his earlier reports to heart. During this IG audit, FBI field personnel minimized the significance of the non-compliance in the use of these highly intrusive FISA warrants.

The IG report dispassionately documents the routine use of FISA against US persons. In this latest report, 7,000 FISA applications targeting US persons over a five-year period were reviewed. There should be outrage in the media—from left as well as right—thousands of Americans are being spied on domestically—yes, "spying" is the correct word—without any recourse. But press reporting was minimal and editorial outrage rare.

Former Attorney General William Barr had correctly characterized as "malfeasance and misfeasance" the abuses identified by the IG in the Carter Page investigation. In speaking with congressional leaders, he urged them to keep this "important tool" as they contemplate reforms to FISA. Yes, let's keep this tool for its original purpose, to gather intelligence on foreign agents, not to spy on Americans.

FBI Director Christopher Wray has been implementing internal reforms at the FBI to address the accuracy of the FISA process. The FBI, in its response to the second IG report, characterize these as "foundational" reforms. Hopefully, their continuing efforts will return the FBI to a culture of rigorous accuracy. Caution should still be maintained: As a current Bureau executive painfully pointed out to me, "But they [the Comey clique] didn't even follow the old rules."

The fundamental need is to return FISA to its original purpose of surveilling foreign agents for intelligence purposes, thus preventing abuses against Americans as we as saw with Carter Page.

ROLE OF CONGRESS

Amending FISA to again prohibit, or stringently limit, targeting US persons is a "foundational reform" congress can make.

The abuse of "unmasking," rampant during the 2016 election cycle, must be addressed. Congress should be notified as to the numbers of unmaskings. Criminal penalties should also be imposed on those who improperly unmask American citizens.

The pernicious "reverse targeting" practice, acknowledged by Brennan, must be ended, as well. The CIA and the NSA are forbidden to spy on Americans. If they accidentally pick up information on an American, while spying on foreigners, they can—and do—pass it on to the FBI. If they set out to deliberately do it by focusing on a foreigner close to an American of interest, it is not truly "incidental" collection. Sanctions for this type of abuse should include criminal penalties.

Congress must look at itself as well. Being a political institution, it has approached oversight issues in a political manner. Recognizing these political realities does not mean they cannot do better. Congressional oversight procedures should forbid one-on-one briefings/meetings with congressional leaders or staff. To avoid memory lapses, all Gang of Eight meetings should be bipartisan and videotaped. Congressional overseers themselves should not standby silently when faced with suspicions of abuse.

NO NEED FOR DOMESTIC TERRORISM LAW

What we don't need from congress is a domestic terrorism law.

Amid understandable public concern over recent political violence and mass shootings, bills have been put forward in both houses of congress to make domestic terrorism a federal crime. But domestic terrorism is not a new problem. US law enforcement already has the legal tools it needs to deal with it, and the proposed law would open the door to future government abuses of Americans' constitutional rights.

Consider the case of domestic terrorist Timothy McVeigh, who killed hundreds in the 1995 Oklahoma City bombing. He was arrested, convicted, and executed under laws that criminalized his violent actions—without regard to his thoughts on the policy or conduct of the government.

The proposed bills, however, would apply to acts when they aim to "intimidate or coerce a civilian population or influence, affect, or retaliate against the policy or conduct of a government." Arrests and convictions under such a law would therefore require investigators to delve into suspects' political beliefs, harking back to some unfortunate chapters in law enforcement history.

The FBI has been engaged successfully in the fight against domestic terrorism for well over half a century. Throughout the 1950s and early '60s, the Bureau waged a campaign against Ku Klux Klan's murders and bombings. Laws making it a crime to conspire to violently deprive other citizens of their constitutional rights were often used in this battle. In the late '60s, attention shifted to the left-wing violence of the Weathermen and similar groups. Federal criminal statutes ranging from conspiracy to wire fraud were invoked to stop their domestic terrorism.

But as the '60s and '70s progressed, there was frequent criticism that groups were being investigated for what they advocated, rather than for their actions. This is the dangerous possibility a domestic terrorism law would again present. The abuses of that time led Attorney General Edward Levi in 1976 to issue the original set of Attorney General Guidelines for the FBI's domestic intelligence investigations. The key guidance is investigations are only to be undertaken of groups advocating or engaging in violence, not simply for their speech or beliefs. Although the AG Guidelines have been amended numerous times over the succeeding decades, that still is—as it should be—the basic standard. Speech that stops short of inciting violence is protected.

Operating under the AG Guidelines for over forty years has constrained FBI operations against domestic terrorism. But then, the Bill of Rights itself hinders investigations against most criminals. Nonetheless, well-trained professionals have led the federal government's successful investigation and prosecution of domestic terrorists. The Black Panther Party and Black Liberation Army, murderers of police officers, have received investigative attention, as have the violent white bigots of the Aryan Nation and the Ku Klux Klan. When confronting such groups, it may be tempting to "take the gloves off," but investigative attention has properly focused on their actions, not their speech or thoughts about government policy.

The current AG Guidelines authorize "a broad examination of groups" for "offenses characteristically understood as terrorism" as described in title 18 US Code § 2332b (5) (B). Under this rubric, investigations have been carried out against groups as diverse as eco-terrorists and the Jewish Defense League. The oft-discussed lone wolf has not escaped attention, either. Ted Kaczynski, the Unabomber, is serving a life sentence in the federal supermax prison in Colorado.

All these terrorists were investigated for their actions—not their beliefs. The existing criminal statutes, which target specific bad behavior, are constitutionally a safer approach to domestic terrorism than the proposed bills in congress. The danger of the proposed legislation is it would inhibit free speech. As ugly as some beliefs are—white supremacy, for example—they are still protected. The mindset of the proposed legislation carries an implicit threat to the First Amendment. Say something out of the mainstream, and you may become a subject for investigation.

State and local police are now closely coordinating with federal authorities in the fight against domestic as well as international terrorism. The Joint Terrorism Task Forces (JTTF), made up of both federal and local offices, is a prime example of this collaboration. The FBI is engaged in preventing mass shootings with projects such as the National Instant Criminal Background Checks (NICS) for firearms purchases, which has the challenging task of keeping firearms from those who would harm us while respecting citizens' Second Amendment rights.

A lot is being done. There is a full menu of federal criminal laws on the books that can and have been invoked. In the understandable urge to "do something," we must do nothing to endanger the Bill of Rights. As former FBI Director William H. Webster frequently reminded us agents, "We must do the work the American people expect of us, in the way the Constitution demands of us." That is what the FBI does and has done. Another federal statute, making some feel good by creating a law against domestic terrorism, is both unnecessary, and worse, a potential threat to the First Amendment.

A great irony is, although Russia's efforts at election interference were clumsy and ineffective, the improper activities of US officials magnified their importance and impact. By undermining Americans confidence in our political processes, these officials have increased the possibility of future foreign interference with our elections.

The intelligence community's house must be put in order.

George Santayana said, "Those who cannot remember the past are condemned to repeat it." We have had major intelligence reforms in the past. Attorney General Barr pointed the way. The reform needs to be continued.

Five Eyes or FVEY
The "Special Relationship"
Further Explanation

The close relationship between British and US intelligence is part of what is known as the Five Eyes, abbreviated in government communications as FVEY. The roots of this group go back to World War II, when the US and Britain began their "special relationship." In the post-war era this group was expanded to include Australia, New Zealand, and Canada. The relationship was formalized by a series of agreements over the decades, many of them secret. As with other aspects of intelligence, these arrangements were intensified in the aftermath of September 11th.

At its most basic, there are two aspects to the Five Eyes arrangement. First, there is an ironclad agreement not to spy on each other. Second is a sharing of all intelligence, including tasking of one another. Information that has been collected on one another's citizens—deliberately or inadvertently—can be shared with each other. Concern has been raised about this most often in the arena of electronic surveillance—carried out by the National Security Agency (NSA) in the US and by the Government Communications Headquarters (GCHQ) in the UK. In this way the "special relationship" elides the intelligence oversight strictures of both countries.

CHAPTER THIRTY-FIVE

FIX THE FBI'S BROKEN CULTURE

I t may seem like the FBI is finally on the mend. Specific lapses have come to light, and each has been thoroughly covered earlier in this book. An IG report, identifying numerous failings, made nine recommendations, which the FBI has embraced. FBI Director Wray has gone further and set forth forty changes that he is implementing at the Bureau. As positive as these developments are, they fall short of the needed fundamental fix. The question is, "Why did so much go off the track?" The answer is a fundamental change in culture at the Bureau.

CULTURE SHIFT

In the wake of the 9/11 attacks, for reasons that may have seemed justified at the time, former FBI Director Robert Mueller set out to mold the FBI into an intelligence organization. Unintended consequences followed.

The FBI's culture had been rooted in law enforcement. A law enforcement agency deals in facts. As a law enforcement officer, you are moving toward the day when you stand up in court, raise your right hand, and swear to tell the truth about those facts. That is why "lack of candor," or lying has always been a firing offense in the FBI. On the other hand, an intelligence agency deals in estimates and best guesses. Guesses are not allowed in court. Intelligence agencies routinely use deception. Hence, bending a rule, or shading the truth, comes naturally to the intelligence culture. These are the behaviors described in the IG reports.

As a result of this change in culture, the FBI fell victim to centralization, politicization, and loss of that bright line between the legal and the extralegal. The FBI always had a counterintelligence role, one rooted in the rule of law. The FBI used criminal statutes, e.g., the espionage act or the treason act, as a basis for this mission. The attitude, the culture, was one of strict adherence to the rule of law.

For several years while in the FBI, I was assigned overseas as a Legal Attaché. There I interacted with my US intelligence agency counterparts on a regular basis. The difference in culture and behavior that springs from our differing missions became evident. Not only did they withhold information, shade the truth, and sometimes lie to our host nation representatives (and this was in allied countries), but they often lied to others in the embassy. Numerous other Legal Attachés have documented similar experiences. One CIA chief of station told me that he had no hesitation in lying to the US Ambassador. That approach was unthinkable to those of us from a "truth-telling" law enforcement culture.

Circular reporting is another common problem for intelligence agencies. It happens when a bit of intelligence appears to come from several sources, but in reality, is the same singular item. This can be caused by a devious originator. But most often it mistakenly happens through simple human error. A piece of information is passed from the original source through other people, agencies, or allied countries, and returns to the originator as corroborating intelligence. But it is not.

Due to the different nature of their business, this problem is much less likely to occur in law enforcement, which deals in evidence (facts).

We know circular reporting happened twice with the 'Steele dossier." First, to corroborate the dossier information in an application for a FISA warrant, statements in a news article were cited. But those statements were based on Steele's information, as well. Earlier, as we now know, the same—or very similar—information and stories were exchanged, in circular fashion, between Steele and his friends and associates, such as Cody Shearer, Sidney Blumenthal, and Jonathan Winer. This is how intelligence agencies get in trouble. It should never happen to a law enforcement agency dealing in facts, facts that must be sworn to in court, in this case the FISC.

CENTRALIZATION

Part of making the FBI more like an intelligence agency was the centralization of case management at FBI headquarters in Washington, rather than in field offices around the country. With this came the placing of operational decisions in the hands of more "politically sensitive" individuals at headquarters.

The 9/11 investigation was the first to be moved from the field to headquarters. But the trend culminated with the investigations into Hillary Clinton's emails and Russian election interference—both run from headquarters. Levels of review—and independent judgment—were eliminated, and thus we got Strzok—a high level headquarters executive—conducting interviews in both of these politically sensitive investigations.

This close compartmentation, typical of an intelligence agency, helps explain—but not excuse—why there were no whistleblowers. While McCabe and Strzok were running it all from headquarters, others in the FBI were kept in the dark. At one point, the Assistant Director in Charge in the NYO was on a phone call with his counterpart in WFO, marveling about the lack of any apparent predicate. They said to each other, "they must have more we don't know about." There wasn't.

As documented earlier in this book, major politically sensitive cases have been successfully run from the field offices in the past. The political "hot potato" of ABSCAM which resulted in the conviction of members of congress is an outstanding example. Large-scale international investigations, such as Scotbom (the bombing of Pan Am flight #103 over Lockerbie, Scotland) and the explosion of Paris-bound TWA flight #800 off Long Island, New York, were also conducted in the traditional field case management system.

In that time-tested model, the case agent, the field supervisor, and the field office's SAC each serve as a level of review. They also have the advantage of knowing the local situation. Independent judgment and oversight was then provided by senior management at FBI headquarters in Washington. Tension between field and headquarters is healthy, and layers of supervision, between field and headquarters levels, help ward off misconduct. This is missing in the Mueller/Comey headquarters-centric model.

The quality of the working FBI field agent should not be overlooked. They are all college-educated men and women, highly trained by the FBI, with many holding law or other advanced degrees.

THE FOREIGN INTELLIGENCE SURVEILLANCE ACT—FISA

After 9/11 there was much talk of the negative consequences of a "wall" between criminal and intelligence investigations. Yes, there was a wall. But you can talk over a wall. It had always been part of our culture to hold a discussion about how to proceed at the outset of a counterintelligence or terrorism investigation. When one would ultimately pursue a prosecution it was considered an abuse to seek a warrant under FISA, with its lower standard of probable cause.[29] It is still an abuse. To shade the truth in a FISA application—as occurred with the "Steele dossier"— is an abuse characteristic of an intelligence agency, not a "swear to tell the truth" law enforcement organization.

---

[29] Title 18, U.S. Code, §2518(1)(b) requires a wiretap application in criminal matters to include "a full and complete statement of facts" relied on in applying for the wiretap, while Title 50, U.S. Code, § 1804 (a)(3) specifies that in applying for a FISA (intelligence) wiretap only a "statement of facts" is required.

John P. O'Neill, who was killed on 9/11 and whose story was featured in *The Looming Tower* TV series, came to Paris several times in the late 1990s to discuss counterterrorism efforts with our French counterparts. I have a vivid memory of him and another agent sitting in my office after the conclusion of a meeting with French officials. The French had just furnished details about a suspected terrorist living in New York City. The back-and-forth discussion was whether to use FISA or the criminal approach to pursue the New York suspect. O'Neill said that in the end the New York FBI would most likely want to prosecute this subject, so we couldn't start down the FISA path and then try to turn it into a prosecutable case. I recall O'Neill concluding it was just not the right way to go.

FISA was taken so seriously that all our applications had to be signed off by the FBI director and then by the attorney general. (Now responsibility is dispersed among a number of officials.) William H. Webster was meticulously demanding about the accuracy of each FISA application. Often, intelligence must be timely, so applications and filings are kept moving even on holidays and weekends. Agents who served during Louis Freeh's tenure as director recall taking applications to his home on the weekend for signing. Even as some of Freeh's young sons called to him in the background, agents recall that he questioned them with specificity as he read though the application, pen in hand. FISA was a tool that was treated with the greatest respect.

FISA was not originally intended to pursue Americans. It was to be used to gather intelligence about agents of a foreign power operating in the US. The aim of this monitoring was to produce intelligence for our national decision-makers. It was never intended to be used in criminal prosecutions. If an American is suspected of operating as an agent of a foreign power, that individual is more properly pursued under the Espionage Act, a criminal statute. The fruits of that monitoring can be used in court for prosecution. The use of FISA to target a US citizen, although now allowed by the Act, is just not the right way to go. Something does not become right just because it's legal. Using FISA, rather than a criminal statute to target a US citizen, as in the Carter

Page matter is an indication of the Bureau drifting away from its law enforcement moorings.

RELATIONS WITH CONGRESS

During my FBI career I spent several years in the Bureau's Office of Congressional and Public Affairs. The deterioration in the Bureau's relationship with congress is shocking. It truly is a change in culture.

Former Directors Webster and Freeh insisted that the FBI respond promptly to any congressional request. In those days, a congressional committee didn't need a subpoena to get information from the FBI. There certainly was no "stonewalling" of congress by the FBI, which was what intelligence agencies might do. With the change in culture, we now hear about "stonewalling" of congress. Yes, we were particularly responsive to the appropriations committees, which are key to the Bureau's funding. But my colleagues and I shared a general sense that responding to congressional requests was the right thing to do.

The Bureau's leaders often reminded us of congress's legitimate oversight role. This was particularly true of the "Gang of Eight,"[30]created by statute to ensure the existence of a secure vehicle through which congressional leaders could be briefed on the most sensitive counterintelligence or terrorism investigations.

When he was director, Judge Webster demanded a smooth relationship with the legislative branch. Those of us who worked for him made sure he and the US congress got it. Congressional Relations at the FBI was always led by a career agent manager, who knew where in the FBIHQ bureaucracy to find the answers to congressional inquiries. Agents can command respect from their peers and have credibility with those in the legislative branch.

The Mueller/Comey years saw outside "professionals" brought in to handle the FBI's Congressional relations. Some were politicians and

---

[30] Consisting of both party leaders in each house of congress and the chairs and ranking minority members of both the Senate and House intelligence committees.

some were media veterans. They lacked the insider's knowledge and identification with the Bureau and its culture. Most recent among this parade of "pros" was Jill C. Tyson, knighted with the title of assistant director. She was slammed in an August 2021 DOJ Inspector General report for carrying on a sexual affair with a subordinate and causing disruption in the workplace. Sadly, the cultural rot continues.

On August 27, 2017, House Intelligence Committee Chairman Devin Nunes asked the FBI to immediately deliver certain documents. The bulk of the documents weren't delivered until January 11, 2018. I cannot imagine Webster or Freeh tolerating such a delay. Delays of this magnitude are not caused by "underlings." Congressional inquiries find their way right to the top of the Bureau pyramid. The director would not only be aware of these requests, he would have ordered the stonewalling. One of the documents Nunes requested was the Electronic Communication (EC) believed to have initiated the counterintelligence investigation of Donald Trump's campaign in July 2016. The FBI had previously provided a redacted text of that communication, but the Intelligence Committee wanted to see it all.

On March 23, 2018, the Bureau essentially told the committee it would not lift the redactions. There are legitimate reasons why the FBI would want certain portions of a sensitive document redacted, such as when information comes from a foreign partner. But there are ways around such difficulties.

On May 1, 2018, we learned some Republican members of Congress were considering articles of impeachment against Deputy Attorney General Rod Rosenstein if he did not hand over certain Bureau documents. In January 2018, House Speaker Paul Ryan had to threaten the Deputy Attorney General and Director Wray with contempt to get them to comply with a House subpoena for documents about the Steele dossier.

Commonly in the past, select members of Congress have been allowed to read highly sensitive documents under specific restrictions. The "Gang of Eight" exists for just this purpose. Comey did not even inform the "Gang of Eight" about the initiation of the counterintelligence investigation of Trump, because of "the sensitivity of the matter." Again, this is not the way a law enforcement agency behaves, but perhaps how an intelligence agency shades around the edges.

The need to tell congress about sensitive matters is the *raison d'être* for the Gang of Eight. The case's origin may have seemed too "sensitive" to disclosure to congress because it involved British intelligence, via the CIA. The FBI continued to withhold the full details of the origin story from congress. Their rationale was likely "protection of sources," in as much as the origin lies with a key international partner. Yes, the FBI has reason to be embarrassed—mainly for being led down a "rabbit hole" of an investigation without sufficient predicate information.

Not using the Gang of Eight was inexplicable at the time. Now it is reasonable to conclude Comey and his cabal did not want congress to discover the flimsy basis for the entire undertaking.

This is not the way a law-enforcement agency should behave under our system of separation of powers. The attorney general and the director must push to get the FBI's relationship with congress back on track. It won't be easy, but the American people deserve it and the Constitution *demands* it.

THE WAY FORWARD—A RENEWAL OF THE CULTURE

A corner may have been turned. The IG has issued several reports, looking at FISA and related abuses. Malefactors have been fired. And since the Russian collusion fiasco, there is a new director and deputy director. Most helpful was having as Attorney General William Barr, who had been in that same role in a pre-9/11 world, until his December 23, 2020 resignation.

The way forward now requires a renewal of culture. A turn away from the "intelligence driven" mindset of the Mueller/Comey years and "back to the future" of a fact-finding, swear-to-tell-the-truth, law enforcement agency. Director Wray has acknowledged there were problems. He has stated to numerous audiences that in running the Bureau he will put an emphasis on process and the "brand." One hopes he means a renewal of the law enforcement culture. Each of the identified problems from the Mueller/Comey years must be addressed.

The centralization of case management at FBI headquarters, a "Headquarters Special" in the words of a Strzok text, must be put behind us. It was Mueller's initial abandonment of the field-office model that set the stage for this mischief. Case management needs to return to the time-tested field office model with its layers of review. Director Wray has wisely tasked the new Deputy Director, Paul Abbate, to review how the Bureau manages sensitive investigations. Part of the answer is avoiding the insular "keep it all at headquarters" Strzok model.

Deputy Director Paul Abbate has been consistent in refusing to refer to the miscreants as former leaders. When he was the Assistant Director-in-Charge of WFO he, and his counterpart in the NYO, were kept in the dark about the basis for the "headquarters special" run by those malefactors. Believing, assuming, "they must have more." They didn't.

The relationship with congress needs to be restored to one of mutual respect. The "Gang of Eight" is the time-tested vehicle for sharing sensitive information. It should be used. The head of the Bureau's Office of Congressional Affairs should come from the agent ranks. During the troublesome Comey years that role was held by a politician. A Special Agent would have the institutional knowledge to respond to congress, and members of congress would afford an agent more credibility.

The FISA process must be reformed. That is something congress must address. But the Bureau—and the DOJ—need not wait for congress to act. An internal standard of avoiding the use of FISA to target an American citizen should be adopted before congress forces even more restrictive controls on counterintelligence investigations. In the wake of the IG's findings, the Bureau has instituted additional rules and guidelines for FISA. These will have to be vigorously enforced. Recall that with the Comey clique, the previously existing guidelines were simply ignored.

In response to congressional questioning about the IG's first two FISA reports, Director Wray told representatives they shouldn't "lose any sleep" over it. With an attitude like that at the top, it's no wonder the IG detected a culture of non-concern about FISA details among field personnel.

A renewed emphasis on the US Constitution as a cornerstone of the Bureau's work is needed. Special agents, in their initial and ongoing training, have always been instructed about our Constitution. After all, it is they who interview suspects and conduct searches. A new category of employee has arisen under the post 9/11 paradigm: Intelligence Analysts (IAs), who don't directly interact with citizens in ways that touch on their constitutional guarantees, now play a major role in the Bureau's mission. These are the employees who deal in estimates and best guesses. Their actions also ultimately affect people's liberty. It is imperative that they, too, receive ongoing training about our Constitution.

When I was in training as a new agent, we were each given a pocket copy of the Constitution by our legal instructor. He told us to keep it in our breast packet. If we did that, we would think about it when interviewing a suspect or conducting a search. If you keep it "close to your heart, you won't go wrong." That may sound corny to some today, but many of us did hold it close to our hearts. I had learned that because of budget reasons some years ago, new agents were no longer being given a copy of the Constitution. Happily, perhaps due to my harping on this point in op-eds and in meetings with Bureau executives, all new FBI employees will be furnished a copy of the Constitution.

A little thing perhaps, but little things mean a lot.

As former FBI Director Webster repeatedly told us: "We must do the work the American people expect of us, in the way the Constitution demands of us." All actions and decisions must once again be viewed though that prism.

During Barr's May 1, 2019 testimony with the Senate Judiciary Committee, it had already been established by the Mueller Report that President Trump had been "falsely accused." The dialog centered on the key question, "How did we get here." Barr's interlocutor, Senator Marsha Blackburn of Tennessee, concluded the explanation for the FBI failings was an "unhealthy work culture" at Bureau headquarters.

To change culture, many things must be done consistently, both big and small. The first would be to recognize the problem. Wray has declined to recognize this by taking shelter in the fact that those who were responsible are no longer employed at the FBI, but there were numerous others in the Bureau, below the dismissed malefactors, who had a role in handling these matters. Some of us have candidly suggested to Wray they need to be asked if they were uneasy or concerned by what they saw. They should have been. If they did not feel any unease or concern, there is a deep cultural problem.

Many of us also found it disappointing when Wray declared that "the Inspector General found in this particular instance, the investigation began with appropriate predication and authorization." That is not much to be proud about. The IG repeatedly noted the bar for opening a counterintelligence investigation is incredibly low. It was the IG's judgment that the referral by a friendly foreign government—relaying the London conversations of George Papadopoulos about Russian "dirt" on Hillary Clinton—met that low standard. The thesis—there was predicate to open the Russian collusion investigation—appears to be where Wray and Attorney General William Barr parted company.

One conversation relating a secondhand rumor should never be enough predicate to justify opening a counterintelligence investigation of any US person, much less a presidential campaign. That is the essence of the concern held by many of us who served in and loved the FBI. One offhand conversation is not sufficient predicate to initiate a full counterintelligence investigation. It should not be, even if the IG says it met that incredibly low bar. FBI management in the past would have said to the investigative team, "We need more."

Politics must also be completely removed from our FBI culture. The Department of Justice already has a policy of not criminally investigating politicians during key portions of the election cycle; this policy needs to be broadened to include counterintelligence investigations. Initiating a counterintelligence investigation is easy. Counterintelligence investigations of any political campaign must be banned.

If an individual campaign member is suspected of being a foreign agent, an investigation of that individual should require the approval of the attorney general. The approval should certify why the investigation cannot be deferred until after the pending election. Procedures must be put in place to ensure that such investigations are rare and would not lead to spying on a campaign.

When explaining the FBI in the past, I and others would often stress how blessed the United States was to have as our domestic security service a law enforcement agency. An organization that works within the guidelines of the law, to protect our democracy. The coin has now flipped, I fear the United States may be cursed to have a domestic intelligence organization with police powers. A once great agency may now have become a threat to democracy.

Christopher A. Wray, or his successor as FBI director, must change this by bending the Bureau away from an intelligence culture and back to a law enforcement culture rooted in the Constitution. A difficult task. But to restore the FBI's brand and credibility, it must be done.

**The Gang of Eight
Further Explanation**

The Gang of Eight is a colloquial term for a set of eight leaders within the United States Congress who are briefed on classified intelligence matters by the executive branch. Specifically, the Gang of Eight includes the leaders of each of the two parties from both the Senate and House of Representatives, and the chairmen and ranking minority members of both the Senate Committee and House Committee on Intelligence. This was established by the Intelligence Oversight Act of 1980 (Title 50, U.S. Code, §3093 (c) (2)).

The President is required, by Title 50, U.S. Code, §3091 (a) (1), to "ensure the congressional intelligence committees are kept fully and currently informed of the intelligence activities of the United States, including any significant anticipated intelligence activity."

The members are "selected" by the leadership without regard to seniority. They must be able to obtain, or already have, a Top Secret or higher security clearance. Their meetings and briefings are conducted in a secure facility within the Capitol.

CHAPTER THIRTY-SIX

CAN THE CULTURE
BE WON BACK?

I t was a painful realization. Some of the Bureau's so-called leaders were totally lacking in character. Strzok and Page were just two individuals whose actions were politicly biased, juvenile, self-centered, and immoral. They're gone, but sadly, similar behavior is still widespread in today's FBI. Numerous incidents point to a deep cultural problem.

On December 14, 2021, the DOJ IG reported the results of an inquiry into the actions of five FBI officials who had engaged in sex with prostitutes overseas. The report also mentioned that one of the FBI officials prepared a package of one hundred white pills to give to an overseas police officer. This reckless behavior opened them up to blackmail and worse. The IG also found—how sadly familiar—they lacked candor. While the investigation of these five officials was underway, two resigned, two retired, and one was removed. More rotten apples out the door, but the cultural rot remains.

In June 2022, US Senator Chuck Grassley sent letters to Director Wray and Attorney General Garland identifying an ASAC in WFO who was manifesting flagrant political bias. According to Senator Grassley, this agent had oversight of political corruption investigations in Washington, DC. He was posting and "liking" deeply partisan rants on social media. Even after the exposure of the Strzok and Page biases, the culture was such that an FBI manager would and could–on twitter and LinkedIn–display hostility towards former President Trump and former Attorney General Bill Barr.

When Bill Barr became the Attorney General on February 2, 2018, Christopher Wray had been FBI director for six months. Barr had a continuing close relationship with several former Bureau executives from his first term as AG. He recognized the cultural problem at the FBI and the ongoing task Wray was facing. Barr proposed an advisory panel to Wray, made up of these former FBI executives, suggesting William Baker and Floyd Clarke. Wray pushed back. Barr, who saw the problem from the outset, was then reduced to using Floyd and Bill as "hip-pocket" resources. It was something, but perhaps too many steps away to be truly effective.

Part of the conflict between Barr and Wray may have been simply that when Barr returned as Attorney General in 2017, he was operating from his pre 9/11 values, while the Bureau and its leadership had moved on to a post-9/11 world of intelligence–not law enforcement–values.

In October 2020, I visited with Deputy Director Paul Abbate at FBIHQ. He provided a cogent briefing of what had been done to "right the ship." I expressed my appreciation. But I stressed that the culture still needs to be fixed. He listened but made no response. At almost the same time, Floyd Clarke, one of the former executives Barr had proposed to Director Wray, was in fact sitting down with Wray in Las Vegas. Their discussion was much the same. Floyd proposed to Wray that those still in the Bureau who worked on the FISA warrants with the dismissed malefactors be asked if they were uncomfortable with what they saw. If they weren't, there is a cultural problem. Wray did not directly respond to Floyd's suggested review, saying only that he was now comfortable with the executives he had around him.

We may never get the Bureau culture back to the one I lived with and loved in the pre-9/11 era. But the effort of reform is worth it, noble, and direly needed.

Judge William H. Webster maintained contact with those who worked with him in the FBI long after he stepped down as Director. Well into his 90s, he continued to be a regular at former agents' gatherings, as pictured here. His oft-repeated admonishment, "We must do the work the American people expect of us, in the way the Constitution demands of us," needs to be heeded today.

CONCLUSION

The professionalism of policing has increased remarkably during the past half century. The FBI National Academy helped greatly with the initial move towards more professional policing, the National Executive Institute enhanced that movement. That a college-educated police officer is no longer remarkable is proof enough of police professionalism. Perhaps more important to the citizenry is that there is no longer the routine corruption, nor the brutality, which were practiced and accepted in the pre-Knapp Commission days.

Law enforcement performance has been enhanced tremendously by innovations in forensics and technology. The FBI's role in that progress is often overlooked, but the Bureau deserves the lion's share of credit for NCIC, CODIS, ViCap, NGI, Rapid-DNA and many other scientific breakthroughs in crime detection and prevention. There are now untold thousands who have not been raped, murdered, maimed, or robbed because of these systems—and they will never know.

An unintended consequence of the response to the September 11 attacks was that the FBI was directed away from its roots in law enforcement and into the ambiguous world of intelligence. The cultural change that began under Mueller's leadership set the stage for the disastrous directorship of Comey. A charlatan who tried to incriminate a president, he now makes money off books celebrating his malign behavior.

The first step in fixing a problem is recognizing the problem. The "few rotten apples" explanation for "what went wrong at the FBI" is a dodge. The culture must be fixed, and to fix it one must acknowledge the problem.

Existing statues, such as FISA, must be reformed to avoid the abuse of Americans' rights. And, please, no new laws against "domestic terrorism," which would present new perils to Americans' civil liberties.

Correcting a widely accepted narrative is very difficult; whether that narrative is about someone's corruption or the difference between a replica and real evidence. That is what I have tried to do in this book. Some readers, I hope, will reconsider their opinions.

EPILOGUE

"MORNING IN AMERICA"

A nne and I experienced a very moving visit to the Ronald Reagan Presidential Library and Museum in Simi Valley, California, on February 5 and 6, 2020. I learned a good bit about how the Presidential Library is organized. It turns out that at this one venue there are several separate, but collaborating, entities.

The library itself is a federal government entity. The archivists who work there are federal employees. The library and the millions of documents it holds are part of the National Archives. On the same campus is the museum, which is privately funded and houses the Reagans' personal and public artifacts.

The Ronald Reagan Foundation and Institute, headquartered on the site, is private. In addition to being a fundraising operation for the other components, it runs special programs and exhibits at the library and the museum.

Thanks to my friend, the journalist James Rosen, I was in contact with Ira Permstein, the supervising archivist for some time concerning a possible collaboration on an oral history of the Reagan assassination attempt. It transpired in the meantime the museum was contemplating upgrading and expanding the small section on their current tour route about the assassination attempt. And separately, the Foundation and Institute were now backing a major temporary exhibit on the FBI itself.

One section of the museum contains 11,000 plus feet of temporary exhibition space on two levels. This has been used in recent years for major exhibitions which do not necessarily have anything to do with the Reagan Presidency. For example, in the past there was an exhibit on the Magna Carta. More recently, the 'Lost Cities of Egypt' was a magnificent display.

The museum planned on having the major exhibit on the FBI running for four or five months. Its opening was pushed back more than a year due to the coronavirus shutdown. They have secured exhibits from the Newseum, the FBI (former tour route artifacts), and the National Archives. And they have interviewed and videotaped several current and former special agents.

When he was FBI Director, Webster made President Ronald Reagan an honorary FBI agent, only months after the attempted assassination. The optimistic 40th President often reminded us, "It is always morning in America."

When the curators on the museum side learned that I was in contact with the archivists' side, they asked that I come to the site sooner rather than later so that they could use my contribution in their temporary exhibition.

It turns out that February 6 is the anniversary of President Reagan's birthday. They have an annual birthday party for the occasion and included us. The staff of all the components of the Presidential Library were incredibly welcoming and made us feel part of their Reagan "family."

On February 5, I was introduced to Jennifer Torres, the registrar of the Presidential Library and Randy Swan, the supervisory curator of the Museum and Library. A docent then gave Anne and me an afternoon-long tour of the museum. This included the private residence that the Reagans used after the White House years—his and her offices, reception/living room, a conference room, and dining room. Not routinely open to the public, this residence area is the property and responsibility of the Foundation and Institute. It was filled with the furnishings, artwork, and mementos of President and Mrs. Reagan.

Also on the 5th, the Medal of Honor Society was meeting on the grounds. The Foundation and Institute have a close relationship with the Medal of Honor Society. One of those present was Tommy Norris, a Medal of Honor recipient, who was also an FBI agent with whom I had worked. Later that day, the curators' team videotaped some of Tommy Norris' FBI recollections for the upcoming exhibition.

That evening we had dinner with our friends Bill and Robin Baker. They live near the Simi Valley site of the library. Bill was—among many other roles—once the assistant director at the Bureau for Public Affairs. Hence, he is very familiar with the upcoming FBI exhibit.

On February 6, we returned to the library. It was Ronald Reagan's 109th birthday. The party started outdoors. The library sits on top of a hill with beautiful views in all directions. The staff had assigned us great seats and we enjoyed the moving music of a Marine band and then a flyover by the Tiger Squadron. The featured speaker was Drew Dix, President of the Medal of Honor Society. A USMC color guard placed a wreath at the graves of the Reagans. We then went inside for lunch. Initially we thought we were having lunch under the wings of Air Force One (yes, the museum is that big), but the staff kindly included us in the small party luncheon in the residence.

After lunch was a working afternoon. In one sitting, for over ninety minutes, I was videotaped by the staff. Some of the resulting material was used in the temporary FBI exhibition. Some of it may be used in a permanent upgrade of their portion of the tour route dealing with the assault on President Reagan. The staff of all the various components at the Reagan Library are committed to telling his story accurately; it is also clear that they want to do the FBI justice as well.

When we were back home after our visit, I packed up and donated all my material from the Reagan assassination attempt to the library—letters, memos, and photographs. Included was the photo of Hinckley just before the shooting started, which Al Fury had gifted to me many decades ago.

It was an honor to contribute my small bit to this history. It was a thrill to visit this wonderful and moving site. Again, I realize how lucky I have been to live in this wonderful country and to have the friends and family I do.

After the long delay caused by the coronavirus shutdown, the Ronald Reagan Presidential Library and Museum reopened to the public on Thursday, July 8, 2021. And the Ronald Reagan Presidential Foundation & Institute's exhibition "The FBI From Al Capone to Al-Qaeda" at the Reagan Library opened on July 9, 2021. An opening reception was held on the evening of Wednesday, July 7, 2021. Anne and I were again honored to be invited and thrilled to attend.

As the 40th president often reminded us: It is always morning in America.

AFTERWORD

I remain an optimist—how could I not be—I have enjoyed the love of a beautiful woman, a meaningful and fun-filled career, many friends, and a truly wonderful family. I live in a free and great country. God has been good to me.

Yet, Bob Levinson died in Iranian captivity, Paul Rico died in chains, and John Connolly sat in prison for twenty years. While Alcee Hastings sat in congress, John Martorano is a free man, Donna Sue's killer lives free in Florida, and David Belfield lives free in Iran. There is much injustice in our world.

BIBLIOGRAPHY

Baker, Thomas. "The Shooting of President Reagan—Lessons for LawEnforcement." *The Grapevine* Vol 77, No 5 (May 2011): 8—11.

"Biometrics for Intelligence-Led Policing: The Coming Trends." *The Police Chief* No 75 (April 2011): 38—45.

"Combating Art Theft: International Cooperation in Action." *The Police Chief* No 10 (October 1996): 19—23.

"Le FBI et le Crime Organisé: le Rôle du Renseignement." *La Criminalité Organisée*, La Documentation Française, Paris, (1996): 219—224.

"La Police Scientifique." *The Review of the French Gendarmerie* No 175, 4th semester, (1995): 39—40.

"The Pacific Training Initiative-Cooperation in Action." *FBI Law Enforcement Bulletin* (April 1993): 1—3.

Barr, William P. *One Damn Thing After Another: Memories of an AttorneyGeneral*. New York: William Morrow, Harper Collins, 2022.

Beauvois, Xavier. Director, *Of Gods and Men*. Armada Films, 2010.

Boeri, David. "The Martyrdom of John Connolly" *Boston Magazine*, August 21, 2008.

Browder, Bill. *Red Notice: A True Story of High Finance, Murder, and One Man's Fight for Justice.* New York: Simon & Schuster, 2015.

Burrough, Bryan. *Vendetta: American Express and the Smearing of Edmond Safra.* New York: Harper Collins, 1992.

Cohen, Herb. *You Can Negotiate Anything: How to Get What You Want.* Secaucus, NJ: Lyle Stuart Inc., 1980.

Cornevin, Christophe and Alice Sedar. "Les Tribulations du Traité de Fontainebleau." *Le Figaro.* (May 31, 1996): 32.

CNN, Crimes of the Century, "The Attempted Assassination of Ronald Reagan," Season 1, Episode # 4. Original broadcast date: July 22, 2013.

DeMille, Nelson. *Night Fall.* New York: Warner Books, 2004.

Depue, Roger L. *Between Good and Evil: A Master Profiler's Hunt for Society's Most Violent Predators.* New York: Warner Books, 2005.

Dillon, Greg. *The Thin Blue Lie: An Honest Cop vs. The FBI.* Nashville: Bombardier, 2022.

Durk, David and Ira Silverman. *The Pleasant Avenue Connection.* New York: Harper & Row, 1976

English, T.J. *Where the Bodies were Buried: Whitey Bulger and the World That Made Him.* New York: William Morrow, 2015.

"The Scapegoat." *Newsweek Magazine* (October 1996): 19—23.

Feliciano, Hector. *The Lost Museum: The Nazi Conspiracy to Steal the World's Greatest Works of Art.* New York: Basic Books, 1997.

Fischer, David. *The Ceremony: The Mafia Initiation Tapes.* Dell Publishing, 1992.

Guisnel, Jean. *Cyber Wars: Espionage on the Internet.* Plenum Trade, 1997.

Halden, Harold and Thomas J. Baker. "Three Quarters of a Million Sex Offenders." *The Associate* No12/5 (September/October 2010): 18-20.

Hemingway, Mollie. *Rigged: How the Media, Big Tech, and the Democrats Seized Our Elections.* Washington D.C.: Regnery Publishing, 2021.

Howard, David. *Chasing Phil: The Adventures of Two Undercover Agents with The World's Most Charming Con Man.* New York: Broadway Books, 2017.

Jett, Philip. *Taking Mr. Exxon: The Kidding of an Oil Giant's President.* John Hunt Publishing, May 1, 2021.

John Baker, July 20, 1992, Response to Christine Chestman's "Affront to description of area where Sidney Reso's body found," Asbury Park Press, July 14, 1992.

Kengor, Paul. *A Pope and A President: John Paul II, Ronald Reagan, and the Extraordinary Untold Story of the 20th Century.* Willington, Delaware: ISI Books, 2017.

Kessler, Ronald. *The First Family Detail: Secret Service Agents Reveal the Hidden Lives of the Presidents.* New York: Crown Publishing, 2014.

In The President's Secret Service: Behind the Scenes with Agents in the Line of Fire and the Presidents They Protect. New York: Crown Publishing, 2009.

Kiser, John. *The Monks of Tibhirine: Faith, Love, and Terror in Algeria.* New York: St. Martin's Press, 2002.

Kwitny, Jonathan. *The Fountain Pen Conspiracy.* New York: Alfred A. Knopf, 1973.

Le Popular du Centre. "La Pêche Miraculeuse de Retour á Aubusson." March 20, 1996, p. 2.

Letersky, Paul. *The Director: My Years Assisting J. Edgar Hoover.* New York: Scribner, 2021.

Levin, Yuval. *A Time to Build: From Family and Community to Congress and the Campus, How Recommitting to Our Institutions Can Revive The American Dream.* New York: Basic Books, 2020.

Marquise, Richard A. *Scotbom: Evidence and the Lockerbie Investigation.* New York: Algora Publishing, 2006.

McCarthy, Andrew C. *Ball of Collusion: The Plot to Rig an Election and Destroy a Presidency.* New York: Encounter Books, 2019.

Meier, Barry. *Missing Man: The American Spy Who Vanished in Iran.* New York: Farrar, Straus, and Giroux, 2016.

Spooked: The Trump Dossier, Black Cube, and the Rise of Private Spies. New York: Harper, 2021.

Miller, John. *The Cell: Inside the 9/11 Plot, and Why the FBI and CIA Failed to Stop It.* New York: Hachette Books, 2002.

Mueller, Robert S. *Report on the Investigation into Russian Interference in the 2016 Presidential Election.* Washington D.C., March 2019.

NBC, Dateline, "Hinckley, Diary of A Dangerous Mind" Season #27, Episode #52. Original broadcast date: August 26, 2019.

Office of the Inspector General, U.S. Department of Justice, "A Review of Various Actions by the Federal Bureau of Investigation and Department of Justice in Advance of the 2016 Election," June 2018.

Picciano, John F. *Liam's Promise.* New York: Page Publishing, 2012.

Pistone, Joseph D. *Donnie Brasco: My Undercover Life in the Mafia: a True Story by an FBI Agent.* New York: Penguin Putnam, 1987.

Powell, Sidney. *Licensed to Lie: Exposing Corruption in The Department of Justice.* Dallas: Brown Book Publishing, 2014.

Rosen, James. *The Strong Man: John Mitchell and the Secrets of Watergate.* New York: Doubleday, 2008.

Ruskin, Marc. *The Pretender: My Undercover Life for the FBI.* New York: St. Martin's Press, 2017.

Strassel, Kimberley. *Resistance (At All Costs): How Trump Haters Are Breaking America.* New York: Twelve, 2019.

Strange, Kenneth R. *A Cop's Son: One G-Man's Fight Against Jihad, Global Fraud, and the Cartels.* Palisades New York: History Publishing Company, 2022.

Stratton, Richard. "Super Rat." *Playboy Magazine* (Nov 2008), 19—20.

"The Fall Guy." *Playboy Magazine* (December 2012), 19—23.

United States v. Sidney J. Gerhart and Joseph Adornato, Mobile, Alabama, Docket No. 82-CR-8.

Van Den Haag, Ernest. *Punishing Criminals: Concerning A Very Old and Painful Question.* New York: Basic Books, 1975.

Wallison, Peter. *Ronald Reagan: The Power of Conviction and the Success of His Presidency.* Boulder Colorado: Westview Press, 2003.

Weiss, Murray. *The Man Who Warned America: The Life and Death of John O'Neill: The FBI's Embattled Counterterror Warrior*. New York: Regan Books, 2003.

Wilson, James Q. *Varieties of Police Behavior: The Management of Law and Order in Eight Communities*. New York: Basic Books, 1968.

Thinking about Crime. Boston: Harvard Press, 1975.

Williams, Jerri, Podcast, Episode #163, *Mackle Kidnapping Case* (April 24, 2019).

Podcast, Episode #167, *The Reagan Shooting* (May 22, 2019).

Wolfinger, Joe, Chris Kerr, Jerry Seper. *Rico: How Politicians, Prosecutors, and The Mob Destroyed One of The FBI's Finest Special Agents*. Telemachus Press, 2010.

Wright, Lawrence. *The Looming Tower: Al-Qaeda and The Road To 9/11*. New York: Alfred A. Knopf, 2006.

GLOSSARY

AFIS—Automated Fingerprint Identification System. A computerized system used to match fingerprints against a database of known and unknown prints.

AO—Auxiliary Office. An FBI field office that is tasked to carry out one or more leads for the Office of Origin, i.e., the office that is running the case.

Apalachin conference—A meeting of about a hundred mobsters in the tiny New York state town on November 14, 1957. Broken up by a police raid, the conference confirmed the existence of a national organized crime network.

ASAC—Assistant Special Agent in Charge. Pronounced "A sack."

ASIO—Australian Security Intelligence Organization. A defensive, i.e., counter-intelligence service.

AUSA—Assistant United States Attorney. A federal prosecutor.

Backstopping—Term for the aliases and false backgrounds for under-cover agents.

Brien McMahon—A US Senator who authored the Atomic Energy Act. A graduate of Fordham University, the Brien McMahon Award is named in his honor. Both Louis Freeh and Saint Mother Teresa of Calcutta are award recipients.

BUCAR—Bureau Car. The official government car used by FBI agents.

BNDD—The Bureau of Narcotics and Dangerous Drugs. A DEA predecessor.

CSIS—The Canadian Security Intelligence Service. A defensive service.

Case Agent—The agent charged with the direction of the case; respon-sible for setting out leads, writing reports, and presenting to an AUSA.

Charge d'affaires—Individual responsible for running an embassy in the absence of an ambassador.

CI—Criminal Informant; term used by most police, as well as FBI.

CJIS—The Criminal Justice Information Services Division. Located in Clarksburg, West Virginia, this FBI Division took over the functions of the old Ident Division. Now it runs NCIC, UCR, NICS, as well as fingerprint services.

CODIS—The Combined DNA Index System. A national database of DNA Information created and maintained by the FBI Laboratory.

COINTELPRO—Counterintelligence Program. A project of ques-tionable legality, conducted by the FBI between 1956–1971, aimed at surveilling, infiltrating, discrediting, and disrupting domestic politi-cal organizations.

COS—Chief of Station. The individual who runs a CIA unit, usually based in an US embassy. Often this person's identity is declared to the host country.

Country Clearance—The permission granted by a US ambassador for a federal employee to enter the host country on official business.

Country Team—The principal officers in a US Embassy, as well as the head of each independent agency represented at that post.

Country Team Meeting—A mandated weekly gathering of the Country Team.

CIP—Criminal Intelligence Program—The FBI's management and development of criminal informants. Begun in the 1960s, its focus was Organized Crime.

CSI—Crime Scene Investigation. Involves protection of crime scenes, collection of physical evidence, and submitting evidence for scientific examination.

DCM—The Deputy Chief of Mission. The number two in a US Embassy.

DNA—Deoxyribonucleic acid. A molecule found in all known organisms and every cell of the human body. Widely accepted for forensic identification.

DEA—The Drug Enforcement Administration. The principal federal agency tasked with combating drug trafficking; part of the Department of Justice.

Démarche—French word meaning "step" or "solicitation." Used in diplomacy as an objection or protest to a foreign government.

DGSE—*Direction Général de la Sécurité Extérieure*—The French intelligence agency; an offensive service much like the CIA.

DST—*Direction de la Surveillance du Territoire*—The division of the French National Police tasked with counterintelligence and counterterrorism. A defensive agency much like the FBI. Since July 1, 2008, it functions under the new name of *Direction Centrale du Renseignements Intérieure* (DGSI).

EC—Electronic Communication—A formatted document, introduced during Louis Freeh's tenure as FBI Director, which replaced almost all the previous forms of paper communications, such as memos and teletypes.

FD-302—A government form used by the FBI to record information, which may be evidence. Often it's interviews, but also other observations or findings.

First Office Agent—An FBI agent in the first field assignment. For decades this had been a fixed term of a year. The practice is no longer followed.

Five Eyes—An intelligence-sharing arrangement between the five nations of Australia, Canada, New Zealand, the United Kingdom, and the United States. Coded as FVEY in government communications.

Gang of Eight—A select group in the US Congress—consisting of the leaders of both parties in the House and the Senate and the chairmen and ranking member of both the House and Senate Intelligence Committees. They are cleared to review the most sensitive intelligence.

IAFIS—Integrated Automated Fingerprint Identification System. The FBI's AFIS, created in 1999, now upgraded to the Next Generation Identification (NGI).

Ident—Identification, as in the old Identification Division.

ILR—International Letters Rotatory. A complex and cumbersome diplomatic process required to collect evidence in many non-common law countries.

JTTF—Joint Terrorism Task Force. Multi-agency partnerships between federal, state, and local law enforcement investigating terrorism-related crimes. Organized by the FBI, the first JTTF was established in NYC in 1980 with ten FBI special agents and ten New York City police (NYPD) detectives.

Knapp Commission—Named after its chairman, Whitman Knapp, the Commission was created to investigate police corruption in New York City. Its final report, on December 27, 1972, documented systematic police corruption.

LCN—*La Cosa Nostra*—"This thing of ours." The principal Italian organized crime group in the USA. More often called the Mafia in the past.

Latents—Latent fingerprints. Marks or traces left at the scene of a crime that may not be immediately visible to the naked eye. To expose them, technicians use fingerprint powder or other techniques.

Legal Attaché—A diplomatic title given to the FBI agent leading the Bureau office in a US Embassy. The first such offices were established during WWII in Ottawa, Mexico City, and London. The FBI, under Director J. Edgar Hoover and with the backing of President FDR, obtained the title Attaché so that the FBI representative would be on an equal footing with the Military attachés.

Legat—The FBI abbreviation for Legal Attaché.

Mafia—A name for Italian organized crime in America. The term derives from the Sicilian Mafia, which is today considered a separate organization.

MI5—The British Security Service. Its name originally was Military Intelligence, Section 5. It is a defensive, counterintelligence service.

MI6—The British Secret Intelligence Service (SIS). The name is from its origin as Military Intelligence, Section 6; an offensive overseas intelligence service.

MPD—Metropolitan Police Department. The Washington DC police.

NA—National Academy. The FBI National Academy in a police training program of three months duration conducted at Quantico, Virginia.

NAA—National Academy Associates—A membership organization made up of the graduates of the FBI National Academy program.

NCIC—The National Crime Information Center. A central database linking federal, state, and local law enforcement agencies in sharing crime-related information. Created in 1967, it is managed by the Criminal Justice Information Services (CJIS) Division of the FBI.

NEI—National Executive Institute—The FBI National Executive Institute is an executive development program for top law enforcement leaders.

NEIA—National Executive Institute Associates—A membership organization made up of the graduates of the FBI National Executive Institute.

New Left—A radical leftist political movement active during the early 1970s, composed largely of college students and young intellectuals. "New," as opposed to the old left of the American Communist Party (CPUSA).

NGI—Next Generation Identification—an enhancement to the FBI's IAFIS, implemented in stages between 2011 and 2015.

NICS—The National Instant Criminal Background Check System. It is a background check system in the United States created by the Brady Handgun Violence Prevention Act (Brady Bill) of 1993 to prevent firearm sales to prohibited individuals. NICS was started in 1998 and is managed by the Criminal Justice Information Services (CJIS) Division of the FBI.

NYO—The New York Office. The unique name for the FBI's NY Division.

OO—Office of Origin. The FBI field office running an investigation. As opposed to the AO, Auxiliary Office, which is assisting in the investigation.

PENTTBOM—Pentagon Twin Towers Bombing. The codename for the FBI Investigation of the September 11, 2001, attacks on the USA.

Place Kléber—A conference center in Paris near the Arch de Triumph in Paris' 16th arrondissement. Famous as the locale where Henry Kissinger in early 1973 concluded negotiations to end the Vietnam War. There Attorney Janet Reno also attended a conference in 1995 and Jim Kallstrom made a presentation in 1996 concerning TWA 800.

Place Vendôme—A luxurious square in Paris' 1st arrondissement, where the French Justice ministry is located. It is where Edmond J. Safra's TDB bank opened its first office outside Geneva. Also the site of the Ritz Hotel.

RA—Resident Agency. A sub-office of an FBI field office.

Relief Supervisor—An agent who assists an FBI field supervisor.

RICO —The Racketeer Influenced and Corrupt Organizations Act. Title IX of the Organized Crime Control Act of 1970. Targeting the criminal enterprise more than the individual, it provides for asset forfeiture and civil damages.

Ritz Hotel—A luxurious hotel on Paris' Place Vendôme. It was here in 1997 that Ambassador Harriman had a stroke that led to her death. And later that same year, it was also from here that Princess Diana departed on her fateful drive.

RCMP—The Royal Canadian Mounted Police. Canada's federal police.

SA—Special Agent. The term "Special" derives from the legal concept of agency, i.e., as opposed to a "general" agent, a special agent is commissioned to act only in specific instances.

SAC—Special Agent in Charge. Most often spoken out as "S_A_C" —seldom pronounced "SACK." Most often the agent in charge of an office.

SAS—Special Air Service. An elite paratrooper component of the British Army.

Scotbom—The FBI's codename for the December 21, 1988, bombing of Pan Am flight #103 over Lockerbie, Scotland. When another Boeing 747, TWA#800, blew up, the lessons of Lockerbie were very much on our minds.

SIOC—Strategic Information and Operations Center. The FBIHQ command post. Now a twenty-four-hour-a-day, seven-day-a-week operation.

STU II—Secure Telephone Unit. An encrypted telephone. II being an upgrade.

Special, a—A major case, which is to receive additional attention and resources.

Street Agent, a—A working level agent. Slang for Special Agent.

Ten Print—The "inked" fingerprint card of an individual's ten fingerprints.

Top Hoodlum Program—The earliest iteration of the FBI's intelligence gathering effort against organized crime. Ran from the late 1950s through the 1960s.

TE—Top Echelon. An extremely well-placed criminal informant.

TWA—Trans World Airlines. Mentioned in two chapters of this book, it was a major US air carrier, which had financial difficulties for years. The lawsuits and bad publicity resulting from the crash of Flight 800 was a final nail in its coffin. It ceased operations as an independent carrier in 2001.

UCA—Undercover Agent.

UCO—Undercover Operation.

USSS—United States Secret Service. Called "the Service" by insiders.

USA—United States Attorney. The chief federal prosecutor in each US district.

ViCap—The Violent Criminal Apprehension Program. A unit created at Quantico in 1985, which focuses on the analysis of serial violent and sexual crimes. Part of the National Center for the Analysis of Violent Crime (NCAVC).

Weathermen—Also known as the Weather Underground, a very violent component of the New Left movement of the early 1970s.

WFO—Washington Field Office. The FBI field office, which now covers DC and Northern Virginia. Part of which territory was formally covered by the Alexandria Field office.

Wire-Room—The location where illegal bookies, using numerous telephones, received bets, odds information, sports scores, and horse race results in real time. Somewhat obsolete in the age of the internet.

APPENDIX

Significant legislation, a brief explanation:

The Omnibus Crime Control and Safe Streets Act of 1968 (Pub. L. 90—351, 82 Stat. 197, enacted June 19, 1968, codified at Title 34, U.S. Code, § 10101 et seq.). It is based on legislation signed into law by President Lyndon B. Johnson. Most significantly, Title III of the Act set rules for legally obtaining wiretap coverage in criminal cases. Title III led to the act being referenced as the "Wire Tap Act." That part of the law is codified as Title 18, U.S. Code, § 2510.

The Organized Crime Control Act of 1970 (Pub. L. 91–452, 84 Stat. 922 October 15, 1970), is an Act of Congress sponsored by Democratic Senator John L. McClellan and signed into law by President Richard Nixon. Title V created the witness protection program. Title VIII made it a federal crime to protect an illegal gambling business. Title IX gave us The Racketeer Influenced and Corrupt Organizations Act—RICO— itself a sweeping criminal statute. RICO provided for asset forfeiture and civil damages, the full extent of which would not be fully realized for decades.

The Foreign Intelligence Surveillance Act of 1978 ("FISA" Pub. L. 95—511, 92 Stat. 1783, Title 50 U.S. Code, ch. 36) is a federal law that establishes procedures for the physical and electronic surveillance and collection of "foreign intelligence information" from "foreign powers" and "agents of foreign powers" suspected of espionage. The Act also created the Foreign Intelligence Surveillance Court (FISC). The act has been expanded to cover terrorism. A widening use of FISA has brought Americans under its purview, contrary to its original intent.

ACKNOWLEDGMENTS

Many people have helped me in the production of this book. I apologize in advance for any I may have unintentionally omitted. Although many named here helped form my thinking on the issues in this book, the conclusions I have arrived at are my own and not completely shared by all those who have helped.

First and foremost, I must thank my publisher, David Bernstein and Bombardier Books, without whose faith this project would never have seen the light of day. Aleigha Kely, my managing editor at Bombardier, was there from the start. Anthony Ziccardi, publisher at Post Hill Press, made it all possible.

My professional editor and friend, Kristina Hart did some serious editing while dealing with the school shutdowns due to Covid-19. Much of the third part of this book, "The Ugly," is based on material that appeared earlier in the *Wall Street Journal*. The *Journal's* features editor, James Taranto, enhanced both the style and substance of those efforts. His able deputy and my fellow Fordham graduate, Matthew Hennessey, assisted as well. I hope what I learned from their writing and editing skills is reflected here.

My son Tom, an editor and features writer for *The Japan News*, provided valuable editorial counsel at several points in the process in spite of his own busy schedule. He put me in touch with the Japan Writers' Conference; their writer's workshops and other sessions were incredibly valuable. My daughter, Virginia, read portions of the manuscript and supplied editorial comments along with her perspective on the events described. I love and cherish all my children and their advice.

The example of two outstanding former directors of the FBI, Louis Freeh and William H. Webster, was front of mind before and through-out the process of writing this book. They were both encouraging in my initial efforts to divine what was happening to our FBI. Former Attorneys General Ed Meese, Janet Reno, and Bill Barr were also prominent in my thoughts throughout this project. It was a privilege to know and work for these five outstanding public servants.

Several authors, who are also friends, helped guide me towards getting published. They include Ron Kessler, David Howard, Phil Jett, James Rosen, Brad Thor, Peter Wallison, and Mark and Mollie Hemingway. Particularly helpful were former FBI agents who had suc-cessfully authored their own books. These included Dick Ayers, Dick Marquise, Roger Depue, Greg Dillon, Steve Gladis, Harry Gossett, Joe Pistone, Paul Letersky, John Picciano, Marc Ruskin, Ken Strange, Bob Pence, John Mindermann, Phil Walter, Joe Wolfinger, and Chris Kerr. All generously shared their insights and experiences. Ernie Porter and Rex Tomb, both veterans of the old FBI's Office of Public and Congressional Affairs, were immensely helpful with research and edit-ing. Kevin Giblin greatly assisted with the precise details of Attorney General Janet Reno's travels to Paris.

Numerous former FBI colleagues shared their recollections and read parts of the early drafts in which they appear or have expertise. These include Jim Siano, Bill Baker, Dick Baker, Guy Berado, Jack Brennan, Kevin Brock, Floyd Clarke, Jim Wedick, John Connolly, Artie Grubert, Jim Greenleaf, Al Hein, Charlie Wroblewski, Tom Renaghan, Willy Reagan, Charlie Rooney, Buck Revell, Tom Sheer, Jerry Pender, Becky Bosley, Robin Stark-Nutter, Bill Tucker, Glenn Tuttle, Allyson Gilliland, Jim Werth, Tom Bush, Rich Garcia, Robin Montgomery, Jack McDermott, Bob Quigley, Frank Waikart, and Gary Penrith. US

District Judge Virginia "Ginnie" Granade provided precision about Gary Steven Krist, the kidnapper of Barbara Jane Mackle.

Other friends and associates read parts of the manuscript and were generous with editorial suggestions. These include Charlie Bailey, John Greaney, Jeanne Grubert, Joe Gannon, Mike Fordyce, Mary Doyle, Claude Dubos, Bob Snow, Ira Selkowitz, Ambassador Mel Sembler, Don Weaver, and Lynne Penrith. Jamie and Maurice Emmer, both outstanding lawyers, were generous with legal and editorial insights.

David Rivkin, another outstanding member of the Bar, shared his analysis of the Russian Collusion narrative, as we collaborated on an article for the *Wall Street Journal*. His guidance and keen insights are greatly appreciated.

Currently serving FBI agents, at every level, who understandably must remain anonymous, also bravely provided valuable insight and interpretation.

In the end, the biggest help of all was my wife Anne. Always my first editor, she certainly qualifies as co-author of this volume. I thank God for her.